Professional Remote Pilot Handbook & ⸹

Published by:

ASSOCIATION of PROFESSIONAL
DRONE PILOTS

118 PINE STREET
RAYNHAM, MA 02767

<u>WWW.PRODRONEPILOTS.ORG</u>

© ASSOCIATION OF PROFESSIONAL DRONE PILOTS, INC.

EDUCATION@PRODRONEPILOTS.ORG

For information about special discounts available for bulk purchases, sales promotions, fund-raising and educational needs, contact the Association of Professional Drone Pilots, Inc. at <u>Education@Prodronepilots.org</u>

First Edition

ISBN-13: 978-1535567305
ISBN-10: 1535567309

Table of Contents

Preface

Thank you for purchasing the Association of Professional Drone Pilots *Pilot's Desk Reference*. Our book was written for professionals in the UAV industry with little to no practical aviation experience and was designed to be a blueprint for drone operators and other professional who are preparing for the FAA's future written exam.

The topics and concepts covered in this text were chosen for their relative importance in the aviation field. Regardless of the pilot certification one seeks, all pilots are required to know and understand such broad topics as: Aviation Definitions, Aerodynamics, Safety, Regulations, Weather, Flight Operations and Human Factors. Other topics were chosen due to their overall importance for UAV Pilots.

This text could not have been written without the support of the Federal Aviation Administration and their own aviation education materials. Publications such as" the *Pilot's Handbook of Aeronautical Knowledge*, the *Helicopter Flying Handbook*, the *Airman's Information Manual*, and the *Federal Aviation Regulations*. For more in depth knowledge, all aviators should become familiar with these texts as well.

We hope that you find this book to be useful, and welcome questions and comments.

Scott Pitta

President

David Price

Vice President

Introduction

The FAA has developed regulations to allow the operation of small unmanned aircraft systems (sUAS) in the National Airspace System (NAS) for purposes other than hobby and recreation. These rules are specified in 14 CFR part 107 and address sUAS classification, certification, and operating rules.

This text is designed for pilots and non-pilots alike who wish to obtain a part 107 remote pilot certificate with an sUAS rating. References to "part 61 pilot certificate holders" specifically refer to holders of pilot certificates other than student pilot certificates. Part 61 pilot certificates include sport pilot, recreational pilot, private pilot, commercial pilot and air transport pilot certificates.

Text Content and Objectives

When you complete this text, you will be able to identify:

- Requirements to obtain a part 107 remote pilot certificate with a small unmanned aircraft system (sUAS) rating
- Characteristics of small unmanned aircraft systems (sUAS) as stipulated in part 107
- Exclusions from the requirements in part 107
- Requirements for sUAS registration, markings, and condition
- Possible supporting crew roles in sUAS operations
- Best practices for crew management
- Recommended maintenance procedures for sUAS
- Inspection requirements to verify that the sUAS is in condition for safe operation
- Restrictions and procedures for safe loading of sUAS
- Procedures for evaluating performance during UAS operations
- Effects of weather on sUAS operations
- Operational requirements and limitations for sUAS
- Procedures for requesting a waiver for eligible requirements in part 107
- Abnormal and emergencies situations that may arise during sUAS operations
- Requirements for reporting accidents resulting from sUAS operations

Chapter 1
Definitions & Acronyms
Abbreviations and Acronyms

AC – Advisory Circular

AGL – Above Ground Level

ACR – Airman Certification Representative

ARC – Aviation Rulemaking Committee

ATC – Air Traffic Control

CAFTA-DR – Dominican Republic-Central America-United States Free Trade Agreement

CAR – Civil Air Regulation

CFI – Certified Flight Instructor

CFR – Code of Federal Regulations

COA – Certificate of Waiver or Authorization

DPE – Designated Pilot Examiner

FR – Federal Register

FSDO – Flight Standards District Office

ICAO – International Civil Aviation Organization

NAFTA – North American Free Trade Agreement

NAS – National Airspace System

NOTAM – Notice to Airmen

NPRM – Notice of Proposed Rulemaking

NTSB – National Transportation Safety Board

PIC – Pilot in Command

Pub. L. – Public Law

PMA – Parts Manufacturer Approval

TFR – Temporary Flight Restriction

TSA – Transportation Security Administration

TSO – Technical Standard Order

UAS – Unmanned Aircraft System

U.S.C. – United States Code

Definitions

Part 107 Definitions

1. <u>Control Station</u>: an interface used by the operator to control the flight path of the small unmanned aircraft.

2. <u>Corrective Lenses</u>: spectacles or contact lenses.

3. <u>Operator and Visual Observer</u>: These positions are discussed further in section III.D.1 of this preamble.

4. <u>Small Unmanned Aircraft</u>: an unmanned aircraft weighing less than 55 pounds, including everything that is on board the aircraft. The FAA proposes to interpret the statutory definition of small unmanned aircraft as referring to total weight at the time of takeoff because heavier aircraft generally pose greater amounts of public risk in the event of an accident. In the event of a crash, a heavier aircraft can do more damage to people and property on the ground.

5. <u>Small Unmanned Aircraft System</u> (small UAS): a small unmanned aircraft and its associated elements (including communication links and the components that control the small unmanned aircraft) that are required for the safe and efficient operation of the small unmanned aircraft in the NAS.

6. <u>Unmanned Aircraft</u>: an aircraft operated without the possibility of direct human intervention from within or on the aircraft.

FAR Part 1, Sec. 1.1

General definitions.

<u>Administrator</u> means the Federal Aviation Administrator or any person to whom he has delegated his authority in the matter concerned.

<u>Air carrier</u> means a person who undertakes directly by lease, or other arrangement, to engage in air transportation.

<u>Air commerce</u> means interstate, overseas, or foreign air commerce or the transportation of mail by aircraft or any operation or navigation of aircraft within the limits of any Federal airway or any operation or navigation of aircraft which directly affects, or which may endanger safety in, interstate, overseas, or foreign air commerce.

<u>Aircraft</u> means a device that is used or intended to be used for flight in the air.

<u>Aircraft engine</u> means an engine that is used or intended to be used for propelling aircraft. It includes turbo-superchargers, appurtenances, and accessories necessary for its functioning, but does not include propellers.

Airplane means an engine-driven fixed-wing aircraft heavier than air, that is supported in flight by the dynamic reaction of the air against its wings.

Airport means an area of land or water that is used or intended to be used for the landing and takeoff of aircraft, and includes its buildings and facilities, if any.

Air traffic clearance means an authorization by air traffic control, for the purpose of preventing collision between known aircraft, for an aircraft to proceed under specified traffic conditions within controlled airspace.

Air traffic control means a service operated by appropriate authority to promote the safe, orderly, and expeditious flow of air traffic.

Air transportation means interstate, overseas, or foreign air transportation or the transportation of mail by aircraft.

Alert Area. An alert area is established to inform pilots of a specific area wherein a high volume of pilot training or an unusual type of aeronautical activity is conducted.

Approved, unless used with reference to another person, means approved by the Administrator.

Area navigation (RNAV) is a method of navigation that permits aircraft operations on any desired flight path.

Area navigation (RNAV) route is an ATS route based on RNAV that can be used by suitably equipped aircraft.

Armed Forces means the Army, Navy, Air Force, Marine Corps, and Coast Guard, including their regular and reserve components and members serving without component status.

Autorotation means a rotorcraft flight condition in which the lifting rotor is driven entirely by action of the air when the rotorcraft is in motion.

Auxiliary rotor means a rotor that serves either to counteract the effect of the main rotor torque on a rotorcraft or to maneuver the rotorcraft about one or more of its three principal axes.

Category:

(1) As used with respect to the certification, ratings, privileges, and limitations of airmen, means a broad classification of aircraft. Examples include: airplane; rotorcraft; glider; and lighter-than-air; and

(2) As used with respect to the certification of aircraft, means a grouping of aircraft based upon intended use or operating limitations. Examples include: transport, normal, utility, acrobatic, limited, restricted, and provisional.

Category A, with respect to transport category rotorcraft, means multiengine rotorcraft designed with engine and system isolation features specified in Part 29 and utilizing scheduled takeoff and landing operations under a critical engine failure concept which assures adequate designated surface area and adequate performance capability for continued safe flight in the event of engine failure.

Category B, with respect to transport category rotorcraft, means single-engine or multiengine rotorcraft which do not fully meet all Category A standards. Category B rotorcraft have no guaranteed stay-up ability in the event of engine failure and unscheduled landing is assumed.

Ceiling means the height above the earth's surface of the lowest layer of clouds or obscuring phenomena that is reported as "broken", "overcast", or "obscuration", and not classified as "thin" or "partial"

Civil aircraft means aircraft other than public aircraft.

Class:

(1) As used with respect to the certification, ratings, privileges, and limitations of airmen, means a classification of aircraft within a category having similar operating characteristics. Examples include: single engine; multiengine; land; water; gyroplane; helicopter; airship; and free balloon; and

(2) As used with respect to the certification of aircraft, means a broad grouping of aircraft having similar characteristics of propulsion, flight, or landing. Examples include: airplane; rotorcraft; glider; balloon; landplane; and seaplane.

Commercial operator means a person who, for compensation or hire, engages in the carriage by aircraft in air commerce of persons or property, other than as an air carrier or foreign air carrier or under the authority of Part 375 of this title. Where it is doubtful that an operation is for "compensation or hire", the test applied is whether the carriage by air is merely incidental to the person's other business or is, in itself, a major enterprise for profit.

Controlled airspace means an airspace of defined dimensions within which air traffic control service is provided to IFR flights and to VFR flights in accordance with the airspace classification.

Note--Controlled airspace is a generic term that covers Class A, Class B, Class C, Class D, and Class E airspace.

Controlled Firing Area. A controlled firing area is established to contain activities, which if not conducted in a controlled environment, would be hazardous to nonparticipating aircraft.

Crewmember means a person assigned to perform duty in an aircraft during flight time.

Extended over-water operation means--

(1) With respect to aircraft other than helicopters, an operation over water at a horizontal distance of more than 50 nautical miles from the nearest shoreline; and

(2) With respect to helicopters, an operation over water at a horizontal distance of more than 50 nautical miles from the nearest shoreline and more than 50 nautical miles from an off-shore heliport structure.

External load means a load that is carried, or extends, outside of the aircraft fuselage.

External-load attaching means the structural components used to attach an external load to an aircraft, including external-load containers, the backup structure at the attachment points, and any quick-release device used to jettison the external load.

Flightcrew member means a pilot, flight engineer, or flight navigator assigned to duty in an aircraft during flight time.

Flight level means a level of constant atmospheric pressure related to a reference datum of 29.92 inches of mercury. Each is stated in three digits that represent hundreds of feet. For example, flight level 250 represents a barometric altimeter indication of 25,000 feet; flight level 255, an indication of 25,500 feet.

Flight plan means specified information, relating to the intended flight of an aircraft, that is filed orally or in writing with air traffic control.

Flight time means:

(1) Pilot time that commences when an aircraft moves under its own power for the purpose of flight and ends when the aircraft comes to rest after landing; or

(2) For a glider without self-launch capability, pilot time that commences when the glider is towed for the purpose of flight and ends when the glider comes to rest after landing.

Flight visibility means the average forward horizontal distance, from the cockpit of an aircraft in flight, at which prominent unlighted objects may be seen and identified by day and prominent lighted objects may be seen and identified by night.

Ground visibility means prevailing horizontal visibility near the earth's surface as reported by the United States National Weather Service or an accredited observer.

Helicopter means a rotorcraft that, for its horizontal motion, depends principally on its engine-driven rotors.

Heliport means an area of land, water, or structure used or intended to be used for the landing and takeoff of helicopters.

IFR conditions means weather conditions below the minimum for flight under visual flight rules.

Indicated airspeed means the speed of an aircraft as shown on its pitot static airspeed indicator calibrated to reflect standard atmosphere adiabatic compressible flow at sea level uncorrected for airspeed system errors.

Load factor means the ratio of a specified load to the total weight of the aircraft. The specified load is expressed in terms of any of the following: aerodynamic forces, inertia forces, or ground or water reactions.

Main rotor means the rotor that supplies the principal lift to a rotorcraft.

Maintenance means inspection, overhaul, repair, preservation, and the replacement of parts, but excludes preventive maintenance.

Major alteration means an alteration not listed in the aircraft, aircraft engine, or propeller specifications--

(1) That might appreciably affect weight, balance, structural strength, performance, powerplant operation, flight characteristics, or other qualities affecting airworthiness; or

(2) That is not done according to accepted practices or cannot be done by elementary operations.

Major repair means a repair:

(1) That, if improperly done, might appreciably affect weight, balance, structural strength, performance, powerplant operation, flight characteristics, or other qualities affecting airworthiness; or

(2) That is not done according to accepted practices or cannot be done by elementary operations.

Medical certificate means acceptable evidence of physical fitness on a form prescribed by the Administrator.

Military operations area. A military operations area (MOA) is airspace established outside Class A airspace to separate or segregate certain nonhazardous military activities from IFR Traffic and to identify for VFR traffic where these activities are conducted.

Minor alteration means an alteration other than a major alteration.

Minor repair means a repair other than a major repair.

Navigable airspace means airspace at and above the minimum flight altitudes prescribed by or under this chapter, including airspace needed for safe takeoff and landing.

Night means the time between the end of evening civil twilight and the beginning of morning civil twilight, as published in the American Air Almanac, converted to local time. Morning civil twilight begins when the geometric center of the sun is 6° below the horizon. Evening civil twilight begins at sunset or when the geometric center of the sun is 0°50' below the horizon, and ends when the geometric center of the sun reaches 6° below the horizon. 33-48 minutes depending on time of year.

Operate, with respect to aircraft, means use, cause to use or authorize to use aircraft, for the purpose (except as provided in Sec. 91.13 of this chapter) of air navigation including the piloting of aircraft, with or without the right of legal control (as owner, lessee, or otherwise).

Operational control, with respect to a flight, means the exercise of authority over initiating, conducting or terminating a flight.

Person means an individual, firm, partnership, corporation, company, association, joint-stock association, or governmental entity. It includes a trustee, receiver, assignee, or similar representative of any of them.

Pilotage means navigation by visual reference to landmarks.

Pilot in command means the person who:

(1) Has final authority and responsibility for the operation and safety of the flight;

(2) Has been designated as pilot in command before or during the flight; and

(3) Holds the appropriate category, class, and type rating, if appropriate, for the conduct of the flight.

Positive control means control of all air traffic, within designated airspace, by air traffic control.

Powered-lift means a heavier-than-air aircraft capable of vertical takeoff, vertical landing, and low speed flight that depends principally on engine-driven lift devices or engine thrust for lift during these flight regimes and on nonrotating airfoil(s) for lift during horizontal flight.

Preventive maintenance means simple or minor preservation operations and the replacement of small standard parts not involving complex assembly operations.

Prohibited area. A prohibited area is airspace designated under part 73 within which no person may operate an aircraft without the permission of the using agency.

Public aircraft means any of the following aircraft when not being used for a commercial purpose or to carry an individual other than a crewmember or qualified non-crewmenber:

(1) An aircraft used only for the United States Government; an aircraft owned by the Government and operated by any person for purposes related to crew training, equipment development, or demonstration; an aircraft owned and operated by the government of a State, the District of Columbia, or a territory or possession of the United States or a political subdivision of one of these governments; or an aircraft exclusively leased for at least 90 continuous days by the government of a State, the District of Columbia, or a territory or possession of the United States or a political subdivision of one of these governments.

(i) For the sole purpose of determining public aircraft status, commercial purposes means the transportation of persons or property for compensation or hire, but does not include the operation of an aircraft by the armed forces for reimbursement when that reimbursement is required by any Federal statute, regulation, or directive, in effect on November 1, 1999, or by one government on behalf of another government under a cost reimbursement agreement if the government on whose behalf the operation is conducted certifies to the Administrator of the Federal Aviation Administration that the operation is necessary to respond to a significant and imminent threat to life or property (including natural resources) and that no service by a private operator is reasonably available to meet the threat.

(ii) For the sole purpose of determining public aircraft status, governmental function means an activity undertaken by a government, such as national defense, intelligence missions, firefighting, search and rescue, law enforcement (including transport of prisoners, detainees, and illegal aliens), aeronautical research, or biological or geological resource management.

(iii) For the sole purpose of determining public aircraft status, qualified non-crewmember means an individual, other than a member of the crew, aboard an aircraft operated by the armed forces or an intelligence agency of the United States Government, or whose presence is required to perform, or is associated with the performance of, a governmental function.

(2) An aircraft owned or operated by the armed forces or chartered to provide transportation to the armed forces if--

(i) The aircraft is operated in accordance with title 10 of the United States Code;

(ii) The aircraft is operated in the performance of a governmental function under title 14, 31, 32, or 50 of the United States Code and the aircraft is not used for commercial purposes; or

(iii) The aircraft is chartered to provide transportation to the armed forces and the Secretary of Defense (or the Secretary of the department in which the Coast Guard is operating) designates the operation of the aircraft as being required in the national interest.

(3) An aircraft owned or operated by the National Guard of a State, the District of Columbia, or any territory or possession of the United States, and that meets the criteria of paragraph (2) of this definition, qualifies as a public aircraft only to the extent that it is operated under the direct control of the Department of Defense.

Rating means a statement that, as a part of a certificate, sets forth special conditions, privileges, or limitations.

Reporting point means a geographical location in relation to which the position of an aircraft is reported.

Restricted area. A restricted area is airspace designated under Part 73 within which the flight of aircraft, while not wholly prohibited, is subject to restriction.

Rotorcraft means a heavier-than-air aircraft that depends principally for its support in flight on the lift generated by one or more rotors.

Rotorcraft-load combination means the combination of a rotorcraft and an external-load, including the external-load attaching means. Rotorcraft-load combinations are designated as Class A, Class B, Class C, and Class D, as follows:

(1) Class A rotorcraft-load combination means one in which the external load cannot move freely, cannot be jettisoned, and does not extend below the landing gear.

(2) Class B rotorcraft-load combination means one in which the external load is jettisonable and is lifted free of land or water during the rotorcraft operation.

(3) Class C rotorcraft-load combination means one in which the external load is jettisonable and remains in contact with land or water during the rotorcraft operation.

(4) Class D rotorcraft-load combination means one in which the external-load is other than a Class A, B, or C and has been specifically approved by the Administrator for that operation.

Second in command means a pilot who is designated to be second in command of an aircraft during flight time.

Show, unless the context otherwise requires, means to show to the satisfaction of the Administrator.

Special VFR conditions mean meteorological conditions that are less than those required for basic VFR flight in controlled airspace and in which some aircraft are permitted fight under visual flight rules.

Special VFR operations means aircraft operating in accordance with clearances within controlled airspace in meteorological conditions less than the basic VFR weather minima. Such operations must be requested by the pilot and approved by ATC.

Standard atmosphere means the atmosphere defined in U.S. Standard Atmosphere, 1962 (Geopotential altitude tables).

Synthetic vision means a computer-generated image of the external scene topography from the perspective of the flight deck that is derived from aircraft attitude, high-precision navigation solution, and database of terrain, obstacles and relevant cultural features.

Synthetic vision system means an electronic means to display a synthetic vision image of the external scene topography to the flight crew.

Traffic pattern means the traffic flow that is prescribed for aircraft landing at, taxiing on, or taking off from, an airport.

United States, in a geographical sense, means (1) the States, the District of Columbia, Puerto Rico, and the possessions, including the territorial waters, and (2) the airspace of those areas.

United States air carrier means a citizen of the United States who undertakes directly by lease, or other arrangement, to engage in air transportation.

Warning area. A warning area is airspace of defined dimensions, extending from 3 nautical miles outward from the coast of the United States, that contains activity that may be hazardous to nonparticipating aircraft. The purpose of such warning areas is to warn nonparticipating pilots of the potential danger. A warning area may be located over domestic or international waters or both.

Chapter 2
Aviation Safety

The Four Tenets of Safety

1. Safety First

Before any flight occurs using your drone, safety must be ensured. This means understanding in advance the geographic location where you will be flying, the characteristics of the aircraft that you will be controlling, and the flight environment (block of air) where the operation will be conducted. Not only is it critical to understand how the weather effects your drone, but you must also understand if you are flying in an airspace that is too close to an airport or other airspace that is a part of the National Airspace System (NAS).

The FAA has developed a safety checklist that you, as a pilot, should use whenever you send a drone into the sky. The FAA wants you to fly safe, fly smart – and have fun.

☐ Fly no higher than the limits of your Certificate of Waiver or Authorization (COA) or 400 feet for recreational flights.

☐ Keep your sUAS in eyesight at all times, and use an observer to assist if needed.

☐ Remain well clear of and do not interfere with manned aircraft operations, and you must see and avoid other aircraft and obstacles at all times.

☐ Do not intentionally fly over unprotected persons or moving vehicles, and remain at least 25 feet away from individuals and vulnerable property.

☐ Contact the airport or control tower before flying within five miles of an airport.

☐ Fly no closer than two nautical miles from a heliport with a published instrument flight procedure.

☐ Do not fly in adverse weather conditions such as in high winds or reduced visibility.

☐ Do not fly under the influence of alcohol or drugs.

☐ Ensure the operating environment is safe and that the operator is competent and proficient in the operation of the sUAS.

☐ Do not fly near or over sensitive infrastructure or property such as power stations, water treatment facilities, correctional facilities, heavily traveled roadways, government facilities, etc. unless you are specifically hired by the facility owner to do so.

☐ Check and follow all local laws and ordinances before flying over private property.

☐ Do not conduct surveillance or photograph persons in areas where there is an expectation of privacy without the individual's permission.

2. Use Good Judgement

Using good judgement can never be emphasized enough. Too often when flying a drone for commercial purposes there is the pressure to complete a mission or project in order to get paid. In manned aircraft this is sometimes referred to as "get home-itis", when the pilot feels pressure to complete a flight into known adverse weather conditions, is flying into an unknown airport, or is piloting an aircraft that is unfamiliar or of questionable reliability.

Get Home-itis is also a very real danger for drone operators. In New England and other northern climates, cold weather alone can dramatically reduce a drone battery life and if the operator is not aware of this problem, and drone could stop working mid-mission and land in an area that is not desirable.

3.   Do Not Harm

The Tenet "Do Not Harm" is one that is both physical and emotion in nature. On the physical side the pilot/operator must be aware that a mid-size drone with four motors is operating each propeller at about 10,000 rpms per motor. If these spinning blades come in contact with another person irreparable harm can occur. Not only is the blame squarely on the operator, but even if insured as all good commercial drone operator ought to be, sometimes insurance will only cover physical damage to property and not physical damage done to another person.

There is another type of harm that occurs when the operator uses their drone for activities that are not ethical or moral in nature. Too often there are stories of drone pilots flying their small UAV's over other people for "spying" types of missions. Either looking over a neighbors' fence or into a window, and even in some cases employers have used drone to spy on their own workers. In the case where a drone operator looks into another person's property without their permission, a violation of privacy laws may occur. One would expect that in today's courts, the violator would receive maximum penalties for breaking these laws since personal privacy is one of the most protected facets of our society.

As a basic rule, a drone operator should never fly over any property without the owner's permission and should never conduct flight over people without their knowledge AND permission.

4.   Open Airspace

For recreational users of sUAV's, flying in open airspace means conducting your flight in an area that is free of risks, and away from people. It means flying over land that the operator either has direct permission to fly over, or in an area that is open to the public, but not congested.

Because the drone industry is so young, and because there are already those in opposition to their recreational use, all drone pilots must act of ambassadors for this field. One suggestion I often tell students is that when they are flying, and there is someone nearby, simply stop flying, walk over to them, and let them know what you are doing. Even asking them if they'd like to get an up close look does wonders for folks that once thought of drone as a dangerous nuisance. Often, it converts them into supporters of this new field.

Aeronautical Decision Making

Introduction

Aeronautical decision-making (ADM) is decision-making in a unique environment—aviation. It is a systematic approach to the mental process used by pilots to consistently determine the best course of action in response to a given set of circumstances. It is what a pilot intends to do based on the latest information he or she has.

ADM is a systematic approach to risk assessment and stress management. To understand ADM is to also understand how personal attitudes can influence decision-making and how those attitudes can be modified to enhance safety in the flight deck. It is important to understand the factors that cause humans to make decisions and how the decision-making process not only works, but can be improved.

This chapter focuses on helping the pilot improve his or her ADM skills with the goal of mitigating the risk factors associated with flight. Advisory Circular (AC) 60-22, Aeronautical Decision-Making, provides background references, definitions, and other pertinent information about ADM training in the general aviation (GA) environment.

Hazard and Risk

Two defining elements of ADM are hazard and risk. Hazard is a real or perceived condition, event, or circumstance that a pilot encounters. When faced with a hazard, the pilot makes an assessment of that hazard based upon various factors. The pilot assigns a value to the potential impact of the hazard, which qualifies the pilot's assessment of the hazard—risk.

Therefore, risk is an assessment of the single or cumulative hazard facing a pilot; however, different pilots see hazards differently. For example, the pilot arrives to preflight and discovers a small, blunt type nick in the leading edge at the middle of the aircraft's prop. Since the aircraft is parked on the tarmac, the nick was probably caused by another aircraft's prop wash blowing some type of debris into the propeller. The nick is the hazard (a present condition). The risk is prop fracture if the engine is operated with damage to a prop blade.

The seasoned pilot may see the nick as a low risk. He realizes this type of nick diffuses stress over a large area, is located in the strongest portion of the propeller, and based on

experience, he doesn't expect it to propagate a crack which can lead to high risk problems. He does not cancel his flight. The inexperienced pilot may see the nick as a high risk factor because he is unsure of the affect the nick will have on the prop's operation and he has been told that damage to a prop could cause a catastrophic failure. This assessment leads him to cancel his flight.

Therefore, elements or factors affecting individuals are different and profoundly impact decision-making. These are called human factors and can transcend education, experience, health, physiological aspects, etc.

Another example of risk assessment was the flight of a Beechcraft King Air equipped with deicing and anti-icing. The pilot deliberately flew into moderate to severe icing conditions while ducking under cloud cover. A prudent pilot would assess the risk as high and beyond the capabilities of the aircraft, yet this pilot did the opposite. Why did the pilot take this action? Past experience prompted the action. The pilot had successfully flown into these conditions repeatedly although the icing conditions were previously forecast 2,000 feet above the surface. This time, the conditions were forecast from the surface. Since the pilot was in a hurry and failed to factor in the difference between the forecast altitudes, he assigned a low risk to the hazard and took a chance. He and the passengers died from a poor risk assessment of the situation.

Recognizing Hazardous Attitudes

Studies have identified five hazardous attitudes that can interfere with the ability to make sound decisions and properly exercise authority: anti-authority, impulsivity, invulnerability, machoism, and resignation. Each attitude is described in more detail below

Remote PICs should be alert for hazardous attitudes (in themselves or in other crewmembers), label it as hazardous, and correct the behavior.

Hazardous Attitudes and Antidotes

Being fit to fly depends on more than just a pilot's physical condition and recent experience. For example, attitude will affect the quality of

The Five Hazardous Attitudes

Anti-Authority: "Don't tell me."

This attitude is found in people who do not like anyone telling them what to do. In a sense, they are saying, "No one can tell me what to do." They may be resentful of someone telling them what to do, or may regard rules, regulations and procedures as silly or unnecessary. However, it is always your prerogative to question authority if you feel it is in error.

Impulsivity: "Do it now!"

This is the attitude of people who frequently feel the need to do something, anything, immediately. They do not stop to think about what they are about to do; they do not select the best alternative, and they do the first thing that comes to mind.

Invulnerability: "It won't happen to me."

Many people falsely believe that accidents happen to others, but never to them. They know accidents can happen, and they know that anyone can be affected. However, they never really feel or believe that they will be personally involved. Pilots who think this war are more likely to take chances and increase risk.

Macho: "I can do it."

Pilots who are always trying to prove that they are better than anyone else think, "I can do it, I'll show them." Pilots with this type of attitude will try to prove themselves by taking risks in order to impress others. While this pattern is thought to be a male characteristic, women are equally susceptible.

Resignation: "What's the use?"

Pilots who think, "What's the use?" do not see themselves as being able to make a great deal of difference in what happens to them. When things go well, the pilot is apt to think that it is good luck. When things go badly, the pilot may feel that someone is out to get them, or attribute it to bad luck. The pilot will leave the action to others, for better or worse. Sometimes, such pilots will

Figure 2-1 *The five hazardous attitudes identified through past and contemporary study.*

decisions. Attitude is a motivational predisposition to respond to people, situations, or events in a given manner. Studies have identified five hazardous attitudes that can interfere with the ability to make sound decisions and exercise authority properly: anti-authority, impulsivity, invulnerability, macho, and resignation. [Figure 2-1]

Hazardous attitudes contribute to poor pilot judgment but can be effectively counteracted by redirecting the hazardous attitude so that correct action can be taken. Recognition of hazardous thoughts is the first step toward neutralizing them. After recognizing a thought as hazardous, the pilot should label it as hazardous, then state the corresponding antidote. Antidotes should be memorized for each of the hazardous attitudes so they automatically come to mind when needed.

Risk

During each flight, the single pilot makes many decisions under hazardous conditions. To fly safely, the pilot needs to assess the degree of risk and determine the best course of action to mitigate risk.

Assessing Risk

For the single pilot, assessing risk is not as simple as it sounds. For example, the pilot acts as his or her own quality control in making decisions. If a fatigued pilot who has flown 16 hours is asked if he or she is too tired to continue flying, the answer may be no. Most pilots are goal oriented and when asked to accept a flight, there is a tendency to deny personal limitations while adding weight to issues not germane to the mission. For example, pilots of helicopter emergency services (EMS) have been known (more than other groups) to

make flight decisions that add significant weight to the patient's welfare. These pilots add weight to intangible factors (the patient in this case) and fail to appropriately quantify actual hazards such as fatigue or weather when making flight decisions. The single pilot who has no other crew member for consultation must wrestle with the intangible factors that draw one into a hazardous position. Therefore, he or she has a greater vulnerability than a full crew.

Examining National Transportation Safety Board (NTSB) reports and other accident research can help a pilot learn to assess risk more effectively. For example, the accident rate during night VFR decreases by nearly 50 percent once a pilot obtains 100 hours, and continues to decrease until the 1,000 hour level. The data suggest that for the first 500 hours, pilots flying VFR at night might want to establish higher personal limitations than are required by the regulations and, if applicable, apply instrument flying skills in this environment.

Several risk assessment models are available to assist in the process of assessing risk. The models, all taking slightly different approaches, seek a common goal of assessing risk in an objective manner. Two are illustrated below.

The most basic tool is the risk matrix. [Figure 2-2] It assesses two items: the likelihood of an event occurring and the consequence of that event.

Likelihood of an Event

Likelihood is nothing more than taking a situation and determining the probability of its occurrence. It is rated as probable, occasional, remote, or improbable. For example, a pilot is flying from point A to point B (50 miles) in marginal visual flight rules (MVFR) conditions. The likelihood of encountering potential instrument meteorological conditions (IMC) is

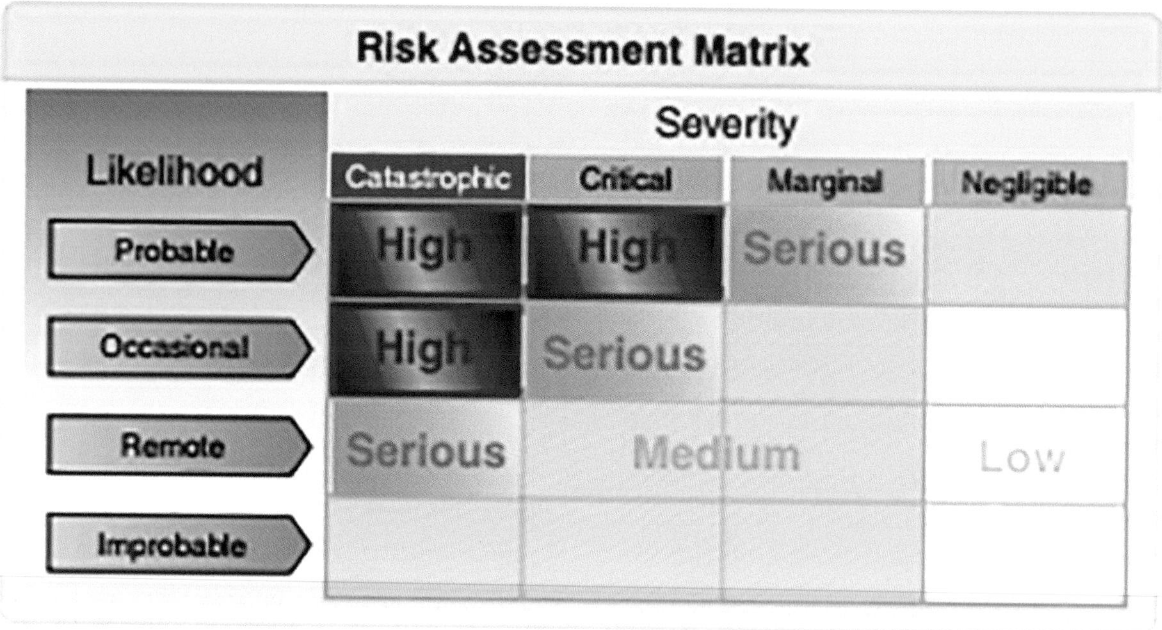

Risk Assessment Matrix

Likelihood	Severity			
	Catastrophic	Critical	Marginal	Negligible
Probable	High	High	Serious	
Occasional	High	Serious		
Remote	Serious	Medium		Low
Improbable				

Figure 2-2 *This risk matrix can be used for almost any operation by assigning likelihood and consequence. In the case presented, the pilot assigned a likelihood of occasional and the severity as catastrophic. As one can see, this falls in the high risk area.*

the first question the pilot needs to answer. The experiences of other pilots coupled with the forecast, might cause the pilot to assign "occasional" to determine the probability of encountering IMC.

The following are guidelines for making assignments.

• Probable—an event will occur several times.

• Occasional—an event will probably occur sometime.

• Remote—an event is unlikely to occur, but is possible.

• Improbable—an event is highly unlikely to occur.

Severity of an Event

The next element is the severity or consequence of a pilot's action(s). It can relate to injury and/or damage. If the individual in the example above is not an instrument flight rules (IFR) pilot, what are the consequences of him or her encountering inadvertent IMC conditions? In this case, because the pilot is not IFR rated, the consequences are catastrophic. The following are guidelines for this assignment.

• Catastrophic—results in fatalities, total loss

• Critical—severe injury, major damage

• Marginal—minor injury, minor damage

• Negligible—less than minor injury, less than minor system damage

Simply connecting the two factors as shown in Figure 2-2 indicates the risk is high and the pilot must either not fly, or fly only after finding ways to mitigate, eliminate, or control the risk.

Although the matrix in Figure 2-2 provides a general viewpoint of a generic situation, a more comprehensive program can be made that is tailored to a pilot's flying. [Figure 2-3] This program includes a wide array of aviation related activities specific to the pilot and assesses health, fatigue, weather, capabilities, etc. The scores are added and the overall score falls into various ranges, with the range

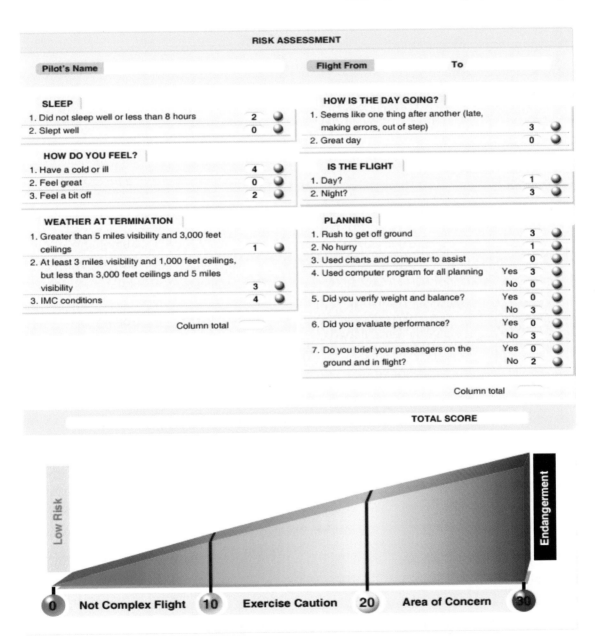

Figure 2-3 *Example of a more comprehensive risk assessment program.*

representative of actions that a pilot imposes upon himself or herself.

Mitigating Risk

Risk assessment is only part of the equation. After determining the level of risk, the pilot needs to mitigate the risk. For example, the pilot flying from point A to point B (50 miles) in MVFR conditions has several ways to reduce risk:

• Wait for the weather to improve to good visual flight rules (VFR) conditions.

• Take a pilot who is certified as an IFR pilot.

• Delay the flight.

• Cancel the flight.

• Drive.

One of the best ways single pilots can mitigate risk is to use the **IMSAFE checklist** to determine physical and mental readiness for flying:

1. Illness / Injury—Am I sick? Illness is an obvious pilot risk. Do I have an injury that limits my ability to fly an aircraft?

2. Medication—Am I taking any medicines that might affect my judgment or make me drowsy?

3. Stress—Am I under psychological pressure from the job? Do I have money, health, or family problems? Stress causes concentration and performance problems. While the regulations list medical conditions that require grounding, stress is not among them. The pilot should consider the effects of stress on performance.

4. Alcohol—Have I been drinking within 8 hours? Within 24 hours? As little as one ounce of liquor, one bottle of beer, or four ounces of wine can impair flying skills. Alcohol also renders a pilot more susceptible to disorientation and hypoxia.

5. Fatigue—Am I tired and not adequately rested? Fatigue continues to be one of the most insidious hazards to flight safety, as it may not be apparent to a pilot until serious errors are made.

6. Eating—Have I eaten enough of the proper foods to keep adequately nourished during the entire flight?

The PAVE Checklist

Another way to mitigate risk is to perceive hazards. By incorporating the PAVE checklist into preflight planning, the pilot divides the risks of flight into four categories: Pilotin-command (PIC), Aircraft, enVironment, and External pressures (PAVE) which form part of a pilot's decision making process.

With the PAVE checklist, pilots have a simple way to remember each category to examine for risk prior to each flight. Once a pilot identifies the risks of a flight, he or she needs to decide whether the risk or combination of risks can be managed safely and successfully. If not, make the decision to cancel the flight. If the pilot decides to continue with the flight, he or she should develop strategies to mitigate the risks. One way a pilot can control the risks is to set personal minimums for items in each risk category. These are limits unique to that individual pilot's current level of experience and proficiency.

For example, the aircraft may have a maximum crosswind component of 15 knots listed in the aircraft flight manual (AFM), and the pilot has experience with 10 knots of direct crosswind. It could be unsafe to exceed a 10 knots crosswind component without additional training. Therefore, the 10 kts crosswind experience level is that pilot's personal limitation until additional training with a certificated flight instructor (CFI) provides the pilot with additional experience for flying in crosswinds that exceed 10 knots.

One of the most important concepts that safe pilots understand is the difference between what is "legal" in terms of the regulations, and what is "smart" or "safe" in terms of pilot experience and proficiency.

P = Pilot in Command (PIC)

The pilot is one of the risk factors in a flight. The pilot must ask, "Am I ready for this trip?" in terms of experience, recency, currency, physical and emotional condition. The IMSAFE checklist provides the answers.

A = Aircraft

What limitations will the aircraft impose upon the trip? Ask the following questions:

• Is this the right aircraft for the flight?

• Am I familiar with and current in this aircraft? Aircraft performance figures and the AFM are based on a brand new aircraft flown by a professional test pilot. Keep that in mind while assessing personal and aircraft performance.

• Is this aircraft equipped for the flight? Instruments? Lights? Navigation and communication equipment adequate?

• Can this aircraft use the runways available for the trip with an adequate margin of safety under the conditions to be flown?

• Can this aircraft carry the planned load?

• Can this aircraft operate at the altitudes needed for the trip?

• Does this aircraft have sufficient fuel capacity, with reserves, for trip legs planned?

• Does the fuel quantity delivered match the fuel quantity ordered?

V = EnVironment

Weather

Weather is a major environmental consideration. Earlier it was suggested pilots set their own personal minimums, especially when it comes to weather. As pilots evaluate the weather for a particular flight, they should consider the following:

• What are the current ceiling and visibility? In mountainous terrain, consider having higher minimums for ceiling and visibility, particularly if the terrain is unfamiliar.

• Consider the possibility that the weather may be different than forecast. Have alternative plans and be ready and willing to divert, should an unexpected change occur.

• Consider the winds at the airports being used and the strength of the crosswind component.

• If flying in mountainous terrain, consider whether there are strong winds aloft. Strong winds in mountainous terrain can cause severe turbulence and downdrafts and be very hazardous for aircraft even when there is no other significant weather.

• Are there any thunderstorms present or forecast?

• If there are clouds, is there any icing, current or forecast? What is the temperature/dew point spread and the current temperature at altitude? Can descent be made safely all along the route?

• If icing conditions are encountered, is the pilot experienced at operating the aircraft's deicing or anti-icing equipment? Is this equipment in good condition and functional? For what icing conditions is the aircraft rated, if any?

Terrain

Evaluation of terrain is another important component of analyzing the flight environment.

• To avoid terrain and obstacles, especially at night or in low visibility, determine safe altitudes in advance by using the altitudes shown on VFR and IFR charts during preflight planning.

• Use maximum elevation figures (MEFs) and other easily obtainable data to minimize chances of an inflight collision with terrain or obstacles.

Airport

• What lights are available at the destination and alternate airports? VASI/PAPI or ILS glideslope guidance? Is the terminal airport equipped with them? Are they working? Will the pilot need to use the radio to activate the airport lights?

• Check the Notices to Airmen (NOTAMS) for closed runways or airports. Look for runway or beacon lights out, nearby towers, etc.

• Choose the flight route wisely. An engine failure gives the nearby airports supreme importance.

• Are there shorter or obstructed fields at the destination and/or alternate airports?

Airspace

• If the trip is over remote areas, are appropriate clothing, water, and survival gear onboard in the event of a forced landing?

• If the trip includes flying over water or unpopulated areas with the chance of losing visual reference to the horizon, the pilot must be prepared to fly IFR.

• Check the airspace and any temporary flight restriction (TFRs) along the route of flight.

E = External Pressures

External pressures are influences external to the flight that create a sense of pressure to complete a flight—often at the expense of safety. Factors that can be external pressures include the following:

• Someone waiting for the drone to get in the air.

• A customer the pilot does not want to disappoint.

• The desire to demonstrate pilot qualifications.

• The desire to impress someone. (Probably the two most dangerous words in aviation are "Watch this!")

• The desire to satisfy a specific personal goal ("get-home-itis," "get-there-itis," and "let's-go-itis").

• The pilot's general goal-completion orientation.

• Emotional pressure associated with acknowledging that skill and experience levels may be lower than a pilot would like them to be. Pride can be a powerful external factor!

Managing External Pressures

Management of external pressure is the single most important key to risk management because it is the one risk factor category that can cause a pilot to ignore all the other risk factors. External pressures put time-related pressure on the pilot and figure into a majority of accidents.

The use of personal standard operating procedures (SOPs) is one way to manage external pressures. The goal is to supply a

Pilot

A pilot must continually make decisions about competency, condition of health, mental and emotional state, level of fatigue, and many other variables. For example, a pilot may be called early in the morning to make a long flight. If a pilot has had only a few hours of sleep and is concerned that the congestion being experienced could be the onset of a cold, it would be prudent to consider if the flight could be accomplished safely.

A pilot had only 4 hours of sleep the night before being asked by the boss to fly to a meeting in a city 750 miles away. The reported weather was marginal and not expected to improve. After assessing fitness as a pilot, it was decided that it would not be wise to make the flight. The boss was initially unhappy, but later convinced by the pilot that the risks involved were unacceptable.

Environment

This encompasses many elements not pilot or airplane related. It can include such factors as weather, air traffic control, navigational aids (NAVAIDS), terrain, takeoff and landing areas, and surrounding obstacles. Weather is one element that can change drastically over time and distance.

A pilot was landing a small airplane just after a heavy jet had departed a parallel runway. The pilot assumed that wake turbulence would not be a problem since landings had been performed under similar circumstances. Due to a combination of prevailing winds and wake turbulence from the heavy jet drifting across the landing runway, the airplane made a hard landing. The pilot made an error when assessing the flight environment.

Aircraft

A pilot will frequently base decisions on the evaluations of the airplane, such as performance, equipment, or airworthiness.

During a preflight, a pilot noticed a small amount of oil dripping from the bottom of the cowling. Although the quantity of oil seemed insignificant at the time, the pilot decided to delay the takeoff and have a mechanic check the source of the oil. The pilot's good judgment was confirmed when the mechanic found that one of the oil cooler hose fittings was loose.

External Pressures

The interaction between the pilot, airplane, and the environment is greatly influenced by the purpose of each flight operation. The pilot must evaluate the three previous areas to decide on the desirability of undertaking or continuing the flight as planned. It is worth asking why the flight is being made, how critical is it to maintain the schedule, and is the trip worth the risks?

On a ferry flight to deliver an airplane from the factory, in marginal weather conditions, the pilot calculated the groundspeed and determined that the airplane would arrive at the destination with only 10 minutes of fuel remaining. The pilot was determined to keep on schedule by trying to "stretch" the fuel supply instead of landing to refuel. After landing with low fuel state, the pilot realized that this could have easily resulted in an emergency landing in deteriorating weather conditions. This was a chance that was not worth taking to keep the planned schedule.

Figure 2-4. *The PAVE checklist.*

release for the external pressures of a flight. These procedures include but are not limited to:

• Allow time on a trip for an extra fuel stop or to make an unexpected landing because of weather.

• Have alternate plans for a late arrival or make backup airline reservations for must-be-there trips.

• For really important trips, plan to leave early enough so that there would still be time to drive to the destination.

• Advise those who are waiting at the destination that the arrival may be delayed. Know how to notify them when delays are encountered.

• Manage passengers' expectations. Make sure passengers know that they might not arrive on

a firm schedule, and if they must arrive by a certain time, they should make alternative plans.

• Eliminate pressure to return home, even on a casual day flight, by carrying a small overnight kit containing prescriptions, contact lens solutions, toiletries, or other necessities on every flight.

The key to managing external pressure is to be ready for and accept delays. Remember that people get delayed when traveling on airlines, driving a car, or taking a bus. The pilot's goal is to manage risk, not create hazards. [Figure 2-4]

Human Behavior

Studies of human behavior have tried to determine an individual's predisposition to taking risks and the level of an individual's involvement in accidents. In 1951, a study regarding injury-prone children was published by Elizabeth Mechem Fuller and Helen B. Baune, of the University of Minnesota. The study was comprised of two separate groups of second grade students. Fifty-five students were considered accident repeaters and 48 students had no accidents. Both groups were from the same school of 600 and their family demographics were similar.

The accident-free group showed a superior knowledge of safety, were considered industrious and cooperative with others, but were not considered physically inclined. The accident-repeater group had better gymnastic skills, were considered aggressive and impulsive, demonstrated rebellious behavior when under stress, were poor losers, and liked to be the center of attention. One interpretation of this data—an adult predisposition to injury stems from childhood behavior and environment—leads to the conclusion that any pilot group should be comprised only of pilots who are safety-conscious, industrious, and cooperative.

Clearly, this is not only an inaccurate inference, it is impossible. Pilots are drawn from the general population and exhibit all types of personality traits. Thus, it is important that good decision-making skills be taught to all pilots.

Historically, the term "pilot error" has been used to describe an accident in which an action or decision made by the pilot was the cause or a contributing factor that led to the accident. This definition also includes the pilot's failure to make a correct decision or take proper action. From a broader perspective, the phrase "human factors related" more aptly describes these accidents. A single decision or event does not lead to an accident, but a series of events and the resultant decisions together form a chain of events leading to an outcome.

In his article "Accident-Prone Pilots," Dr. Patrick R. Veillette uses the history of "Captain Everyman" to demonstrate how aircraft accidents are caused more by a chain of poor choices rather than one single poor choice. In the case of Captain Everyman, after a gear-up landing accident, he became involved in another accident while taxiing a Beech 58P Baron out of the ramp. Interrupted by a radio call from the 17-11 dispatcher, Everyman neglected to complete the fuel crossfeed check before taking off. Everyman, who was flying solo, left the right-fuel selector in the cross-feed position. Once aloft and cruising, he noticed a right roll tendency and corrected with aileron trim. He did not realize that both engines were feeding off the left wing's tank, making the wing lighter.

After two hours of flight, the right engine quit when Everyman was flying along a deep canyon gorge. While he was trying to troubleshoot the cause of the right engine's failure, the left engine quit. Everyman landed the aircraft on a river sand bar but it sank into ten feet of water.

Several years later Everyman flew a de Havilland Twin Otter to deliver supplies to a remote location. When he returned to home base and landed, the aircraft veered sharply to the left, departed the runway, and ran into a marsh 375 feet from the runway. The airframe and engines sustained considerable damage. Upon inspecting the wreck, accident investigators found the nose wheel steering tiller in the fully deflected position. Both the after takeoff and before landing checklists required the tiller to be placed in the neutral position. Everyman had overlooked this item.

Now, is Everyman accident prone or just unlucky? Skipping details on a checklist appears to be a common theme in the preceding accidents. While most pilots have made similar mistakes, these errors were probably caught prior to a mishap due to extra margin, good warning systems, a sharp copilot, or just good luck. What makes a pilot less prone to accidents?

The successful pilot possesses the ability to concentrate, manage workloads, monitor and perform several simultaneous tasks. Some of the latest psychological screenings used in aviation test applicants for their ability to multitask, measuring both accuracy, as well as the individual's ability to focus attention on several subjects simultaneously. The FAA oversaw an extensive research study on the similarities and dissimilarities of accident-free pilots and those who were not. The project surveyed over 4,000 pilots, half of whom had "clean" records while the other half had been involved in an accident.

Five traits were discovered in pilots prone to having accidents. These pilots:

• Have disdain toward rules.

• Have very high correlation between accidents on their flying records and safety violations on their driving records.

• Frequently fall into the "thrill and adventure seeking" personality category.

• Are impulsive rather than methodical and disciplined, both in their information gathering and in the speed and selection of actions to be taken.

• A disregard for or underutilization of outside sources of information, including copilots, flight attendants, flight service personnel, flight instructors, and air traffic controllers.

The Decision-Making Process

An understanding of the decision-making process provides the pilot with a foundation for developing ADM and SRM skills. While some

situations, such as engine failure, require an immediate pilot response using established procedures, there is usually time during a flight to analyze any changes that occur, gather information, and assess risk before reaching a decision.

Risk management and risk intervention is much more than the simple definitions of the terms might suggest. Risk management and risk intervention are decision-making processes designed to systematically identify hazards, assess the degree of risk, and determine the best course of action. These processes involve the identification of hazards, followed by assessments of the risks, analysis of the controls, making control decisions, using the controls, and monitoring the results.

The DECIDE Model

Using the acronym "DECIDE," the six-step process DECIDE Model is another continuous loop process that provides the pilot with a logical way of making decisions. [Figure **2-5**] DECIDE means to Detect, Estimate, Choose a course of action, Identify solutions, Do the necessary actions, and Evaluate the effects of the actions.

First, consider a recent accident involving a Piper Apache (PA- 23). The aircraft was substantially damaged during impact with terrain at a local airport in Alabama. The certificated airline transport pilot (ATP) received minor injuries and the certificated private pilot was not injured. The private pilot was receiving a checkride from the ATP (who was also a designated examiner) for a commercial pilot certificate with a multi-engine rating. After performing air work at altitude, they returned to the airport and the private pilot performed a single-engine approach to a full stop landing. He then taxied back for takeoff, performed a short field takeoff, and then joined the traffic pattern to return for another landing. During the approach for the second landing, the ATP simulated a right engine failure by reducing power on the right engine to zero thrust. This caused the aircraft to yaw right.

The procedure to identify the failed engine is a two-step process. First, bring power to maximum controllable on both engines. Because the left engine is the only engine delivering thrust, the yaw increases to the right, which necessitates application of additional left rudder application. The failed engine is the side that requires no rudder pressure, in this case the right engine. Second, having identified the failed right engine, the procedure is to feather the right engine and adjust power to maintain descent angle to a landing.

However, in this case the pilot feathered the left engine because he assumed the engine failure was a left engine failure. During twin-engine training, the left engine out is emphasized more than the right engine because the left engine on most light twins is the critical engine. This is due to multiengine airplanes being subject to P-factor, as are single engine airplanes. The descending propeller blade of each engine will produce greater thrust than the ascending blade when the airplane is operated under power and at positive angles of attack. The descending propeller blade of the right engine is also a greater distance from the center of gravity, and therefore has a longer moment arm than the descending propeller blade of the left engine. As a result, failure of the left engine will result in the most asymmetrical thrust (adverse yaw) because the right engine will be providing the remaining thrust. Many twins are designed with a counter-rotating right engine. With this design, the degree of asymmetrical thrust is the same with either engine inoperative. Neither engine is more critical than the other.

Since the pilot never executed the first step of identifying which engine failed, he feathered the left engine and set the right engine at zero thrust. This essentially restricted the aircraft to a controlled glide. Upon realizing that he was not going to make the runway, the pilot increased power to both engines causing an enormous yaw to the left (the left propeller was feathered) whereupon the aircraft started to turn left. In desperation, the instructor closed both throttles and the aircraft hit the ground and was substantially damaged.

This case is interesting because it highlights two particular issues. First, taking action without forethought can be just as dangerous as taking no action at all. In this case, the pilot's actions were incorrect; yet, there was sufficient time to take the necessary steps to analyze the simulated emergency. The second and subtler issue is that decisions made under pressure are sometimes executed based upon limited experience and the actions taken may be incorrect, incomplete, or insufficient to handle the situation.

Detect (the Problem)

Problem detection is the first step in the decision-making process. It begins with recognizing a change occurred or an expected change did not occur. A problem is perceived first by the senses and then it is distinguished through insight and experience. These same abilities, as well as an objective analysis of all available information, are used to determine the nature and severity of the problem. One critical error made during the decision-making process is incorrectly detecting the problem. In the example above, the change that occurred was a yaw.

Estimate (the Need To React)

In the engine-out example, the aircraft yawed right, the pilot was on final approach, and the problem warranted a prompt solution. In many cases, overreaction and fixation excludes a safe outcome. For example, what if the cabin door of a Mooney suddenly opened in flight while the aircraft climbed through 1,500 feet on a clear sunny day? The sudden opening would be alarming, but the perceived hazard the open door presents is quickly and effectively assessed as minor. In fact, the door's opening would not impact safe flight and can almost be

disregarded. Most likely, a pilot would return to the airport to secure the door after landing.

The pilot flying on a clear day faced with this minor problem may rank the open cabin door as a low risk. What about the pilot on an IFR climb out in IMC conditions with light intermittent turbulence in rain who is receiving

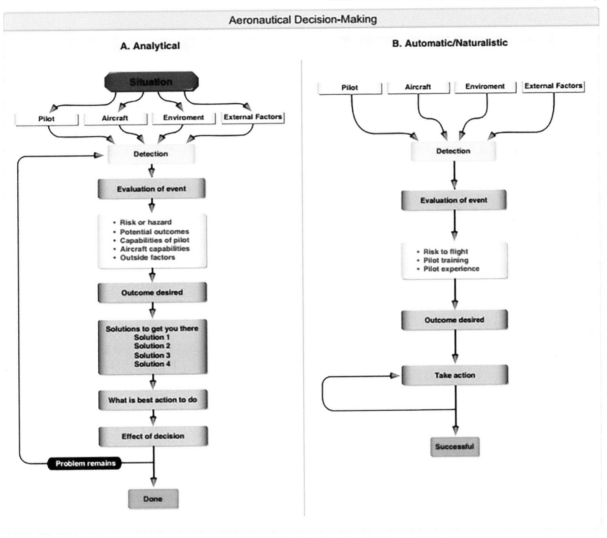

The DECIDE Model

1. **Detect.** The decision maker detects the fact that change has occurred.
2. **Estimate.** The decision maker estimates the need to counter or react to the change.
3. **Choose.** The decision maker chooses a desirable outcome (in terms of success) for the flight.
4 **Identify.** The decision maker identifies actions which could successfully control the change.
5. **Do.** The decision maker takes the necessary action.
6. **Evaluate.** The decision maker evaluates the effect(s) of his/her action countering the change.

Figure 2-5. The DECIDE model has been recognized worldwide. Its application is illustrated in A while automatic/naturalistic decision-making is shown in B.

an amended clearance from air traffic control (ATC)? The open cabin door now becomes a higher risk factor. The problem has not changed, but the perception of risk a pilot assigns it changes because of the multitude of ongoing tasks and the environment. Experience, discipline, awareness, and knowledge will influence how a pilot ranks a problem.

Choose (a Course of Action)

After the problem has been identified and its impact estimated, the pilot must determine the desirable outcome and choose a course of action. In the case of the multiengine pilot given the simulated failed engine, the desired objective is to safely land the airplane.

Identify (Solutions)

The pilot formulates a plan that will take him or her to the objective. Sometimes, there may be only one course of action available. In the case of the engine failure, already at 500 feet or below, the pilot solves the problem by identifying one or more solutions that lead to a successful outcome. It is important for the pilot not to become fixated on the process to the exclusion of making a decision.

Do (the Necessary Actions)

Once pathways to resolution are identified, the pilot selects the most suitable one for the situation. The multiengine pilot given the simulated failed engine must now safely land the aircraft.

Evaluate (the Effect of the Action)

Finally, after implementing a solution, evaluate the decision to see if it was correct. If the action taken does not provide the desired results, the process may have to be repeated.

Situational Awareness

Situational awareness is the accurate perception and understanding of all the factors and conditions within the five fundamental risk elements (flight, pilot, aircraft, environment, and type of operation that comprise any given aviation situation) that affect safety before, during, and after the flight. Monitoring radio communications for traffic, weather discussion, and ATC communication can enhance situational awareness by helping the pilot develop a mental picture of what is happening.

Maintaining situational awareness requires an understanding of the relative significance of all flight related factors and their future impact on the flight. When a pilot understands what is going on and has an overview of the total operation, he or she is not fixated on one perceived significant factor. Not only is it important for a pilot to know the aircraft's geographical location, it is also important he or she understand what is happening. For instance, while flying above Richmond, Virginia, toward Dulles Airport or Leesburg, the pilot should know why he or she is being vectored and be able to anticipate spatial location. A pilot who is simply making turns without understanding why has added an additional burden to his or her management in the event of an emergency. To maintain situational awareness, all of the skills involved in ADM are used.

Situational Awareness and Decision Making

The Remote PIC attains situational awareness by obtaining as much information as possible prior to a flight and becoming familiar with the performance capabilities of the sUAS, weather conditions, surrounding airspace, and Air Traffic Control (ATC) requirements. Sources of information include a weather briefing, ATC, FAA, local pilots, and landowners. Technology, such as global positioning systems (GPS), mapping systems, and computer applications, can assist in collecting and managing information to improve your situational awareness and risk-based aeronautical decision making (ADM).

Obstacles to Maintaining Situational Awareness

Fatigue, stress, and work overload can cause a pilot to fixate on a single perceived important item and reduce an overall situational awareness of the flight. A contributing factor in many accidents is a distraction that diverts the pilot's attention from monitoring the instruments or scanning outside the aircraft. Many flight deck distractions begin as a minor problem, such as a gauge that is not reading correctly, but result in accidents as the pilot diverts attention to the perceived problem and neglects to properly control the aircraft.

Workload Management

Effective workload management ensures essential operations are accomplished by planning, prioritizing, and sequencing tasks to avoid work overload. As experience is gained, a pilot learns to recognize future workload requirements and can prepare for high workload periods during times of low workload. Reviewing the appropriate chart and setting radio frequencies well in advance of when they are needed helps reduce workload as the flight nears the airport. In addition, a pilot should listen to ATIS, Automated Surface Observing System (ASOS), or Automated Weather Observing System (AWOS), if available, and then monitor the tower frequency or Common Traffic Advisory Frequency (CTAF) to get a good idea of what traffic conditions to expect. Checklists should be performed well in advance so there is time to focus on traffic and ATC instructions. These procedures are especially important prior to entering a high density traffic area, such as Class B airspace.

Recognizing a work overload situation is also an important component of managing workload.

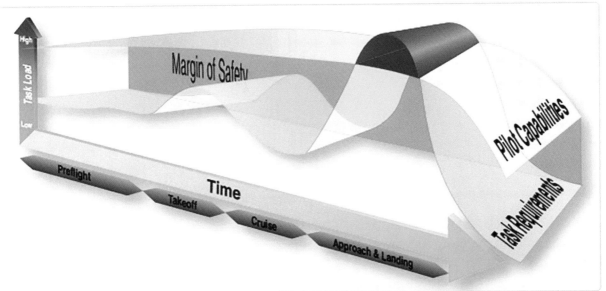

Figure 2-6. *The pilot has a certain capacity of doing work and handling tasks. However, there is a point where the tasking exceeds the pilot's capability. When this happens, tasks are either not done properly or some are not done at all.*

The first effect of high workload is that the pilot may be working harder but accomplishing less. As workload increases, attention cannot be devoted to several tasks at one time, and the pilot may begin to focus on one item. When a pilot becomes task saturated, there is no awareness of input from various sources, so decisions may be made on incomplete information and the possibility of error increases. [Figure 2-6]

When a work overload situation exists, a pilot needs to stop, think, slow down, and prioritize. It is important to understand how to decrease workload. For example, in the case of the cabin door that opened in VFR flight, the impact on workload should be insignificant. If the cabin door opens under IFR different conditions, its impact on workload will change. Therefore, placing a situation in the proper perspective, remaining calm, and thinking rationally are key elements in reducing stress and increasing the capacity to fly safely. This ability depends upon experience, discipline, and training.

Managing Risks: The ability to manage risk begins with preparation. Here are some things a pilot can do to manage overall risk:

• Assess the flight's risk based upon experience. Use some form of risk assessment. For example, if the weather is marginal and the pilot has low IMC training, it is probably a good idea to cancel the flight

• In addition to the SAFETY list, discuss with passengers whether or not smoking is permitted, flight route altitudes, time en route, destination, weather during flight, expected weather at the destination, controls and what they do, and the general capabilities and limitations of the aircraft.

• Use a sterile flight deck (one that is completely silent with no pilot communication with passengers or by passengers) from the

time of departure to the first intermediate altitude and clearance from the local airspace.

• Use a sterile flight deck during arrival from the first radar vector for approach or descent for the approach.

• Keep the passengers informed during times when the workload is low.

• Consider using the passenger in the right seat for simple tasks such as holding the chart. This relieves the pilot of a task.

Crew Resource Management

Crew resource management (CRM) is the effective use of all available resources—human, hardware, and information—prior to and during flight to ensure a successful outcome of the operation. The Remote PIC must integrate crew resource management techniques into all phases of the sUAS operation.

Many of the crew resource management techniques traditionally used in manned aircraft operations are also applicable for sUAS, such as the ability to:

- Delegate operational tasks and manage crewmembers

- Recognize and address hazardous attitudes

- Establish effective team communication procedures

Task Management

The Remote PIC identifies, delegates, and manages tasks for each sUAS operation.

Tasks can vary greatly depending on the complexity of the sUAS operation. Supporting crewmembers can help accomplish those tasks and ensure the safety of flight. For example, visual observers and other ground crew can provide valuable information about traffic, airspace, weather, equipment, and aircraft loading and performance.

The Remote PIC:

- Assesses the operating environment (airspace, surrounding terrain, weather, hazards, etc.)

- Determines the appropriate number of crewmembers that are needed to safely conduct a given operation. The Remote PIC must ensure sufficient crew support so that no one on the team becomes over-tasked, which increases the possibility of an incident or accident.

- Informs participants of delegated tasks and sets expectations

- Manages and supervises the crew to ensure that everyone completes their assigned tasks

Effective Communication

The FAA requires that the Remote PIC and other crewmembers coordinate to:

- Scan the airspace in the operational area for any potential collision hazard; and

- Maintain awareness of the position of the sUAS through direct visual observation.

To achieve this goal, the Remote PIC should:

- Foster an environment where open communication is encouraged and expected between the entire crew to maximize team performance

- Establish effective communication procedures prior to flight

- Select an appropriate method of communication, such as the use of hand-held radio or other effective means that would not create a distraction and allows all crewmembers to understand each other

- Inform the crew as conditions change about any needed adjustments to ensure a safe outcome of the operation

Chapter Summary

This chapter focused on helping the pilot improve his or her ADM skills with the goal of mitigating the risk factors associated with flight in both classic and automated aircraft. In the end, the discussion is not so much about aircraft, but about the people who fly them.

Chapter 3 Aerodynamics

Aerodynamics of Flight

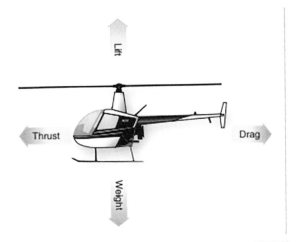

Figure 3-1. *Four forces acting on a helicopter in forward flight.*

Once a helicopter leaves the ground, it is acted upon by four aerodynamic forces; thrust, drag, lift and weight. Understanding how these forces work and knowing how to control them with the use of power and flight controls are essential to flight. [Figure 3-1] They are defined as follows:

Thrust—the forward force produced by the power plant/propeller or rotor. It opposes or overcomes the force of drag. As a general rule, it acts parallel to the longitudinal axis. However, this is not always the case, as explained later.

Drag—a rearward, retarding force caused by disruption of airflow by the wing, rotor, fuselage, and other protruding objects. Drag opposes thrust and acts rearward parallel to the relative wind.

Weight—the combined load of the aircraft itself, the crew, the fuel, and the cargo or baggage. Weight pulls the aircraft downward because of the force of gravity. It opposes lift and acts vertically downward through the aircraft's center of gravity (CG).

Lift—opposes the downward force of weight, is produced by the dynamic effect of the air acting on the airfoil, and acts perpendicular to the flightpath through the center of lift.

Lift

Lift is generated when an object changes the direction of flow of a fluid or when the fluid is forced to move by the object passing through it. When the object and fluid move relative to each other and the object turns the fluid flow in a direction perpendicular to that flow, the force required to do this work creates an equal and opposite force that is lift. The object may be moving through a stationary fluid, or the fluid may be flowing past a stationary object—these two are effectively identical as, in principle, it is only the frame of reference of the viewer which differs. The lift generated by an airfoil depends on such factors as:

• Speed of the airflow

• Density of the air

• Total area of the segment or airfoil

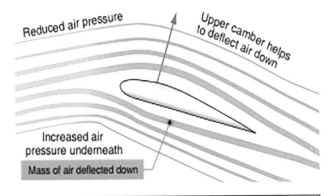

Figure 3-2. *Production of Lift*

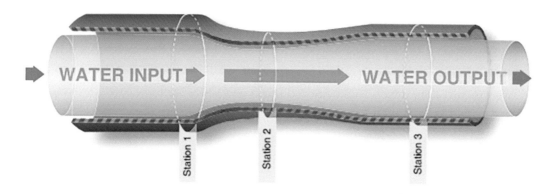

Figure 3-3. *Constant flow rate*

• Angle of attack (AOA) between the air and the airfoil

The AOA is the angle at which the airfoil meets the oncoming airflow (or vice versa). In the case of a helicopter, the object is the rotor blade (airfoil) and the fluid is the air. Lift is produced when a mass of air is deflected, and it always acts perpendicular to the resultant relative wind. A symmetric airfoil must have a positive AOA to generate positive lift. At a zero AOA, no lift is generated. At a negative AOA, negative lift is generated. A cambered or nonsymmetrical airfoil may produce positive lift at zero, or even small negative AOA.

The basic concept of lift is simple. However, the details of how the relative movement of air and airfoil interact to produce the turning action that generates lift are complex. In any case causing lift, an angled flat plate, revolving cylinder, airfoil, etc., the flow meeting the leading edge of the object is forced to split over and under the object. The sudden change in direction over the object causes an area of low pressure to form behind the leading edge on the upper surface of the object. In turn, due to this pressure gradient and the viscosity of the fluid, the flow over the object is accelerated down along the upper surface of the object. At

the same time, the flow forced under the object is rapidly slowed or stagnated causing an area of high pressure. This also causes the flow to accelerate along the upper surface of the object. The two sections of the fluid each leave the trailing edge of the object with a downward component of momentum, producing lift. [Figure 3-2]

Bernoulli's Principle

Bernoulli's principle describes the relationship between internal fluid pressure and fluid velocity. It is a statement of the law of conservation of energy and helps explain why an airfoil develops an aerodynamic force. The concept of conservation of energy states energy cannot be created or destroyed and the amount of energy entering a system must also exit. A simple tube with a constricted portion near the center of its length illustrates this principle. An example is running water through a garden hose. The mass of flow per unit area (cross-sectional area of tube) is the mass flow rate. In Figure 3-3, the flow into the tube is constant, neither accelerating nor decelerating; thus, the mass flow rate through the tube must be the same at stations 1, 2, and 3. If the cross sectional area at any one of these stations—or

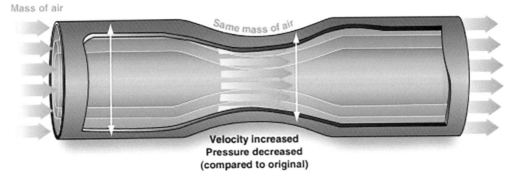

Cross-section of cylinder

Mass of air

Same mass of air

Velocity increased
Pressure decreased
(compared to original)

Figure 3-4. *Bernoulli's Principle*

any given point—in the tube is reduced, the fluid velocity must increase to maintain a constant mass flow rate to move the same amount of fluid through a smaller area. Fluid speeds up in direct proportion to the reduction in area. Venturi effect is the term used to describe this phenomenon. *Figure 3-4* illustrates what happens to mass flow rate in the constricted tube as the dimensions of the tube change.

Venturi Flow

While the amount of total energy within a closed system (the tube) does not change, the form of the energy may be altered. Pressure of flowing air may be compared to energy in that the total pressure of flowing air always remains constant unless energy is added or removed.

Fluid flow pressure has two components—static and dynamic pressure. Static pressure is the pressure component measured in the flow but not moving with the flow as pressure is measured. Static pressure is also known as the force per unit area acting on a surface. Dynamic pressure of flow is that component existing as a result of movement of the air. The sum of these two pressures is total pressure. As air flows through the constriction, static pressure decreases as velocity increases. This increases dynamic pressure. Figure 3-5 depicts the bottom half of the constricted area of the tube, which resembles the top half of an airfoil. Even with the top half of the tube removed, the air still accelerates over the curved area because the upper air layers restrict the flow—just as the top half of the constricted tube did. This acceleration causes decreased static pressure

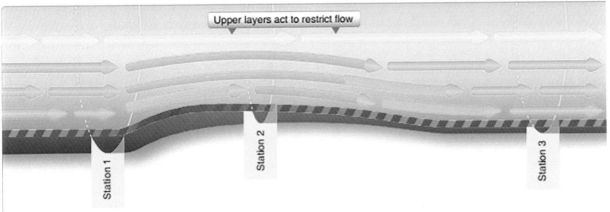

Upper layers act to restrict flow

Station 1

Station 2

Station 3

Figure 3-5. *Venturi Flow*

above the curved portion and creates a pressure differential caused by the variation of static and dynamic pressures.

Newton's Third Law of Motion

Additional lift is provided by the rotor blade's lower surface as air striking the underside is deflected downward. According to Newton's Third Law of Motion, "for every action there is an equal and opposite reaction," the air that is deflected downward also produces an upward (lifting) reaction.

Since air is much like water, the explanation for this source of lift may be compared to the planing effect of skis on water. The lift that supports the water skis (and the skier) is the force caused by the impact pressure and the deflection of water from the lower surfaces of the skis.

Under most flying conditions, the impact pressure and the deflection of air from the lower surface of the rotor blade provides a comparatively small percentage of the total lift. The majority of lift is the result of decreased pressure above the blade, rather than the increased pressure below it.

Weight

Normally, weight is thought of as being a known, fixed value, such as the weight of the helicopter, fuel, and occupants. To lift the helicopter off the ground vertically, the rotor system must generate enough lift to overcome or offset the total weight of the helicopter and its occupants. Newton's First Law states: "Every object in a state of uniform motion tends to remain in that state of motion unless an external force is applied to it." In this case, the object is the helicopter whether at a hover or on the ground and the external force applied to it is lift, which is accomplished by increasing the pitch angle of the main rotor blades. This action

forces the helicopter into a state of motion, without it the helicopter would either remain on the ground or at a hover.

The weight of the helicopter can also be influenced by aerodynamic loads. When you bank a helicopter while maintaining a constant altitude, the "G" load or load factor increases. The load factor is the actual load on the rotor blades at any time, divided by the normal load or gross weight (weight of the helicopter and its contents). Any time a helicopter flies in a constant altitude curved flightpath, the load supported by the rotor blades is greater than the total weight of the helicopter. The tighter the curved flightpath is, the steeper the bank is; the more rapid the flare or pullout from a dive is, the greater the load supported by the rotor. Therefore, the greater the load factor must be. [Figure 3-6]

To overcome this additional load factor, the helicopter must be able to produce more lift. If excess engine power is not available, the helicopter either descends or has to decelerate in order to maintain the same altitude. The load factor and, hence, apparent gross weight increase is relatively small in banks up to 30°. Even so, under the right set of adverse circumstances, such as high density altitude, turbulent air, high gross weight, and poor pilot

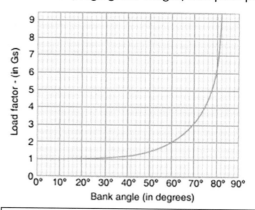

Figure 3-6. *The load factor diagram allows a pilot to calculate the amount of "G" loading exerted with various angles of bank.*

technique, sufficient or excess power may not be available to maintain altitude and airspeed. Pilots must take all of these factors into consideration throughout the entire flight from the point of ascending to a hover to landing.

Above 30° of bank, the apparent increase in gross weight soars. At 30° of bank, or pitch, the apparent increase is only 16 percent, but at 60°, it is twice the load on the wings and rotor system. For example, if the weight of the helicopter is 1,600 pounds, the weight supported by the rotor disk in a 30° bank at a constant altitude would be 1,856 pounds (1,600 + 16 percent (or 256)). In a 60° bank, it would be 3,200 pounds; in an 80° bank, it would be almost six times as much, or 8,000 pounds. It is important to note that each rotor blade must support a percentage of the gross weight. In a two bladed system, each blade of the 1,600 pound helicopter as stated above would have to lift 50 percent or 800 pounds. If this same helicopter had three rotor blades, each blade would have to lift only 33 percent, or 533 pounds. One additional cause of large load factors is rough or turbulent air. The severe vertical gusts produced by turbulence can cause a sudden increase in AOA, resulting in increased rotor blade loads that are resisted by the inertia of the helicopter.

Each type of helicopter has its own limitations which are based on the aircraft structure, size, and capabilities. Regardless of how much weight one can carry or the engine power that it may have, they are all susceptible to aerodynamic overloading. Unfortunately, if the pilot attempts to push the performance envelope the consequence can be fatal. Aerodynamic forces effect every movement in a helicopter, whether it is increasing the collective or a steep bank angle. Anticipating results from a particular maneuver or adjustment of a flight control is not good piloting technique. Instead pilots need to truly understand the capabilities of the helicopter under any and all circumstances and plan to never exceed the flight envelope for any situation.

Thrust

Thrust, like lift, is generated by the rotation of the main rotor system. In a helicopter, thrust can be forward, rearward, sideward, or vertical. The resultant lift and thrust determines the direction of movement of the helicopter.

The solidity ratio is the ratio of the total rotor blade area, which is the combined area of all the main rotor blades, to the total rotor disk area. This ratio provides a means to measure the potential for a rotor system to provide thrust and lift. The mathematical calculations needed to calculate the solidity ratio for each helicopter may not be of importance to most pilots but what should be are the capabilities of the rotor system to produce and maintain lift. Many helicopter accidents are caused from the rotor system being overloaded. Simply put, pilots attempt maneuvers that require more lift than the rotor system can produce or more power than the helicopter's powerplant can provide. Trying to land with a nose high attitude along with any other unfavorable condition (i.e., high gross weight or wind gusts) is most likely to end in disaster.

The tail rotor also produces thrust. The amount of thrust is variable through the use of the antitorque pedals and is used to control the helicopter's yaw.

Drag

The force that resists the movement of a helicopter through the air and is produced when lift is developed is called drag. Drag must be overcome by the engine to turn the rotor. Drag always acts parallel to the relative wind.

Total drag is composed of three types of drag: profile, induced, and parasite.

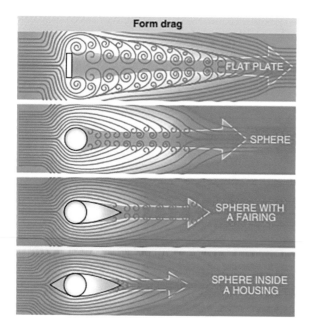

Figure 3-7 *It is easy to visualize the creation of form drag by examining the airflow around a flat plate. Streamlining decreases form drag by reducing the airflow separation.*

Profile Drag

Profile drag develops from the frictional resistance of the blades passing through the air. It does not change significantly with the airfoil's AOA, but increases moderately when airspeed increases. Profile drag is composed of form drag and skin friction. Form drag results from the turbulent wake caused by the separation of airflow from the surface of a structure. The amount of drag is related to both the size and shape of the structure that protrudes into the relative wind. *[Figure 3-7]*

Skin friction is caused by surface roughness. Even though the surface appears smooth, it may be quite rough when viewed under a microscope. A thin layer of air clings to the rough surface and creates small eddies that contribute to drag.

Induced Drag

Induced drag is generated by the airflow circulation around the rotor blade as it creates lift. The high pressure area beneath the blade joins the low pressure area above the blade at the trailing edge and at the rotor tips. This causes a spiral, or vortex, which trails behind each blade whenever lift is being produced. These vortices deflect the airstream downward in the vicinity of the blade, creating an increase in downwash. Therefore, the blade operates in an average relative wind that is inclined downward and rearward near the blade. Because the lift produced by the blade is perpendicular to the relative wind, the lift is inclined aft by the same amount. The component of lift that is acting in a rearward direction is induced drag. [Figure 3-8]

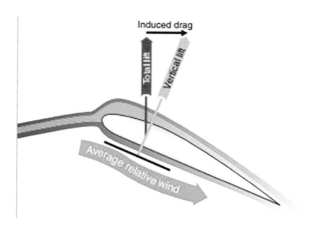

Figure 3-8 *The formation of induced drag is associated with the downward deflection of the airstream near the rotor blade.*

As the air pressure differential increases with an increase in AOA, stronger vortices form, and induced drag increases. Since the blade's AOA is usually lower at higher airspeeds, and higher at low speeds, induced drag decreases as airspeed increases and increases as airspeed decreases.

Induced drag is the major cause of drag at lower airspeeds.

Parasite Drag

Parasite drag is present any time the helicopter is moving through the air. This type of drag increases with airspeed. Non-lifting components of the helicopter, such as the cabin, rotor mast, tail, and landing gear, contribute to parasite drag. Any loss of momentum by the airstream, due to such things as openings for engine cooling, creates additional parasite drag. Because of its rapid increase with increasing airspeed, parasite drag is the major cause of drag at higher airspeeds. Parasite drag varies with the square of the velocity; therefore, doubling the airspeed increases the parasite drag four times.

Total Drag

Total drag for a helicopter is the sum of all three drag forces. [Figure 3-9] As airspeed increases, parasite drag increases, while induced drag decreases. Profile drag remains relatively constant throughout the speed range with some increase at higher airspeeds. Combining all drag forces results in a total drag curve. The low point on the total drag curve shows the airspeed at which drag is minimized. This is the point where the lift-to-drag ratio is greatest and is referred to as L/DMAX. At this speed, the total lift capacity of the helicopter, when compared to the total drag of the helicopter, is most favorable. This is an important factor in helicopter performance.

Airfoil

Helicopters are able to fly due to aerodynamic forces produced when air passes around the airfoil. An airfoil is any surface producing more lift than drag when passing through the air at a suitable angle. Airfoils are most often associated with production of lift. Airfoils are

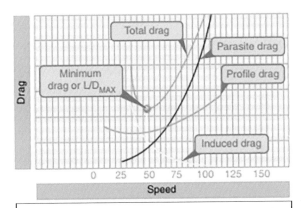

Figure 3-9 *The total drag curve represents the combined forces of parasite, profile, and induced drag and is plotted against airspeed.*

also used for stability (fin), control (elevator), and thrust or propulsion (propeller or rotor). Certain airfoils, such as rotor blades, combine some of these functions. The main and tail rotor blades of the helicopter are airfoils, and air is forced to pass around the blades by mechanically powered rotation. In some conditions, parts of the fuselage, such as the vertical and horizontal stabilizers, can become airfoils. Airfoils are carefully structured to accommodate a specific set of flight characteristics.

Airfoil Terminology and Definitions

• Blade span—the length of the rotor blade from center of rotation to tip of the blade.

• Chord line—a straight line intersecting leading and trailing edges of the airfoil. [Figure 3-10]

• Chord—the length of the chord line from leading edge to trailing edge; it is the characteristic longitudinal dimension of the airfoil section.

• Mean camber line—a line drawn halfway between the upper and lower surfaces of the airfoil. [Figure 3-10]

The chord line connects the ends of the mean camber line. Camber refers to curvature of the

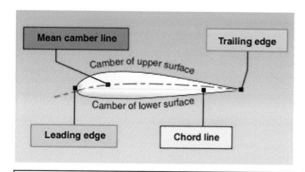

Figure 3-10 *Aerodynamic terms of an airfoil*

airfoil and may be considered curvature of the mean camber line. The shape of the mean camber is important for determining aerodynamic characteristics of an airfoil section. Maximum camber (displacement of the mean camber line from the chord line) and its location help to define the shape of the mean camber line. The location of maximum camber and its displacement from the chord line are expressed as fractions or percentages of the basic chord length. By varying the point of maximum camber, the manufacturer can tailor an airfoil for a specific purpose. The profile thickness and thickness distribution are important properties of an airfoil section.

• Leading edge—the front edge of an airfoil. [Figure 2-10]

• Flightpath velocity—the speed and direction of the airfoil passing through the air. For airfoils on an airplane, the flightpath velocity is equal to true airspeed (TAS). For helicopter rotor blades, flightpath velocity is equal to rotational velocity, plus or minus a component of directional airspeed. The rotational velocity of the rotor blade is lowest closer to the hub and increases outward towards the tip of the blade during rotation.

• Relative wind—defined as the airflow relative to an airfoil and is created by movement of an airfoil through the air. This is rotational relative wind for rotary-wing aircraft and is covered in detail later. As an induced airflow may modify

flightpath velocity, relative wind experienced by the airfoil may not be exactly opposite its direction of travel.

• Trailing edge—the rearmost edge of an airfoil.

• Induced flow—the downward flow of air through the rotor disk.

• Resultant relative wind—relative wind modified by induced flow.

• Angle of attack (AOA)—the angle measured between the resultant relative wind and chord line.

• Angle of incidence (AOI)—the angle between the chord line of a blade and rotor hub. It is usually referred to as blade pitch angle. For fixed airfoils, such as vertical fins or elevators, angle of incidence is the angle between the chord line of the airfoil and a selected reference plane of the helicopter.

• Center of pressure—the point along the chord line of an airfoil through which all aerodynamic forces are considered to act. Since pressures vary on the surface of an airfoil, an average location of pressure variation is needed. As the AOA changes, these pressures change and center of pressure moves along the chord line.

Airfoil Types

Symmetrical Airfoil

The symmetrical airfoil is distinguished by having identical upper and lower surfaces. [Figure 3-11] The mean camber line and chord line are the same on a symmetrical airfoil, and it produces no lift at zero AOA. Most light helicopters incorporate symmetrical airfoils in the main rotor blades.

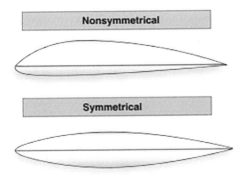

Figure 3-11 *The upper and lower curvatures are the same on a symmetrical airfoil and vary on a nonsymmetrical airfoil.*

Nonsymmetrical Airfoil (Cambered)

The nonsymmetrical airfoil has different upper and lower surfaces, with a greater curvature of the airfoil above the chord line than below. [Figure 3-11] The mean camber line and chord line are different. The nonsymmetrical airfoil design can produce useful lift at zero AOA. A nonsymmetrical design has advantages and disadvantages. The advantages are more lift production at a given AOA than a symmetrical design, an improved lift-to-drag ratio, and better stall characteristics. The disadvantages are center of pressure travel of up to 20 percent of the chord line (creating undesirable torque on the airfoil structure) and greater production costs.

Blade Twist

Because of lift differential due to differing rotational relative wind values along the blade, the blade should be designed with a twist to alleviate internal blade stress and distribute the lifting force more evenly along the blade. Blade twist provides higher pitch angles at the root where velocity is low and lower pitch angles nearer the tip where velocity is higher. This increases the induced air velocity and blade loading near the inboard section of the blade. [Figure 3-12]

Rotor Blade and Hub Definitions

• Hub—on the mast is the center point and attaching point for the root of the blade

• Tip—the farthest outboard section of the rotor blade

• Root—the inner end of the blade and is the point that attaches to the hub

• Twist—the change in blade incidence from the root to the outer blade

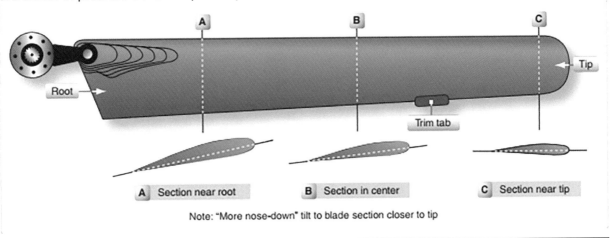

Figure 3-12 *Blade Twist*

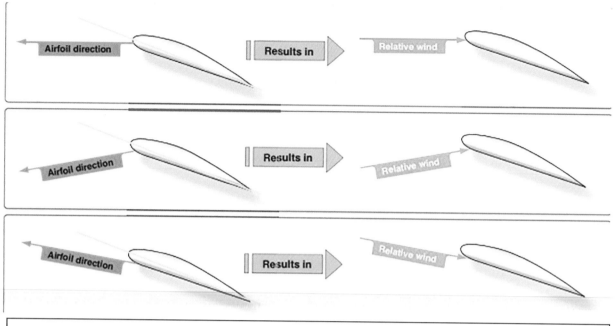

Figure 3-13 *Relative wind.*

The angular position of the main rotor blades is measured from the helicopter's longitudinal axis, which is usually the nose position and the blade. The radial position of a segment of the blade is the distance from the hub as a fraction of the total distance.

Airflow and Reactions in the Rotor System

Relative Wind

Knowledge of relative wind is essential for an understanding of aerodynamics and its practical flight application for the pilot. Relative wind is airflow relative to an airfoil. Movement of an airfoil through the air creates relative wind. Relative wind moves in a parallel but opposite direction to movement of the airfoil. [Figure 3-13]

There are two components to wind passing a rotor blade:

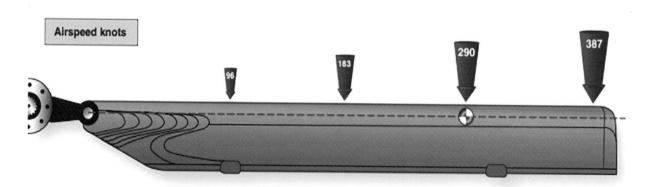

Figure 3-14 *Horizontal component of* relative wind.

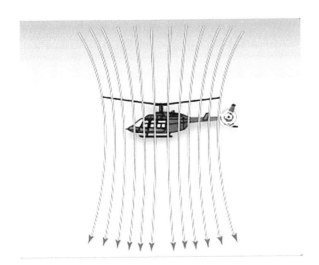

• Horizontal component—caused by the blades turning plus movement of the helicopter through the air [Figure 3-14]

• Vertical component—caused by the air being forced down through the rotor blades plus any movement of the air relative to the blades caused by the helicopter climbing or descending [Figures 3-15 and 3-16]

Induced Flow (Downwash)

At flat pitch, air leaves the trailing edge of the rotor blade in the same direction it moved across the leading edge; no lift or induced flow is being produced. As blade pitch angle is increased, the rotor system induces a downward flow of air through the rotor blades creating a downward component of air that is

Axis of rotation

Figure 3-16 *Normal induced flow velocities along the blade span during hovering flight. Downward velocity is highest at the blade tip where blade speed is highest. As blade speed decreases nearer the center of the disk, downward velocity is less.*

added to the rotational relative wind. Because the blades are moving horizontally, some of the air is displaced downward. The blades travel along the same path and pass a given point in rapid succession. Rotor blade action changes the still air to a column of descending air. Therefore, each blade has a decreased AOA due to the downwash. This downward flow of air is called induced flow (downwash). It is most pronounced at a hover under no-wind conditions. [Figure 3-19]

Rotational Relative Wind (Tip-Path Plane)

The rotation of rotor blades as they turn about the mast produces rotational relative wind (tip-path plane). The term rotational refers to the method of producing relative wind. Rotational relative wind flows opposite the physical flightpath of the airfoil, striking the blade at 90° to the leading edge and parallel to the plane of rotation; and it is constantly changing in

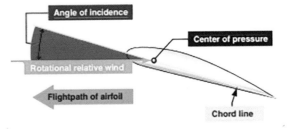

Figure 3-17 *Rotational relative wind.*

direction during rotation. Rotational relative wind velocity is highest at blade tips, decreasing uniformly to zero at the axis of rotation (center of the mast). [Figure 3-17]

Resultant Relative Wind

The resultant relative wind at a hover is rotational relative wind modified by induced flow. This is inclined downward at some angle and opposite the effective flightpath of the airfoil, rather than the physical flightpath (rotational relative wind). The resultant relative wind also serves as the reference plane for

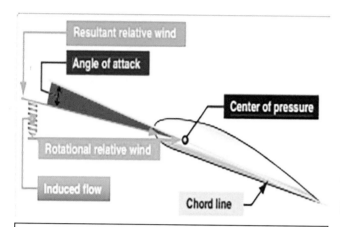

Figure 3-18 *Resultant relative wind*

development of lift, drag, and total aerodynamic force (TAF) vectors on the airfoil. [Figure 3-18] When the helicopter has horizontal motion, airspeed further modifies the resultant relative wind. The airspeed component of relative wind results from the helicopter moving through the air. This airspeed component is added to, or subtracted from, the rotational relative wind depending on whether the blade is advancing or retreating in relation to helicopter movement. Introduction of airspeed relative wind also modifies induced

flow. Generally, the downward velocity of induced flow is reduced. The pattern of air circulation through the disk changes when the aircraft has horizontal motion. As the helicopter gains airspeed, the addition of forward velocity results in decreased induced flow velocity. This change results in an improved efficiency (additional lift) being produced from a given blade pitch setting.

In Ground Effect (IGE)

Ground effect is the increased efficiency of the rotor system caused by interference of the airflow when near the ground. The air pressure or density is increased, which acts to decrease the downward velocity of air. Ground effect permits relative wind to be more horizontal, lift vector to be more vertical, and induced drag to be reduced. These conditions allow the rotor system to be more efficient. Maximum ground effect is achieved when hovering over smooth hard surfaces. When hovering over surfaces as tall grass, trees, bushes, rough terrain, and water, maximum ground effect is reduced. Rotor efficiency is increased by ground effect to

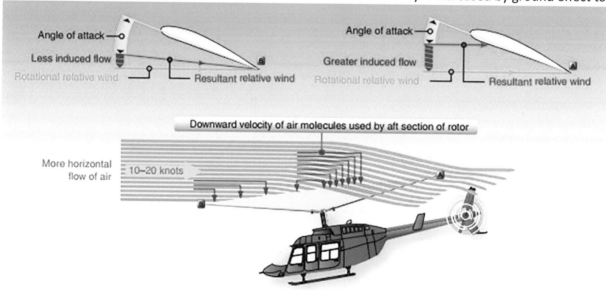

Figure 3-19 *A helicopter in forward flight, or hovering with a headwind or crosswind, has more molecules of air entering the aft portion of the rotor blade. Therefore, the angle of attack is less and the induced flow is greater at the rear of the disk.*

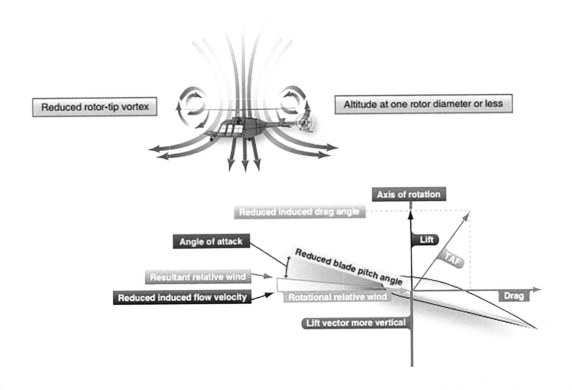

Reduced rotor-tip vortex

Altitude at one rotor diameter or less

Axis of rotation

Reduced induced drag angle

Angle of attack

Lift

Reduced blade pitch angle

TAF

Resultant relative wind

Reduced induced flow velocity

Rotational relative wind

Drag

Lift vector more vertical

Figure 3-20 *In ground effect (IGE)*

a height of about one rotor diameter (measured from the ground to the rotor disk) for most helicopters. Since the induced flow velocities are decreased, the AOA is increased, which requires a reduced blade pitch angle and a reduction in induced drag. This reduces the power required to hover IGE. [Figure 3-20]

Out of Ground Effect (OGE)

The benefit of placing the helicopter near the ground is lost above IGE altitude. Above this altitude, the power required to hover remains nearly constant, given similar conditions (such as wind). Induced flow velocity is increased, resulting in a decrease in AOA and a decrease in lift. Under the correct circumstances, this downward flow can become so localized that the helicopter and locally disturbed air will sink at alarming rates. This effect is called settling with power and is discussed at length in a later chapter. A higher blade pitch angle is required to maintain the same AOA as in IGE hover. The

increased pitch angle also creates more drag. This increased pitch angle and drag requires more power to hover OGE than IGE. [Figure 3-21]

Rotor Blade Angles

There are two angles that enable a rotor system to produce the lift required for a helicopter to fly: angle of incidence and angle of attack.

Angle of Incidence

Angle of incidence is the angle between the chord line of a main or tail rotor blade and the rotor hub. It is a mechanical angle rather than an aerodynamic angle and is sometimes referred to as blade pitch angle. [Figure 3-22] In the absence of induced flow, AOA and angle of incidence are the same. Whenever induced flow, up flow (inflow), or airspeed modifies the relative wind, the AOA is different from the angle of incidence. Collective input and cyclic

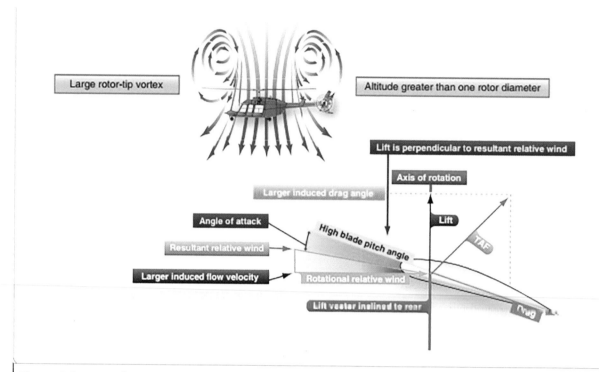

Figure 3-21 *Out of ground effect (OGE)*

feathering change the angle of incidence. A change in the angle of incidence changes the AOA, which changes the coefficient of lift, thereby changing the lift produced by the airfoil.

Angle of Attack

AOA is the angle between the airfoil chord line and resultant relative wind. [Figure 3-23] AOA is an aerodynamic angle and not easy to measure. It can change with no change in the blade pitch angle (angle of incidence, discussed earlier).

When the AOA is increased, air flowing over the airfoil is diverted over a greater distance, resulting in an increase of air velocity and more lift. As the AOA is increased further, it becomes more difficult for air to flow smoothly across the top of the airfoil. At this point, the airflow begins to separate from the airfoil and enters a burbling or turbulent pattern. The turbulence results in a large increase in drag and loss of lift in the area where it is taking place. Increasing the AOA increases lift until the critical angle of

attack is reached. Any increase in the AOA beyond this point produces a stall and a rapid decrease in lift.

Several factors may change the rotor blade AOA. The pilot has little direct control over AOA except indirectly through the flight control input. Collective and cyclic feathering help to make these changes. Feathering is the rotation of the blade about its spanwise axis by collective/cyclic inputs causing changes in blade pitch angle. Collective feathering changes angle of incidence equally and in the same direction on all rotor blades simultaneously. This action

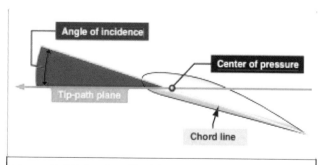

Figure 3-22 *Angle of incidence*

55

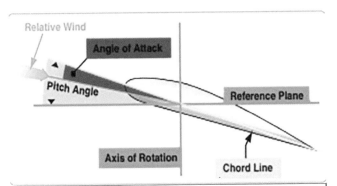

Figure 3-23 *The AOA is the angle between the airfoil chord line and resultant relative wind.*

changes AOA, which changes coefficient of lift (CL), and affects overall lift of the rotor system.

Cyclic feathering changes angle of incidence differentially around the rotor system. Cyclic feathering creates a differential lift in the rotor system by changing the AOA differentially across the rotor system. Aviators use cyclic feathering to control attitude of the rotor system. It is the means to control rearward tilt of the rotor (blowback) caused by flapping action and (along with blade flapping) counteract dissymmetry of lift. Cyclic feathering causes attitude of the rotor disk to change but does not change the amount of lift the rotor system is producing.

Most of the changes in AOA come from change in airspeed and rate of climb or descent; others such as flapping occur automatically due to rotor system design. Flapping is the up and down movement of rotor blades about a hinge on a fully articulated rotor system. The semi-rigid system does not have a hinge but flap as a unit. The rigid rotor system has no vertical or horizontal hinges so the blades cannot flap or drag, but they can flex. By flexing, the blades themselves compensate for the forces which previously required rugged hinges. It occurs in response to changes in lift due to changing velocity or cyclic feathering. No flapping occurs when the tip path plane is perpendicular to the mast. The flapping action alone, or along with

cyclic feathering, controls dissymmetry of lift. Flapping is the primary means of compensating for dissymmetry of lift.

Pilots adjust AOA through normal control manipulation of the pitch angle of the blades. If the pitch angle is increased, the AOA increases; if the pitch angle is reduced, the AOA is reduced.

Powered Flight

In powered flight (hovering, vertical, forward, sideward, or rearward), the total lift and thrust forces of a rotor are perpendicular to the tip-path plane or plane of rotation of the rotor.

Hovering Flight

Hovering is the most challenging part of flying a helicopter. This is because a helicopter generates its own gusty air while in a hover, which acts against the fuselage and flight control surfaces. The end result is constant control inputs and corrections by the pilot to keep the helicopter where it is required to be. Despite the complexity of the task, the control inputs in a hover are simple. The cyclic is used to eliminate drift in the horizontal plane, controlling forward, backward, right and left movement or travel. The throttle, if not governor controlled, is used to control revolutions per minute (rpm). The collective is used to maintain altitude. The pedals are used to control nose direction or heading. It is the interaction of these controls that makes hovering difficult, since an adjustment in any one control requires an adjustment of the other two, creating a cycle of constant correction. During hovering flight, a helicopter maintains a constant position over a selected point, usually a few feet above the ground. The ability of the helicopter to hover comes from the both the lift component, which is the force developed by the main rotor(s) to overcome gravity and aircraft weight, and the thrust component, which acts horizontally to accelerate or decelerate the helicopter in the desired direction. Pilots direct the thrust of the rotor system by using the cyclic to change the tip-path plane as compared to the visible horizon to induce travel or compensate for the wind and hold a position. At a hover in a no-wind condition, all opposing forces (lift, thrust, drag, and weight) are in balance; they are equal and opposite. Therefore, lift and weight are equal, resulting in the helicopter remaining at a stationary hover. [Figure 3-24]

While hovering, the amount of main rotor thrust can be changed to maintain the desired hovering altitude. This is done by changing the angle of incidence (by moving the collective) of the rotor blades and hence the angle of attack (AOA) of the main rotor blades. Changing the AOA changes the drag on the rotor blades, and the power delivered by the engine must change as well to keep the rotor speed constant.

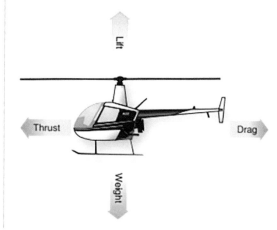

Figure 3-24 *To maintain a hover at a constant altitude, the lift must equal the weight of the helicopter. Thrust must equal any wind and tail rotor thrust to maintain position. The power must be sufficient to turn the rotors and overcome the various drags and frictions involved.*

The weight that must be supported is the total weight of the helicopter and its occupants. If the amount of lift is greater than the actual weight, the helicopter accelerates upwards until the lift force equals the weight gain altitude; if thrust is less than weight, the helicopter accelerates downward. When operating near the ground, the effects of the proximity to the surface change this response.

The drag of a hovering helicopter is mainly induced drag incurred while the blades are producing lift. There is, however, some profile drag on the blades as they rotate through the air and a small amount of parasite drag from the non-lift-producing surfaces of the helicopter, such as the rotor hub, cowlings, and landing gear. Throughout the rest of this discussion, the term "drag" includes induced, profile and parasite drag.

An important consequence of producing thrust is torque. As discussed in Chapter 2, Newton's Third Law, for every action there is an equal and opposite reaction. Therefore, as the engine turns the main rotor system in a counterclockwise direction, the helicopter fuselage wants to turn clockwise. The amount of torque is directly related to the amount of engine power being used to turn the main rotor system. Remember, as power changes, torque changes.

To counteract this torque-induced turning tendency, an antitorque rotor or tail rotor is incorporated into most helicopter designs. A pilot can vary the amount of thrust produced by the tail rotor in relation to the amount of torque produced by the engine. As the engine supplies more power to the main rotor, the tail rotor must produce more thrust to overcome the increased torque effect. This control change is accomplished through the use of antitorque pedals.

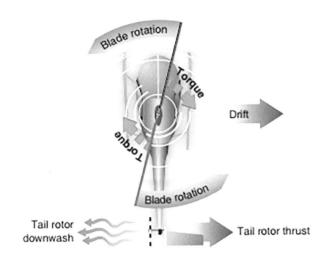

Blade rotation

Torque

Drift

Torque

Blade rotation

Tail rotor
downwash

Tail rotor thrust

Figure 3-25 *A tail rotor is designed to produce thrust in a direction opposite torque. The thrust produced by the tail rotor is sufficient to move the helicopter laterally.*

Translating Tendency (Drift)

During hovering flight, a single main rotor helicopter tends to move in the direction of tail rotor thrust. This lateral (or sideward) movement is called translating tendency. [Figure 3-25]

To counteract this tendency, one or more of the following features may be used. All examples are for a counterclockwise rotating main rotor system.

• The main transmission is mounted at a slight angle to the left (when viewed from behind) so that the rotor mast has a built-in tilt to oppose the tail rotor thrust.

• Flight controls can be rigged so that the rotor disk is tilted to the left slightly when the cyclic is centered. Whichever method is used, the tip-path plane is tilted slightly to the left in the hover.

• If the transmission is mounted so the rotor shaft is vertical with respect to the fuselage, the helicopter "hangs" left skid low in the hover. The opposite is true for rotor systems turning

clockwise when viewed from above. The helicopter fuselage will also be tilted when the tail rotor is below the main rotor disk and supplying antitorque thrust. The fuselage tilt is caused by the imperfect balance of the tail rotor thrust against the main rotor torque in the same plane. The helicopter tilts due to two separate forces, the main rotor disk tilt to neutralize the translating tendency and the lower tail rotor thrust below the plane of the torque action.

• In forward flight, the tail rotor continues to push to the right, and the helicopter makes a small angle with the wind when the rotors are level and the slip ball is in the middle. This is called inherent sideslip. For some larger helicopters, the vertical fin or stabilizer is often designed with the tail rotor mounted on them to correct this side slip and to eliminate some of the tilting at a hover. Also, by mounting the tail rotor on top of the vertical fin or pylon, the antitorque is more in line with or closer to the horizontal plane of torque, resulting in less airframe (or body) lean from the tail rotor. Having the tail rotor higher off the ground reduces the risk of objects coming in contact with the blades, but at the cost of increased weight and complexity.

Pendular Action

Since the fuselage of the helicopter, with a single main rotor, is suspended from a single point and has considerable mass, it is free to oscillate either longitudinally or laterally in the same way as a pendulum. This pendular action can be exaggerated by overcontrolling;

Calm wind hover

Initial rearward flight

Initial forward flight

Figure 3-26 *Because the helicopter's body has mass and is suspended from a single point (the rotor mast head), it tends to act much like a pendulum.*

therefore, control movements should be smooth and not exaggerated. [Figure 3-26]

The horizontal stabilizer tends to level the airframe in forward flight. However, in rearward flight, the horizontal stabilizer can press the tail downward, resulting in a tail strike if the helicopter is moved into the wind. Normally, with the helicopter mostly into the wind, the horizontal stabilizer experiences less headwind component as the helicopter begins rearward travel (downwind). When rearward flight groundspeed equals the windspeed, then the helicopter is merely hovering in a no-wind condition. However, rearward hovering into the wind requires considerable care and caution to prevent tail strikes.

Coning

In order for a helicopter to generate lift, the rotor blades must be turning. Rotor system rotation drives the blades into the air, creating a relative wind component without having to

move the airframe through the air as with an airplane or glider. Depending on the motion of the blades and helicopter airframe, many factors cause the relative wind direction to vary. The rotation of the rotor system creates centrifugal force (inertia), which tends to pull the blades straight outward from the main rotor hub. The faster the rotation is, the greater the centrifugal force; and the slower the rotation is, the smaller the centrifugal force. This force gives the rotor blades their rigidity and, in turn, the strength to support the weight of the helicopter. The maximum centrifugal force generated is determined by the maximum operating rotor revolutions per minute (rpm).

As lift on the blades is increased (in a takeoff, for example), two major forces are acting at the same time—centrifugal force acting outward, and lift acting upward. The result of these two forces is that the blades assume a conical path instead of remaining in the plane perpendicular to the mast. This can be seen in any helicopter when it takes off; the rotor disk changes from flat to a slight cone shape. [Figure 3-27]

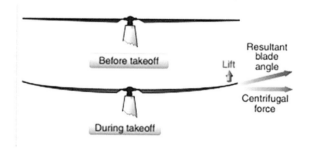

Before takeoff

During takeoff

Lift

Resultant blade angle

Centrifugal force

Figure 3-27 *During takeoff, the combination of centrifugal force and lift cause the rotor disk to cone upward.*

If the rotor rpm is allowed to go too low (below the minimum power-on rotor rpm, for example), the centrifugal force becomes smaller and the coning angle becomes much larger. In other words, should the rpm decrease too much, at some point the rotor blades fold up with no chance of recovery.

Coriolis Effect (Law of Conservation of Angular Momentum)

The Coriolis Effect is also referred to as the law of conservation of angular momentum. It states that the value of angular momentum of a rotating body does not change unless an external force is applied. In other words, a rotating body continues to rotate with the same rotational velocity until some external force is applied to change the speed of rotation. Angular momentum is the moment of inertia (mass times distance from the center of rotation squared) multiplied by the speed of rotation.

Changes in angular velocity, known as angular acceleration and deceleration, take place as the mass of a rotating body is moved closer to or farther away from the axis of rotation. The speed of the rotating mass varies proportionately with the square of the radius.

An excellent example of this principle in action is a figure skater performing a spin on ice skates. The skater begins rotation on one foot, with the other leg and both arms extended. The rotation of the skater's body is relatively slow. When a skater draws both arms and one leg inward, the moment of inertia (mass times radius squared) becomes much smaller and the body is rotating almost faster than the eye can follow. Because the angular momentum must, by law of nature, remain the same (no external force applied), the angular velocity must increase.

The rotor blade rotating about the rotor hub possesses angular momentum. As the rotor begins to cone due to G-loading maneuvers, the diameter or the rotor disk shrinks. Due to conservation of angular momentum, the blades continue to travel the same speed even though the blade tips have a shorter distance to travel due to reduced disk diameter. The action results in an increase in rotor rpm which causes a slight increase in lift. Most pilots arrest this increase of rpm with an increase in collective pitch. This increase in blade rpm lift is somewhat negated by the slightly smaller disk area as the blades cone upward.

Phase Lag ("Gyroscopic Precession")

The spinning main rotor of a helicopter acts like a gyroscope. As such, it has the properties of gyroscopic action, one of which is precession. Gyroscopic precession is the resultant action or deflection of a spinning object when a force is applied to this object. This action occurs approximately 90° in the direction of rotation from the point where the force is applied (or 90° later in the rotation cycle). [Figure 3-28] Examine a two-bladed rotor system to see how gyroscopic precession affects the movement of the tip-path plane. Moving the cyclic pitch control increases the angle of incidence of one rotor blade with the result of a greater lifting force being applied at that point in the plane of rotation. This same control movement simultaneously decreases the angle of incidence of the other blade the same amount, thus decreasing the lifting force applied at that point in the plane of rotation. The blade with the

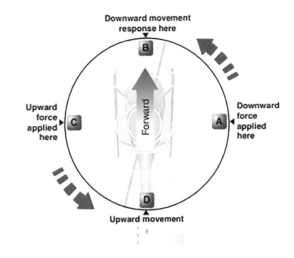

Figure 3-28 *Phase Lag or Gyroscopic precession.*

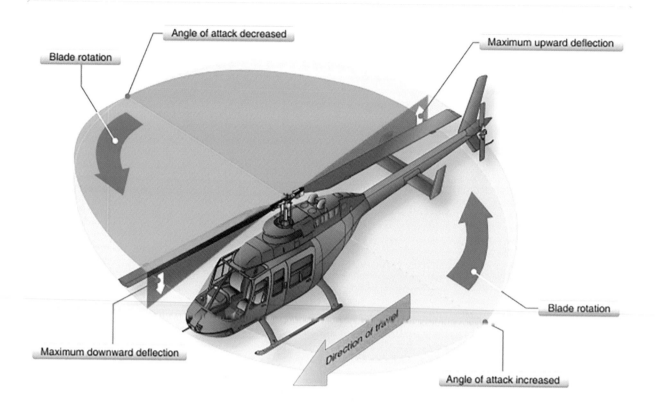

Blade rotation

Angle of attack decreased

Maximum upward deflection

Maximum downward deflection

Direction of travel

Blade rotation

Angle of attack increased

Figure 3-29 *As each blade passes the 90° position on the left in a counterclockwise main rotor blade rotation, the maximum increase in angle of incidence occurs. As each blade passes the 90° position to the right, the maximum decrease in angle of incidence occurs. Maximum deflection takes place 90° later—maximum upward deflection at the rear and maximum downward deflection at the front—and the tip-path plane tips forward.*

increased angle of incidence tends to flap up; the blade with the decreased angle of incidence tends to flap down. Because the rotor disk acts like a gyro, the blades reach maximum deflection at a point approximately 90° later in the plane of rotation. Figure 3-29 illustrates the result of a forward cyclic input. The retreating blade angle of incidence is increased and the advancing blade angle of incidence is decreased resulting in a tipping forward of the tip-path plane, since maximum deflection takes place 90° later when the blades are at the rear and front, respectively.

In a rotor system using three or more blades, the movement of the cyclic pitch control changes the angle of incidence of each blade an appropriate amount so that the end result is the same.

Vertical Flight

Hovering is actually an element of vertical flight. Increasing the angle of incidence of the rotor blades (pitch) while keeping their rotation speed constant generates additional lift and the helicopter ascends. Decreasing the pitch causes the helicopter to descend. In a no-wind condition in which lift and thrust are less than weight and drag, the helicopter descends vertically. If lift and thrust are greater than weight and drag, the helicopter ascends vertically. [Figure 3-30]

Forward Flight

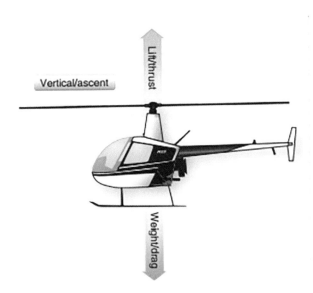

Figure 3-30 *Balanced forces: hovering in a no-wind condition.*

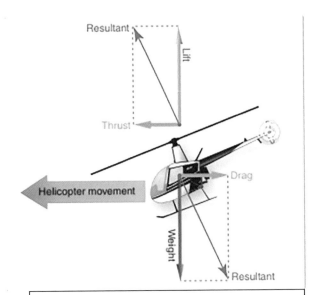

Figure 3-31 *To transition to forward flight, more lift and thrust must be generated to overcome the forces of weight and drag.*

In steady forward flight, with no change in airspeed or vertical speed, the four forces of lift, thrust, drag, and weight must be in balance. Once the tip-path plane is tilted forward, the total lift-thrust force is also tilted forward. This resultant lift-thrust force can be resolved into two components—lift acting vertically upward and thrust acting horizontally in the direction of flight. In addition to lift and thrust, there is weight (the downward acting force) and drag (the force opposing the motion of an airfoil through the air). [Figure 3-31]

In straight-and-level, unaccelerated forward flight (straight and-level flight is flight with a constant heading and at a constant altitude), lift equals weight and thrust equals drag. If lift exceeds weight, the helicopter accelerates vertically until the forces are in balance; if thrust is less than drag, the helicopter slows down until the forces are in balance. As the helicopter moves forward, it begins to lose altitude because lift is lost as thrust is diverted forward. However, as the helicopter begins to accelerate from a hover, the rotor system becomes more efficient due to translational lift (see translational lift on page 3-19). The result is

excess power over that which is required to hover. Continued acceleration causes an even larger increase in airflow, to a point, through the rotor disk and more excess power. In order to maintain unaccelerated flight, the pilot must understand that with any changes in power or in cyclic movement, the helicopter begins either

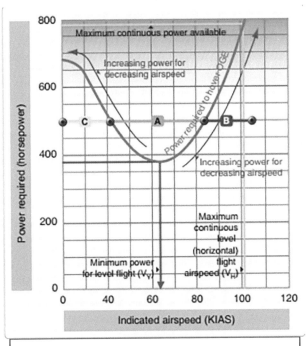

Figure 3-32 *Power versus airspeed chart.*

to climb or to descend. Once straight-and-level flight is obtained, the pilot should make note of the power (torque setting) required and not make major adjustments to the flight controls. [Figure 3-32]

Airflow in Forward Flight

Airflow across the rotor system in forward flight varies from airflow at a hover. In forward flight, air flows opposite the aircraft's flightpath. The velocity of this air flow equals the helicopter's forward speed. Because the rotor blades turn in a circular pattern, the velocity of airflow across a blade depends on the position of the blade in the plane of rotation at a given instant, its rotational velocity, and airspeed of the helicopter. Therefore, the airflow meeting each blade varies continuously as the blade rotates. The highest velocity of airflow occurs over the right side (3 o'clock position) of the helicopter (advancing blade in a rotor system that turns counterclockwise) and decreases to rotational velocity over the nose. It continues to decrease until the lowest velocity of airflow occurs over the left side (9 o'clock position) of the helicopter (retreating blade). As the blade continues to rotate, velocity of the airflow then increases to rotational velocity over the tail. It continues to increase until the blade is back at the 3 o'clock position. The advancing blade in Figure 3-33, position A, moves in the same direction as the helicopter. The velocity of the air meeting this blade equals rotational velocity of the blade plus wind velocity resulting from forward airspeed. The retreating blade (position C) moves in a flow of air moving in the opposite direction of the helicopter. The velocity of airflow meeting this blade equals rotational velocity of the blade minus wind velocity resulting from forward airspeed. The blades (positions B and D) over the nose and tail move essentially at right angles to the airflow created by forward airspeed; the velocity of airflow meeting these blades equals the rotational

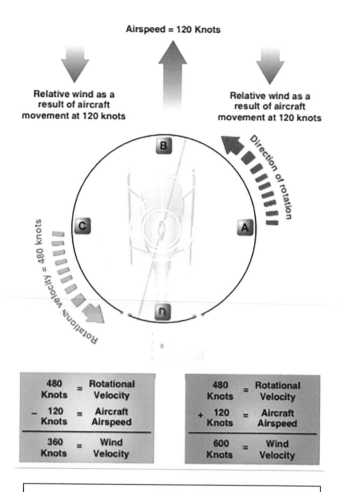

Figure 3-33 *Airflow in forward flight*

velocity. This results in a change to velocity of airflow all across the rotor disk and a change to the lift pattern of the rotor system.

Advancing Blade

As the relative wind speed of the advancing blade increases, the blade gains lift and begins to flap up. It reaches its maximum upflap velocity at the 3 o'clock position, where the wind velocity is the greatest. This upflap creates a downward flow of air and has the same effect as increasing the induced flow velocity by imposing a downward vertical velocity vector to the relative wind which decreases the AOA.

Retreating Blade

As relative wind speed of the retreating blade decreases, the blade loses lift and begins to flap down. It reaches its maximum down flap velocity at the 9 o'clock position, where wind velocity is the least. This down flap creates an upward flow of air and has the same effect as decreasing the induced flow velocity by imposing an upward velocity vertical vector to the relative wind which increases the AOA.

Dissymmetry of Lift

Dissymmetry of lift is the differential (unequal) lift between advancing and retreating halves of the rotor disk caused by the different wind flow velocity across each half. This difference in lift would cause the helicopter to be uncontrollable in any situation other than hovering in a calm wind. There must be a means of compensating, correcting, or eliminating this unequal lift to attain symmetry of lift.

When the helicopter moves through the air, the relative airflow through the main rotor disk is different on the advancing side than on the retreating side. The relative wind encountered by the advancing blade is increased by the forward speed of the helicopter, while the relative wind speed acting on the retreating blade is reduced by the helicopter's forward airspeed. Therefore, as a result of the relative wind speed, the advancing blade side of the rotor disk can produce more lift than the retreating blade side. [Figure 3-34]

If this condition were allowed to exist, a helicopter with a counterclockwise main rotor blade rotation would roll to the left because of the difference in lift. In reality, the main rotor blades flap and feather automatically to equalize lift across the rotor disk. Articulated rotor systems, usually with three or more blades, incorporate a horizontal hinge (flapping hinge) to allow the individual rotor blades to

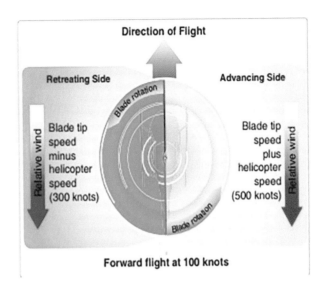

Figure 3-34 *The blade tip speed of this helicopter is approximately 400 knots. If the helicopter is moving forward at 100 knots, the relative windspeed on the advancing side is 400 knots. On the retreating side, it is only 200 knots. This difference in speed causes a dissymmetry of lift.*

move, or flap up and down as they rotate. A semi-rigid rotor system (two blades) utilizes a teetering hinge, which allows the blades to flap as a unit. When one blade flaps up, the other blade flaps down.

As shown in Figure 3-35, as the rotor blade reaches the advancing side of the rotor disk (A), it reaches its maximum up flap velocity. When the blade flaps upward, the angle between the chord line and the resultant relative wind decreases. This decreases the AOA, which reduces the amount of lift produced by the blade. At position (C), the rotor blade is now at its maximum down flapping velocity. Due to down flapping, the angle between the chord line and the resultant relative wind increases. This increases the AOA and thus the amount of lift produced by the blade.

The combination of blade flapping and slow relative wind acting on the retreating blade normally limits the maximum forward speed of a helicopter. At a high forward speed, the

64

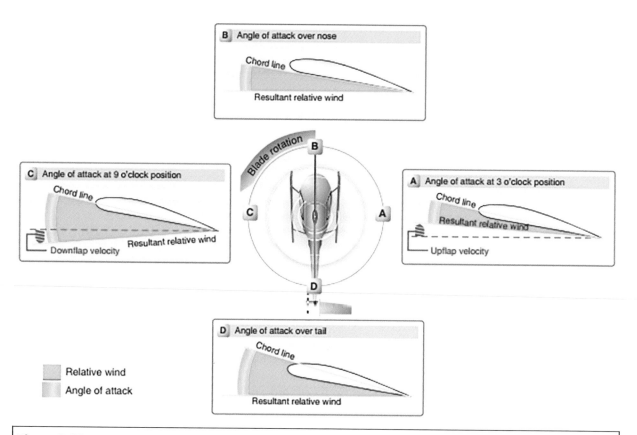

| B | Angle of attack over nose |
Chord line
Resultant relative wind

| C | Angle of attack at 9 o'clock position |
Chord line
Downflap velocity
Resultant relative wind

Blade rotation

| A | Angle of attack at 3 o'clock position |
Chord line
Resultant relative wind
Upflap velocity

| D | Angle of attack over tail |
Chord line
Resultant relative wind

Relative wind
Angle of attack

Figure 3-35 *The combined upward flapping (reduced lift) of the advancing blade and downward flapping (increased lift) of the retreating blade equalizes lift across the main rotor disk, counteracting dissymmetry of lift.*

retreating blade stalls because of a high AOA and slow relative wind speed. This situation is called retreating blade stall and is evidenced by a nose pitch up, vibration, and a rolling tendency—usually to the left in helicopters with counterclockwise blade rotation.

Pilots can avoid retreating blade stall by not exceeding the never-exceed speed. This speed is designated VNE and is indicated on a placard and marked on the airspeed indicator by a red line.

Blade flapping compensates for dissymmetry of lift in the following way. At a hover, equal lift is produced around the rotor system with equal pitch (AOI) on all the blades and at all points in the rotor system (disregarding compensation for translating tendency). The rotor disk is parallel to the horizon. To develop a thrust force, the rotor system must be tilted in the desired direction of movement. Cyclic feathering changes the angle of incidence differentially around the rotor system. Forward cyclic movements decrease the angle of incidence at one part on the rotor system while increasing the angle in another part.

When transitioning to forward flight either from a hover or taking off from the ground, pilots

Figure 3-36 *To compensate for blowback, you must move the cyclic forward.*

65

must be aware that as the helicopter speed increases, translational lift becomes more effective and causes the nose to rise, or pitch up (sometimes referred to as blowback). This tendency is caused by the combined effects of dissymmetry of lift and transverse flow. Pilots must correct for this tendency to maintain a constant rotor disk attitude that will move the helicopter through the speed range in which blowback occurs. If the nose is permitted to pitch up while passing through this speed range, the aircraft may also tend to roll to the right. To correct for this tendency, the pilot must continuously move the cyclic forward as velocity of the helicopter increases until the takeoff is complete and the helicopter has transitioned into forward flight.

Figure 3-36 illustrates the changes in pitch angle as the cyclic is moved forward at increased airspeeds. At a hover, the cyclic is centered and the pitch angle on the advancing and retreating blades is the same. At low forward speeds, moving the cyclic forward reduces pitch angle on the advancing blade and increases pitch angle on the retreating blade. This causes a slight rotor tilt. At higher forward speeds, the pilot must continue to move the cyclic forward. This further reduces pitch angle on the

advancing blade and further increases pitch angle on the retreating blade. As a result, there is even more tilt to the rotor than at lower speeds.

A horizontal lift component (thrust) generates higher helicopter airspeed. The higher airspeed induces blade flapping to maintain symmetry of lift. The combination of flapping and cyclic feathering maintains symmetry of lift and desired attitude on the rotor system and helicopter.

Translational Lift

Improved rotor efficiency resulting from directional flight is called translational lift. The efficiency of the hovering rotor system is greatly improved with each knot of incoming wind gained by horizontal movement of the aircraft or surface wind. As the incoming wind produced by aircraft movement or surface wind enters the rotor system, turbulence and vortices are left behind and the flow of air becomes more horizontal. In addition, the tail rotor becomes more aerodynamically efficient during the transition from hover to forward flight. Figures 3-37 and 3-38 show the different airflow patterns at different speeds and how airflow affects the efficiency of the tail rotor.

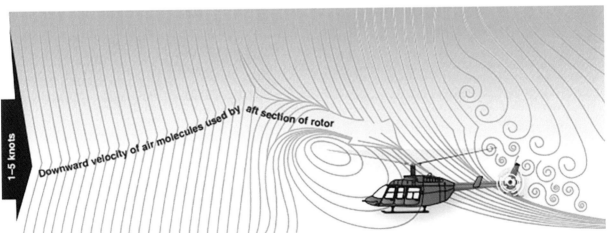

Figure 3-37 *The airflow pattern for 1–5 knots of forward airspeed. Note how the downwind vortex is beginning to dissipate and induced flow down through the rear of the rotor system is more horizontal.*

Effective Translational Lift (ETL)

While transitioning to forward flight at about 16 to 24 knots, the helicopter goes through effective translational lift (ETL). As mentioned earlier in the discussion on translational lift, the rotor blades become more efficient as forward airspeed increases. Between 16 and 24 knots, the rotor system completely outruns the recirculation of old vortices and begins to work in relatively undisturbed air. The flow of air through the rotor system is more horizontal; therefore, induced flow and induced drag are reduced. The AOA is effectively increased, which makes the rotor system operate more efficiently. This increased efficiency continues with increased airspeed until the best climb airspeed is reached, and total drag is at its lowest point.

As speed increases, translational lift becomes more effective, nose rises or pitches up, and aircraft rolls to the right. The combined effects of dissymmetry of lift, gyroscopic precession, and transverse flow effect cause this tendency. It is important to understand these effects and anticipate correcting for them. Once the helicopter is transitioning through ETL, the pilot needs to apply forward and left lateral cyclic input to maintain a constant rotor-disk attitude. [Figure 3-39]

Translational Thrust

Translational thrust occurs when the tail rotor becomes more aerodynamically efficient during the transition from hover to forward flight. As the tail rotor works in progressively less turbulent air, this improved efficiency produces more anti-torque thrust, causing the nose of the aircraft to yaw left (with a main rotor turning counterclockwise) and forces the pilot to apply right pedal (decreasing the AOA in the tail rotor blades) in response. In addition, during this period, the airflow affects the horizontal components of the stabilizer found on most helicopters which tends to bring the nose of the helicopter to a more level attitude.

When a helicopter is hovering, the tail rotor is operating in very disturbed airflow. As the helicopter achieves ETL, the tail rotor begins to generate much more thrust because of the less disturbed airflow. The helicopter reacts to the increased thrust by yawing. Therefore, as the helicopter achieves ETL, you must reduce tail rotor thrust by pedal input at about the same

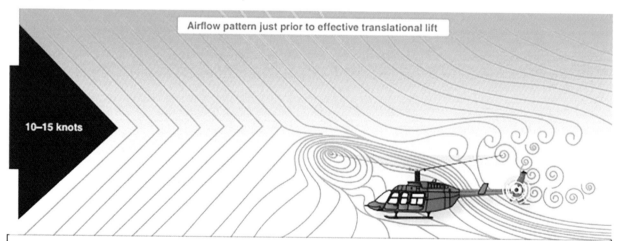

Figure 3-38 *An airflow pattern at a speed of 10–15 knots. At this increased airspeed, the airflow continues to become more horizontal. The leading edge of the downwash pattern is being overrun and is well back under the nose of the helicopter.*

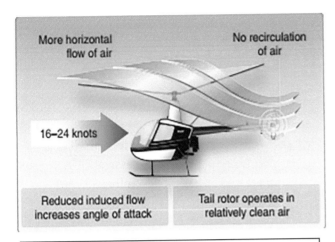

Figure 3-39 *Effective translational lift is easily recognized in actual flight by a transient induced aerodynamic vibration and increased performance of the helicopter*

time that you need to make cyclic adjustments for lateral tracking, acceleration, and climb.

Induced Flow

As the rotor blades rotate, they generate what is called rotational relative wind. This airflow is characterized as flowing parallel and opposite the rotor's plane of rotation and striking

perpendicular to the rotor blade's leading edge. This rotational relative wind is used to generate lift. As rotor blades produce lift, air is accelerated over the foil and projected downward. Anytime a helicopter is producing lift, it moves large masses of air vertically and down through the rotor system. This downwash or induced flow can significantly change the efficiency of the rotor system. Rotational relative wind combines with induced flow to form the resultant relative wind. As induced flow increases, resultant relative wind becomes less horizontal. Since AOA is determined by measuring the difference between the chord line and the resultant relative wind, as the resultant relative wind becomes less horizontal, AOA decreases. [Figure 3-40]

Transverse Flow Effect

As the helicopter accelerates in forward flight, induced flow drops to near zero at the forward disk area and increases at the aft disk area. These differences in lift between the fore and aft portions of the rotor disk are called transverse flow effect. [Figure 3-39] This

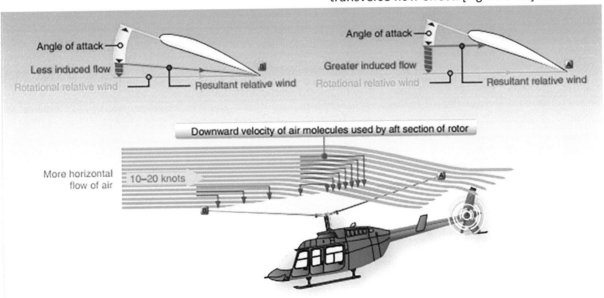

Figure 3-40 *A helicopter in forward flight, or hovering with a headwind or crosswind, has more molecules of air entering the aft portion of the rotor blade. Therefore, the angle of attack is less and the induced flow is greater at the rear of the rotor disk.*

increases the AOA at the front disk area causing the rotor blade to flap up, and reduces AOA at the aft disk area causing the rotor blade to flap down. Because the rotor acts like a gyro, maximum displacement occurs 90° in the direction of rotation. The result is a tendency for the helicopter to roll slightly to the right as it accelerates through approximately 20 knots or if the headwind is approximately 20 knots. Transverse flow effect is recognized by increased vibrations of the helicopter at airspeeds just below ETL on takeoff and after passing through ETL during landing. To counteract transverse flow effect, a cyclic input to the left may be needed.

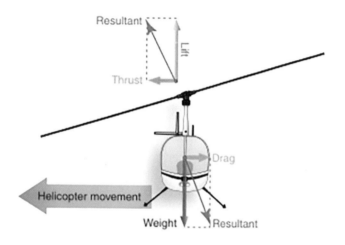

Figure 3-41 *Forces acting on the helicopter during sideward flight*

Sideward Flight

In sideward flight, the tip-path plane is tilted in the direction that flight is desired. This tilts the total lift-thrust vector sideward. In this case, the vertical or lift component is still straight up and weight straight down, but the horizontal or thrust component now acts sideward with drag acting to the opposite side. [Figure 3-41]

Sideward flight can be a very unstable condition due to the parasitic drag of the fuselage combined with the lack of horizontal stabilizer for that direction of flight. Increased altitudes help with control and the pilot must always scan in the direction of flight. Movement of the cyclic in the intended direction of flight causes the helicopter to move, controls the rate of speed, and ground track, but the collective and pedals are key to successful sideward flight. Just as in forward flight, the collective keeps the helicopter from contacting the ground and the pedals help maintain the correct heading; even in sideward flight, the tail of the helicopter should remain behind you. Inputs to the cyclic should be smooth and controlled, and the pilot should always be aware of the tip-path plane in relation to the ground. [Figure 3-42]

Contacting the ground with the skids during sideward flight will most likely result in a dynamic rollover event before the pilot has a chance to react. Extreme caution should be

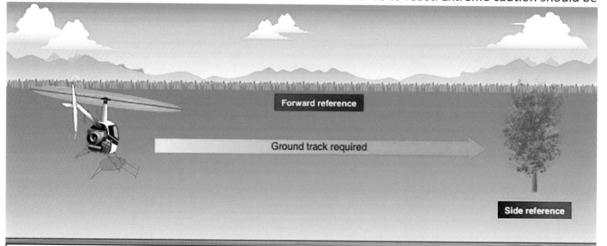

Figure 3-42 *Extreme caution should be used when maneuvering the helicopter sideways to avoid hazards*

used when maneuvering the helicopter sideways to avoid such hazards from happening.

Rearward Flight

For rearward flight, the tip-path plane is tilted rearward, which, in turn, tilts the lift-thrust vector rearward. Drag now acts forward with the lift component straight up and weight straight down. [Figure 3-43]

Pilots must be aware of the hazards of rearward flight. Because of the position of the horizontal stabilizer, the tail end of the helicopter tends to pitch downward in rearward flight, causing the probability of hitting the ground to be greater than in forward flight. Another factor to consider in rearward flight is skid design. Most helicopter skids are not turned upward in the back, and any contact with the ground during rearward flight can put the helicopter in an uncontrollable position leading to tail rotor contact with the ground. Pilots must do a thorough scan of the area before attempting to hover rearward, looking for obstacles and terrain changes. Slower airspeeds can help

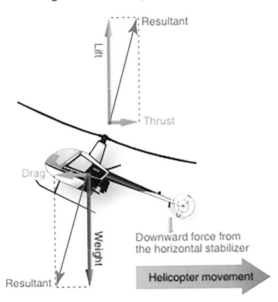

Figure 3-43. *Forces acting on the helicopter during rearward flight*

mitigate risk and maintain a higher-than-normal hover altitude.

Turning Flight

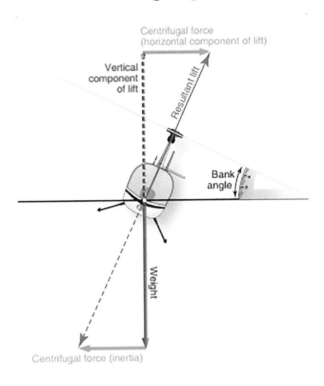

Figure 3-44 *Forces acting on the helicopter during turning flight.*

In forward flight, the rotor disk is tilted forward, which also tilts the total lift-thrust force of the rotor disk forward. When the helicopter is banked, the rotor disk is tilted sideward resulting in lift being separated into two components. Lift acting upward and opposing weight is called the vertical component of lift. Lift acting horizontally and opposing inertia (centrifugal force) is the horizontal component of lift (centripetal force). [Figure 3-44]

As the angle of bank increases, the total lift force is tilted more toward the horizontal, thus causing the rate of turn to increase because more lift is acting horizontally. Since the resultant lifting force acts more horizontally, the effect of lift acting vertically is decreased.

Figure 3-45 *Vortex Ring State*

To compensate for this decreased vertical lift, the AOA of the rotor blades must be increased in order to maintain altitude. The steeper the angle of bank is, the greater the AOA of the rotor blades required to maintain altitude. Thus, with an increase in bank and a greater AOA, the resultant lifting force increases and the rate of turn is higher. Simply put, collective pitch must be increased in order to maintain altitude and airspeed while turning. Collective pitch controls the angle of incidence and along with other factors, determines the overall AOA in the rotor system.

Emergency Procedures

Settling With Power (Vortex Ring State)

Vortex ring state describes an aerodynamic condition in which a helicopter may be in a vertical descent with 20 percent up to maximum power applied, and little or no climb performance. The term "settling with power" comes from the fact that the helicopter keeps settling even though full engine power is applied.

In a normal out-of-ground-effect (OGE) hover, the helicopter is able to remain stationary by propelling a large mass of air down through the main rotor. Some of the air is recirculated near the tips of the blades, curling up from the bottom of the rotor system and rejoining the air entering the rotor from the top. This phenomenon is common to all airfoils and is known as tip vortices. Tip vortices generate drag and degrade airfoil efficiency. As long as the tip vortices are small, their only effect is a small loss in rotor efficiency. However, when the helicopter begins to descend vertically, it settles into its own downwash, which greatly enlarges the tip vortices. In this vortex ring state, most of the power developed by the engine is wasted in circulating the air in a doughnut pattern around the rotor.

In addition, the helicopter may descend at a rate that exceeds the normal downward induced-flow rate of the inner blade sections. As a result, the airflow of the inner blade sections is upward relative to the disk. This produces a secondary vortex ring in addition to the normal tip vortices. The secondary vortex ring is generated about the point on the blade where the airflow changes from up to down. The result is an unsteady turbulent flow over a large area of the disk. Rotor efficiency is lost even though power is still being supplied from the engine.

A fully developed vortex ring state is characterized by an unstable condition in which the helicopter experiences uncommanded pitch and roll oscillations, has little or no collective authority, and achieves a descent rate that may approach 6,000 feet per minute (fpm) if allowed to develop.

A vortex ring state may be entered during any maneuver that places the main rotor in a condition of descending in a column of disturbed air and low forward airspeed. Airspeeds that are below translational lift airspeeds are within this region of susceptibility to settling with power aerodynamics. This condition is sometimes seen during quick-stop type maneuvers or during recovery from autorotation.

The following combination of conditions is likely to cause settling in a vortex ring state in any helicopter:

1. A vertical or nearly vertical descent of at least 300 fpm. (Actual critical rate depends on the gross weight, rpm, density altitude, and other pertinent factors.)

2. The rotor system must be using some of the available engine power (20–100 percent).

3. The horizontal velocity must be slower than effective translational lift.

Some of the situations that are conducive to a settling with power condition are: any hover above ground effect altitude, specifically attempting to hover OGE at altitudes above the hovering ceiling of the helicopter, attempting to hover OGE without maintaining precise altitude control, pinnacle or rooftop helipads when the wind is not aligned with the landing direction, and downwind and steep power approaches in which airspeed is permitted to drop below 10 knots depending on the type of helicopter.

When recovering from a settling with power condition, the pilot tends first to try to stop the descent by increasing collective pitch. However, this only results in increasing the stalled area of the rotor, thereby increasing the rate of descent. Since inboard portions of the blades are stalled, cyclic control may be limited. Recovery is accomplished by increasing airspeed, and/or partially lowering collective pitch. In many helicopters, lateral cyclic combined with lateral tailrotor thrust will produce the quickest exit from the hazard assuming that there are no barriers in that direction. In a fully developed vortex ring state, the only recovery may be to enter autorotation to break the vortex ring state.

Figure 3-45 *Ground Resonance*

Tandem rotor helicopters should maneuver laterally to achieve clean air in both rotors at the same time.

For settling with power demonstrations and training in recognition of vortex ring state conditions, all maneuvers should be performed at an altitude of 2000–3000 feet AGL to allow sufficient altitude for entry and recovery.

To enter the maneuver, come to an OGE hover, maintaining little or no airspeed (any direction), decrease collective to begin a vertical descent, and as the turbulence begins, increase collective. Then allow the sink rate to increase to 300 fpm or more as the attitude is adjusted to obtain airspeed of less than 10 knots. When the aircraft begins to shudder, the application of additional up collective increases the vibration and sink rate. As the power is increased, the rate of sink of the aircraft in the column of air will increase.

If altitude is sufficient, sometime can be spent in the vortices, to enable the pilot to develop a healthy knowledge of the maneuver. However, helicopter pilots would normally initiate recovery at the first indication of settling with power. Recovery should be initiated at the first sign of vortex ring state by applying forward cyclic to increase airspeed and/ or simultaneously reducing collective. The recovery is complete when the aircraft passes through effective translational lift and a normal climb is established.

Common Errors

1. Too much lateral speed for entry into settling with power.

2. Excessive decrease of collective pitch.

Retreating Blade Stall

In forward flight, the relative airflow through the main rotor disk is different on the advancing and retreating side. The relative airflow over the advancing side is higher due to the forward speed of the helicopter, while the relative airflow on the retreating side is lower. This dissymmetry of lift increases as forward speed increases.

To generate the same amount of lift across the rotor disk, the advancing blade flaps up while the retreating blade flaps down. This causes the AOA to decrease on the advancing blade, which reduces lift, and increase on the retreating blade, which increases lift. At some point as the forward speed increases, the low blade speed on the retreating blade, and its high AOA cause a stall and loss of lift.

Retreating blade stall is a major factor in limiting a helicopter's never-exceed speed (VNE) and its development can be felt by a low frequency vibration, pitching up of the nose, and a roll in the direction of the retreating blade. High weight, low rotor rpm, high density altitude, turbulence and/ or steep, abrupt turns are all conducive to retreating blade stall at high forward airspeeds. As altitude is increased, higher blade angles are required to maintain lift at a given airspeed. Thus, retreating blade stall is encountered at a lower forward airspeed at

altitude. Most manufacturers publish charts and graphs showing a VNE decrease with altitude.

When recovering from a retreating blade stall condition, moving the cyclic aft only worsens the stall as aft cyclic produces a flare effect, thus increasing the AOA. Pushing forward on the cyclic also deepens the stall as the AOA on the retreating blade is increased. Correct recovery from retreating blade stall requires the collective to be lowered first, which reduces blade angles and thus AOA. Aft cyclic can then be used to slow the helicopter.

Common Errors

1. Failure to recognize the combination of contributing factors leading to retreating blade stall.

2. Failure to compute VNE limits for altitudes to be flown.

Ground Resonance

Helicopters with articulating rotors (usually designs with three or more main rotor blades) are subject to ground resonance, a destructive vibration phenomenon that occurs at certain rotor speeds when the helicopter is on the ground. Ground resonance is a mechanical design issue that results from the helicopter's airframe having a natural frequency that can be intensified by an out-of-balance rotor. The unbalanced rotor system vibrates at the same frequency or multiple of the airframe's resonant frequency and the harmonic oscillation increases because the engine is adding power to the system, increasing the magnitude (or amplitude) of the vibrations until the structure or structures fail. This condition can cause a helicopter to self-destruct in a matter of seconds.

Hard contact with the ground on one corner (and usually with wheel-type landing gear) can send a shockwave to the main rotor head, resulting in the blades of a three-blade rotor system moving from their normal 120° relationship to each other. This movement occurs along the drag hinge and could result in something like 122°, 122°, and 116° between blades. When one of the other landing gear strikes the surface, the unbalanced condition could be further aggravated. If the rpm is low, the only corrective action to stop ground resonance is to close the throttle immediately and fully lower the collective to place the blades in low pitch. If the rpm is in the normal operating range, fly the helicopter off the ground, and allow the blades to rephase themselves automatically. Then, make a normal touchdown. If a pilot lifts off and allows the helicopter to firmly re-contact the surface before the blades are realigned, a second shock could move the blades again and aggravate the already unbalanced condition. This could lead to a violent, uncontrollable oscillation.

This situation does not occur in rigid or semi-rigid rotor systems because there is no drag hinge. In addition, skid-type landing gear is not as prone to ground resonance as wheel type landing gear since the rubber tires are not

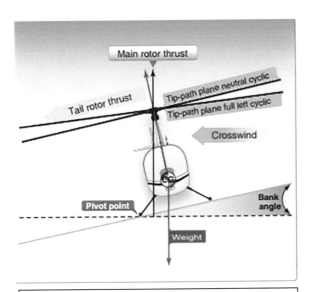

Figure 3-46 *Dynamic Rollover*

present and change the rebound characteristics.

Dynamic Rollover

A helicopter is susceptible to a lateral rolling tendency, called dynamic rollover, when the helicopter is in contact with the surface during takeoffs or landings. For dynamic rollover to occur, some factor must first cause the helicopter to roll or pivot around a skid or landing gear wheel, until its critical rollover angle is reached. (5–8° depending on helicopter, winds, and loading) Then, beyond this point, main rotor thrust continues the roll and recovery is impossible. After this angle is achieved, the cyclic does not have sufficient range of control to eliminate the thrust component and convert it to lift. If the critical rollover angle is exceeded, the helicopter rolls on its side regardless of the cyclic corrections made.

Dynamic rollover begins when the helicopter starts to pivot laterally around its skid or wheel. This can occur for a variety of reasons, including the failure to remove a tie down or skid-securing device, or if the skid or wheel contacts a fixed object while hovering sideward, or if the gear is stuck in ice, soft asphalt, or mud. Dynamic rollover may also occur if you use an improper landing or takeoff technique or while performing slope operations. Whatever the cause, if the gear or skid becomes a pivot point, dynamic rollover is possible if not using the proper corrective technique.

Once started, dynamic rollover cannot be stopped by application of opposite cyclic control alone. For example, the right skid contacts an object and becomes the pivot point while the helicopter starts rolling to the right. Even with full left cyclic applied, the main rotor thrust vector and its moment follows the aircraft as it continues rolling to the right. Quickly reducing collective pitch is the most effective way to stop dynamic rollover from developing. Dynamic rollover can occur with any type of landing gear and all types of rotor systems.

It is important to remember rotor blades have a limited range of movement. If the tilt or roll of the helicopter exceeds that range (5–8°), the controls (cyclic) can no longer command a vertical lift component and the thrust or lift becomes a lateral force that rolls the helicopter over. When limited rotor blade movement is coupled with the fact that most of a helicopter's weight is high in the airframe, another element of risk is added to an already slightly unstable center of gravity. Pilots must remember that in order to remove thrust, the collective must be lowered as this is the only recovery technique available.

Critical Conditions

Certain conditions reduce the critical rollover angle, thus increasing the possibility for dynamic rollover and reducing the chance for recovery. The rate of rolling motion is also a consideration because, as the roll rate increases, there is a reduction of the critical rollover angle at which recovery is still possible. Other critical conditions include operating at high gross weights with thrust (lift) approximately equal to the weight.

Refer to Figure 11-7. The following conditions are most critical for helicopters with counterclockwise rotor rotation:

1. Right side skid or landing wheel down, since translating tendency adds to the rollover force.

2. Right lateral center of gravity (CG).

3. Crosswinds from the left.

4. Left yaw inputs.

For helicopters with clockwise rotor rotation, the opposite conditions would be true.

Cyclic Trim

When maneuvering with one skid or wheel on the ground, care must be taken to keep the helicopter cyclic control carefully adjusted. For example, if a slow takeoff is attempted and the cyclic is not positioned and adjusted to account for translating tendency, the critical recovery angle may be exceeded in less than two seconds. Control can be maintained if the pilot maintains proper cyclic position, and does not allow the helicopter's roll and pitch rates to become too great. Fly the helicopter into the air smoothly while keeping movements of pitch, roll, and yaw small; do not allow any abrupt cyclic pressures.

Normal Takeoffs and Landings

Dynamic rollover is possible even during normal takeoffs and landings on relatively level ground, if one wheel or skid is on the ground and thrust (lift) is approximately equal to the weight of the helicopter. If the takeoff or landing is not performed properly, a roll rate could develop around the wheel or skid that is on the ground. When taking off or landing, perform the maneuver smoothly and carefully adjust the cyclic so that no pitch or roll movement rates build up, especially the roll rate. If the bank angle starts to increase to an angle of

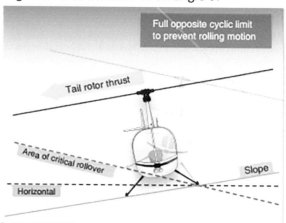

Figure 3-47 *Dynamic Rollover. Slope Operations*

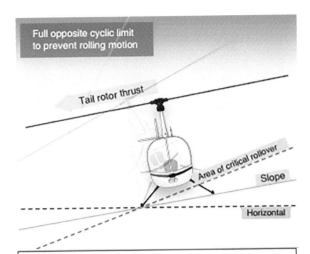

Full opposite cyclic limit to prevent rolling motion

Tail rotor thrust

Area of critical rollover

Slope

Horizontal

Figure 3-48 *Dynamic Rollover. Slope Operations*

approximately 5–8°, and full corrective cyclic does not reduce the angle, the collective should be reduced to diminish the unstable rolling condition. Excessive bank angles can also be caused by landing gear caught in a tie down strap, or a tie down strap still attached to one side of the helicopter. Lateral loading imbalance (usually outside published limits) is another contributing factor.

Slope Takeoffs and Landings

During slope operations, excessive application of cyclic control into the slope, together with excessive collective pitch control, can result in the downslope skid or landing wheel rising sufficiently to exceed lateral cyclic control limits, and an upslope rolling motion can occur.

When performing slope takeoff and landing maneuvers, follow the published procedures and keep the roll rates small. Slowly raise the downslope skid or wheel to bring the helicopter level, and then lift off. During landing, first touch down on the upslope skid or wheel, then slowly lower the downslope skid or wheel using combined movements of cyclic and collective. If the helicopter rolls approximately 5–8° to the upslope side, decrease collective to correct the

bank angle and return to level attitude, then start the landing procedure again.

Use of Collective

The collective is more effective in controlling the rolling motion than lateral cyclic, because it reduces the main rotor thrust (lift). A smooth, moderate collective reduction, at a rate of less than approximately full up to full down in two seconds, may be adequate to stop the rolling motion. Take care, however, not to dump collective at an excessively high rate, as this may cause a main rotor blade to strike the fuselage. Additionally, if the helicopter is on a slope and the roll starts toward the upslope side, reducing collective too fast may create a high roll rate in the opposite direction. When the upslope skid or wheel hits the ground, the dynamics of the motion can cause the helicopter to bounce off the upslope skid or wheel, and the inertia can cause the helicopter to roll about the downslope ground contact point and over on its side. [Figure 11-9]

Under normal conditions, the collective should not be pulled suddenly to get airborne because a large and abrupt rolling moment in the opposite direction could occur. Excessive application of collective can result in the upslope skid or wheel rising sufficiently to exceed lateral cyclic control limits. This movement may be uncontrollable. If the helicopter develops a roll rate with one skid or wheel on the ground, the helicopter can roll over on its side.

Precautions

To help avoid dynamic rollover:

1. Always practice hovering autorotations into the wind, and be wary when the wind is gusty or greater than 10 knots.

2. Use extreme caution when hovering close to fences, sprinklers, bushes, runway/taxi lights,

tiedown cables, deck nets, or other obstacles that could catch a skid or wheel. Aircraft parked on hot asphalt over night might find the landing gear sunk in and stuck as the ramp cooled during the evening.

3. Always use a two-step lift-off. Pull in just enough collective pitch control to be light on the skids or landing wheels and feel for equilibrium, then gently lift the helicopter into the air.

4. Hover high enough to have adequate skid or landing wheel clearance with any obstacles when practicing hovering maneuvers close to the ground, especially when practicing sideways or rearward flight.

5. Remember that when the wind is coming from the upslope direction, less lateral cyclic control is available.

6. Avoid tailwind conditions when conducting slope operations.

7. Remember that less lateral cyclic control is available due to the translating tendency of the tail rotor when the left skid or landing wheel is upslope. (This is true for counterclockwise rotor systems.)

8. Keep in mind that the lateral cyclic requirement changes when passengers or cargo are loaded or unloaded.

9. Be aware that if the helicopter utilizes interconnecting fuel lines that allow fuel to automatically transfer from one side of the helicopter to the other, the gravitational flow of fuel to the downslope tank could change the CG, resulting in a different amount of cyclic control application to obtain the same lateral result.

10. Do not allow the cyclic limits to be reached. If the cyclic control limit is reached, further

lowering of the collective may cause mast bumping. If this occurs, return to a hover and select a landing point with a lesser degree of slope.

11. During a takeoff from a slope, begin by leveling the main rotor disk with the horizon or very slightly into the slope to ensure vertical lift and only enough lateral thrust to prevent sliding on the slope. If the upslope skid or wheel starts to leave the ground before the downslope skid or wheel, smoothly and gently lower the collective and check to see if the downslope skid or wheel is caught on something. Under these conditions, vertical ascent is the only acceptable method of lift-off.

12. Be aware that dynamic rollover can be experienced during flight operations on a floating platform if the platform is pitching/rolling while attempting to land or takeoff. Generally, the pilot operating on floating platforms (barges, ships, etc.) observes a cycle of seven during which the waves increase and then decrease to a minimum. It is that time of minimum wave motion that the pilot needs to use for the moment of landing or takeoff on floating platforms. Pilots operating from floating platforms should also exercise great caution concerning cranes, masts, nearby boats (tugs) and nets.

Chapter Summary

Emergencies should always be anticipated. Knowledge of the helicopter, possible malfunctions and failures, and methods of recovery can help the pilot avoid accidents and be a safer pilot. Helicopter pilots should always expect the worse hazards and possible aerodynamic effects and plan for a safe exit path or procedure to compensate for the hazard.

Chapter 4 - Global Positioning System (GPS)

Global Navigation Satellite System (GNSS)

The Global Navigation Satellite System (GNSS) is a constellation of satellites providing a high-frequency signal that contains time and distance that is picked up by a receiver. The receiver that picks up multiple signals from different satellites is able to triangulate its position from these satellites.

Three GNSSs exist today: the GPS, a United States system; the Russian GNSS (GLONASS); and Galileo, a European system.

> 1. GLONASS is a network of 24 satellites that can be picked up by any GLONASS receiver, allowing the user to pinpoint their position.

> 2. Galileo planned to be a network of 30 satellites that continuously transmit high-frequency radio signals containing time and distance data that can be picked up by a Galileo receiver with operational expectancy by 2013.

> 3. The GPS came on line in 1992 with 24 satellites and today utilizes 30 satellites.

Global Positioning System (GPS) The GPS is a satellite-based radio navigation system that broadcasts a signal that is used by receivers to determine precise position anywhere in the world. The receiver tracks multiple satellites and determines a measurement that is then used to determine the user location. [Figure 4-1]

The Department of Defense (DOD) developed and deployed GPS as a space-based positioning, velocity, and time system. The DOD is responsible for operation of the GPS satellite constellation, and constantly monitors the satellites to ensure proper operation. The GPS system permits Earth-centered coordinates to be determined and provides aircraft position referenced to the DOD World Geodetic System of 1984 (WGS-84). Satellite navigation systems are unaffected by weather and provide global navigation coverage that fully meets the civil requirements for use as the primary means of navigation in oceanic airspace and certain remote areas. Properly certified GPS equipment may be used as a supplemental means of IFR navigation for domestic en route, terminal operations and certain IAPs. Navigational values, such as distance and bearing to a WP and groundspeed, are computed from the aircraft's current position (latitude and longitude) and the location of the next WP. Course guidance is provided as a linear deviation from the desired track of a Great Circle route between defined WPs.

GPS may not be approved for IFR use in other countries. Prior to its use, pilots should ensure that GPS is authorized by the appropriate countries.

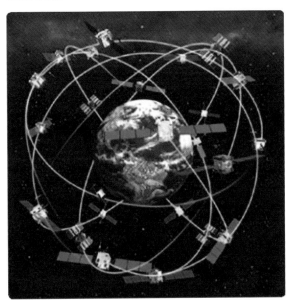

Fig. 4-1 *GPS Satellite Constellation*

GPS Components

GPS consists of three distinct functional elements: space, control, and user.

The space element consists of over 30 Navstar satellites. This group of satellites is called a constellation. The space element consists of 24 Navigation System using Timing and Ranging (NAVSTAR) satellites in 6 orbital planes. The satellites in each plane are spaced 60° apart for complete coverage and are located (nominally) at about 11,000 miles above the Earth. The planes are arranged so that there are always five satellites in view at any time on the Earth. Presently, there are at least 31 Block II/IIA/IIR and IIR-M satellites in orbit with the additional satellites representing replacement satellites (upgraded systems) and spares. Recently, the Air Force received funding for procurement of 31 Block IIF satellites. The GPS constellation broadcasts a pseudo-random code timing signal and data message that the aircraft equipment processes to obtain satellite position and status data. By knowing the precise location of each satellite and precisely matching timing with the atomic clocks on the satellites, the aircraft receiver/processor can accurately measure the time each signal takes to arrive at the receiver and, therefore, determine aircraft position.

The control element consists of a network of ground-based GPS monitoring and control stations that ensure the accuracy of satellite positions and their clocks. In its present form, it has five monitoring stations, three ground antennas, and a master control station.

The user element consists of antennas and receiver/processors on board the aircraft that provide positioning, velocity, and precise timing to the user. GPS equipment used while operating under IFR must meet the standards set forth in Technical Standard Order (TSO) C-129 (or equivalent); meet the airworthiness installation requirements; be "approved" for

that type of IFR operation; and be operated in accordance with the applicable POH/AFM or flight manual supplement.

An updatable GPS database that supports the appropriate operations (e.g., en route, terminal, and instrument approaches) is required when operating under IFR. The aircraft GPS navigation database contains WPs from the geographic areas where GPS navigation has been approved for IFR operations. The pilot selects the desired WPs from the database and may add user-defined WPs for the flight.

Equipment approved in accordance with TSO C-115a, visual flight rules (VFR), and hand-held GPS systems do not meet the requirements of TSO C-129 and are not authorized for IFR navigation, instrument approaches, or as a principal instrument flight reference. During IFR operations, these units (TSO C-115a) may be considered only an aid to situational awareness.

Prior to GPS/WAAS IFR operation, the pilot must review appropriate NOTAMs and aeronautical information. This information is available on request from an flight service station (FSS). The FAA does provide NOTAMs to advise pilots of the status of the WAAS and level of service available.

Function of GPS

GPS operation is based on the concept of ranging and triangulation from a group of satellites in space that act as precise reference points. The receiver uses data from a minimum of four satellites above the mask angle (the lowest angle above the horizon at which it can use a satellite).

The aircraft GPS receiver measures distance from a satellite using the travel time of a radio signal. Each satellite transmits a specific code, called a course/acquisition (CA) code, which contains information about satellite position, the GPS system time, and the health and accuracy of the transmitted data. Knowing the speed at which the signal traveled (approximately 186,000 miles per second) and the exact broadcast time, the distance traveled by the signal can be computed from the arrival time. The distance derived from this method of computing distance is called a pseudo-range because it is not a direct measurement of distance, but a measurement based on time. In addition to knowing the distance to a satellite, a receiver needs to know the satellite's exact position in space, its ephemeris. Each satellite transmits information about its exact orbital location. The GPS receiver uses this information to establish the precise position of the satellite.

Using the calculated pseudo-range and position information supplied by the satellite, the GPS receiver/processor mathematically determines its position by triangulation from several satellites. The GPS receiver needs at least four satellites to yield a three-dimensional position (latitude, longitude, and altitude) and time solution. The GPS receiver computes navigational values (distance and bearing to a WP, groundspeed, etc.) by using the aircraft's known latitude/longitude and referencing these to a database built into the receiver.

The GPS receiver verifies the integrity (usability) of the signals received from the GPS constellation through receiver autonomous integrity monitoring (RAIM) to determine if a satellite is providing corrupted information. RAIM needs a minimum of five satellites in view or four satellites and a barometric altimeter baro-aiding to detect an integrity anomaly. For receivers capable of doing so, RAIM needs six satellites in view (or five satellites with baro-aiding) to isolate a corrupt satellite signal and remove it from the navigation solution.

Generally, there are two types of RAIM messages. One type indicates that there are not enough satellites available to provide RAIM and another type indicates that the RAIM has

detected a potential error that exceeds the limit for the current phase of flight. Without RAIM capability, the pilot has no assurance of the accuracy of the GPS position.

Aircraft using GPS navigation equipment under IFR for domestic en route, terminal operations, and certain IAPs, must be equipped with an approved and operational alternate means of navigation appropriate to the flight. The avionics necessary to receive all of the ground-based facilities appropriate for the route to the destination airport and any required alternate airport must be installed and operational. Ground-based facilities necessary for these routes must also be operational. Active monitoring of alternative navigation equipment is not required if the GPS receiver uses RAIM for integrity monitoring. Active monitoring of an alternate means of navigation is required when the RAIM capability of the GPS equipment is lost. In situations where the loss of RAIM capability is predicted to occur, the flight must rely on other approved equipment, delay departure, or cancel the flight.

GPS Errors

Normally, with 30 satellites in operation, the GPS constellation is expected to be available continuously worldwide. Whenever there are fewer than 24 operational satellites, GPS navigational capability may not be available at certain geographic locations. Loss of signals may also occur in valleys surrounded by high terrain, and any time the aircraft's GPS antenna is "shadowed" by the aircraft's structure (e.g., when the aircraft is banked).

Certain receivers, transceivers, mobile radios, and portable receivers can cause signal interference. Some VHF transmissions may cause "harmonic interference." Pilots can isolate the interference by relocating nearby portable receivers, changing frequencies, or turning off suspected causes of the interference while monitoring the receiver's signal quality data page.

GPS position data can be affected by equipment characteristics and various geometric factors, which typically cause errors of less than 100 feet. Satellite atomic clock inaccuracies, receiver/processors, signals reflected from hard objects (multi-path), ionospheric and tropospheric delays, and satellite data transmission errors may cause small position errors or momentary loss of the GPS signal.

System Status

The status of GPS satellites is broadcast as part of the data message transmitted by the GPS satellites. GPS status information is also available by means of the United States Coast Guard navigation information service: (703) 313-5907 or on the internet at www.navcen.uscg.gov. Additionally, satellite status is available through the NOTAM system.

The GPS receiver verifies the integrity (usability) of the signals received from the GPS constellation through RAIM to determine if a satellite is providing corrupted information. At least one satellite, in addition to those required for navigation, must be in view for the receiver to perform the RAIM function; thus, RAIM needs a minimum of five satellites in view or four satellites and a barometric altimeter (baro-aiding) to detect an integrity anomaly. For receivers capable of doing so, RAIM needs six satellites in view (or five satellites with baro-aiding) to isolate the corrupt satellite signal and remove it from the navigation solution.

RAIM messages vary somewhat between receivers; however, there are two most commonly used types. One type indicates that there are not enough satellites available to provide RAIM integrity monitoring and another type indicates that the RAIM integrity monitor has detected a potential error that exceeds the limit for the current phase of flight. Without RAIM capability, the pilot has no assurance of the accuracy of the GPS position. Selective Availability. Selective availability is a method by which the accuracy of GPS is intentionally degraded. This feature is designed to deny hostile use of precise GPS positioning data. Selective availability was discontinued on May 1, 2000, but many GPS receivers are designed to assume that selective availability is still active. New receivers may take advantage of the discontinuance of selective availability based on the performance values in ICAO Annex 10 and do not need to be designed to operate outside of that performance.

GPS Familiarization

Pilots should practice GPS approaches under VMC until thoroughly proficient with all aspects of their equipment (receiver and installation) prior to attempting flight in the NAS. Some of the tasks which the pilot should practice are:

1. Utilizing the RAIM prediction function;

2. Inserting a DP into the flight plan, including setting terminal CDI sensitivity, if required, and the conditions under which terminal RAIM is available for departure (some receivers are not DP or STAR capable);

3. Programming the Home Point or destination;

4. Programming and flying the route;

5. Changing to another route after selecting and activating a route;

6. Entering, flying, and exiting holding patterns;

7. Programming and flying a "route";

8. Indication of the actions required for RAIM failure; and

9. Programming a radial and distance from an airports, heliport, or VOR.

Differential Global Positioning Systems (DGPS)

Differential global positioning systems (DGPS) are designed to improve the accuracy of GNSS by measuring changes in variables to provide satellite positioning corrections.

Because multiple receivers receiving the same set of satellites produce similar errors, a reference receiver placed at a known location can compute its theoretical position accurately and can compare that value to the measurements provided by the navigation satellite signals. The difference in measurement between the two signals is an error that can be

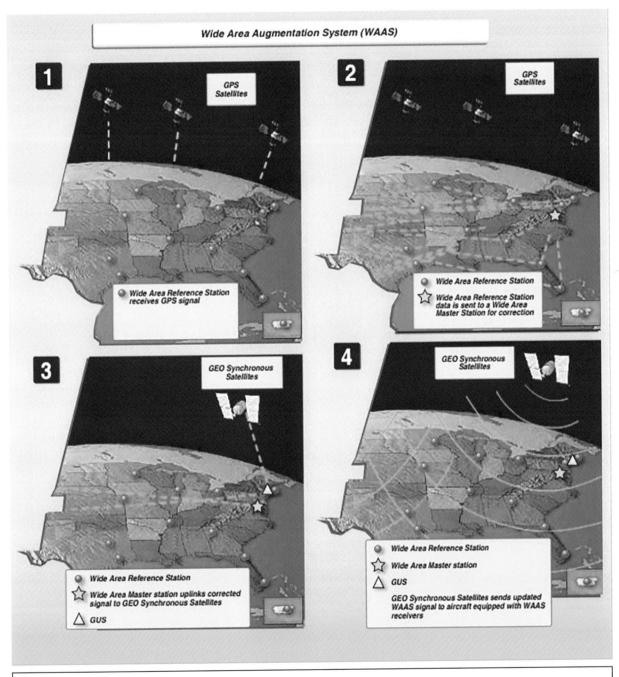

Wide Area Augmentation System (WAAS)

1 GPS Satellites

Wide Area Reference Station receives GPS signal

2 GPS Satellites

Wide Area Reference Station

Wide Area Reference Station data is sent to a Wide Area Master Station for correction

3 GEO Synchronous Satellites

Wide Area Reference Station

Wide Area Master station uplinks corrected signal to GEO Synchronous Satellites

GUS

4 GEO Synchronous Satellites

Wide Area Reference Station

Wide Area Master station

GUS

GEO Synchronous Satellites sends updated WAAS signal to aircraft equipped with WAAS receivers

Fig. 4-2 *WAAS satellite representation.*

corrected by providing a reference signal correction.

As a result of this differential input accuracy of the satellite system can be increased to meters. The Wide Area Augmentation System (WAAS) and Local Area Augmentation System (LAAS) are examples of differential global positioning systems.

Wide Area Augmentation System (WAAS)

The WAAS is designed to improve the accuracy, integrity, and availability of GPS signals. WAAS allows GPS to be used as the aviation navigation system from takeoff through Category I precision approaches. ICAO has defined Standards for satellite-based augmentation systems (SBAS), and Japan and Europe are building similar systems that are planned to be interoperable with WAAS: EGNOS, the European Geostationary Navigation Overlay System, and MSAS, the Japanese Multifunctional Transport Satellite (MTSAT) Satellite-based Augmentation System. The result will be a worldwide seamless navigation capability similar to GPS but with greater accuracy, availability, and integrity.

Unlike traditional ground-based navigation aids, WAAS will cover a more extensive service area in which surveyed wide-area ground reference stations are linked to the WAAS network. Signals from the GPS satellites are monitored by these stations to determine satellite clock and ephemeris corrections. Each station in the network relays the data to a wide-area master station where the correction information is computed. A correction message is prepared and uplinked to a geostationary satellite (GEO) via a ground uplink and then broadcast on the same frequency as GPS to WAAS receivers within the broadcast coverage area. [Figure 4-2]

In addition to providing the correction signal, WAAS provides an additional measurement to the aircraft receiver, improving the availability of GPS by providing, in effect, an additional GPS satellite in view. The integrity of GPS is improved through real-time monitoring, and the accuracy is improved by providing differential corrections to reduce errors. [Figure 4-3] As a result, performance improvement is sufficient to enable approach procedures with GPS/WAAS glidepaths. At this time the FAA has completed installation of 25 wide area ground

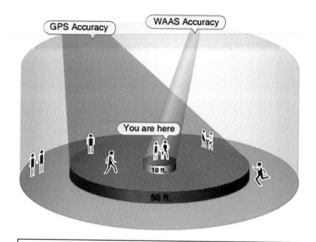

Fig. 4-3 *WAAS provides performance enhancement for GPS approach procedures through real-time monitoring.*

reference systems, two master stations, and four ground uplink stations.

General Requirements

WAAS avionics must be certified in accordance with TSO-C145A, Airborne Navigation Sensors Using the GPS Augmented by the WAAS; or TSO-146A for stand-alone systems. GPS/WAAS operation must be conducted in accordance with the FAA-approved aircraft flight manual (AFM) and flight manual supplements. Flight manual supplements must state the level of approach procedure that the receiver supports.

Local Area Augmentation System (LAAS)

LAAS is a ground-based augmentation system that uses a GPS-reference facility located on or in the vicinity of the airport being serviced. This facility has a reference receiver that measures GPS satellite pseudo-range and timing and retransmits the signal. Aircraft landing at LAAS-equipped airports are able to conduct approaches to Category I level and above for properly equipped aircraft. Figure 4-4

Inertial Navigation System (INS)

Inertial Navigation System (INS) is a system that navigates precisely without any input from outside of the aircraft. It is fully self-contained. The INS is initialized by the pilot, who enters into the system the exact location of the aircraft on the ground before the flight. The INS is also programmed with WPs along the desired route of flight.

INS Components

INS is considered a stand-alone navigation system, especially when more than one independent unit is onboard. The airborne equipment consists of an accelerometer to measure acceleration—which, when integrated with time, gives velocity—and gyros to measure direction.

Later versions of the INS, called inertial reference systems (IRS), utilize laser gyros and more powerful computers; therefore, the accelerometer mountings no longer need to be kept level and aligned with true north. The computer system can handle the added workload of dealing with the computations necessary to correct for gravitational and directional errors. Consequently, these newer systems are sometimes called strap down systems, as the accelerometers and gyros are strapped down to the airframe rather than

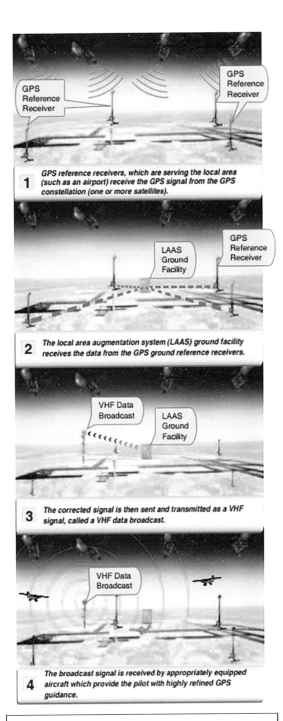

1 GPS reference receivers, which are serving the local area (such as an airport) receive the GPS signal from the GPS constellation (one or more satellites).

2 The local area augmentation system (LAAS) ground facility receives the data from the GPS ground reference receivers.

3 The corrected signal is then sent and transmitted as a VHF signal, called a VHF data broadcast.

4 The broadcast signal is received by appropriately equipped aircraft which provide the pilot with highly refined GPS guidance.

Fig. 4-4 LAAS *representation.*

being mounted on a structure that stays fixed with respect to the horizon and true north.

INS Errors

The principal error associated with INS is degradation of position with time. INS computes position by starting with accurate position input which is changed continuously as accelerometers and gyros provide speed and direction inputs. Both accelerometers and gyros are subject to very small errors; as time passes, those errors probably accumulate.

While the best INS/IRS display errors of 0.1 to 0.4 NM after flights across the North Atlantic of 4 to 6 hours, smaller and less expensive systems are being built that show errors of 1 to 2 NM per hour. This accuracy is more than sufficient for a navigation system that can be combined with and updated by GPS. The synergy of a navigation system consisting of an INS/IRS unit in combination with a GPS resolves the errors and weaknesses of both systems. GPS is accurate all the time it is working but may be subject to short and periodic outages. INS is made more accurate because it is continually updated and continues to function with good accuracy if the GPS has moments of lost signal.

Selective Availability

Selective Availability (SA) is a method by which the accuracy of GPS is intentionally degraded. This feature is designed to deny hostile use of precise GPS positioning data. SA was discontinued on May 1, 2000, but many GPS receivers are designed to assume that SA is still active.

The GPS constellation of 24 satellites is designed so that a minimum of five satellites are always observable by a user anywhere on earth. The receiver uses data from a minimum of four satellites above the mask angle (the lowest angle above the horizon at which a receiver can use a satellite).

VFR Use of GPS

GPS navigation has become a great asset to VFR pilots, providing increased navigation capability and enhanced situational awareness, while reducing operating costs due to greater ease in flying direct routes. While GPS has many benefits to the VFR pilot, care must be exercised to ensure that system capabilities are not exceeded.

Types of receivers used for GPS navigation under VFR are varied, from a full IFR installation being used to support a VFR flight, to a VFR only installation (in either a VFR or IFR capable aircraft) to a hand-held receiver. The limitations of each type of receiver installation or use must be understood by the pilot to avoid misusing navigation information. In all cases, VFR pilots should never rely solely on one system of navigation. GPS navigation must be integrated with other forms of electronic navigation as well as pilotage and dead reckoning. Only through the integration of these techniques can the VFR pilot ensure accuracy in navigation. 15-33 Some critical concerns in VFR use of GPS include RAIM capability, database currency and antenna location.

Tips for Using GPS for VFR Operations

Always check to see if the unit has RAIM capability. If no RAIM capability exists, be suspicious of a GPS displayed position when any disagreement exists with the position derived from other radio navigation systems, pilotage, or dead reckoning.

Check the currency of the database, if any. If expired, update the database using the current revision. If an update of an expired database is not possible, disregard any moving map display of airspace for critical navigation decisions. Be aware that named waypoints may no longer exist or may have been relocated since the database expired. At a minimum, the waypoints planned to be used should be checked against a current official source, such as the A/FD, or a Sectional Aeronautical Chart.

While a hand-held GPS receiver can provide excellent navigation capability to VFR pilots, be prepared for intermittent loss of navigation signal, possibly with no RAIM warning to the pilot. If mounting the receiver in the aircraft, be sure to comply with 14 CFR part 43.

Plan flights carefully before taking off. If navigating to user defined waypoints, enter them before flight, not on the fly. Verify the planned flight against a current source, such as a current sectional chart. There have been cases in which one pilot used waypoints created by another pilot that were not where the pilot flying was expecting. This generally resulted in a navigation error. Minimize head-down time in the aircraft and keep a sharp lookout for traffic, terrain, and obstacles. Just a few minutes of preparation and planning on the ground makes a great difference in the air.

Another way to minimize head-down time is to become very familiar with the receiver's operation. Most receivers are not intuitive. The pilot must take the time to learn the various keystrokes, knob functions, and displays that are used in the operation of the receiver. Some manufacturers provide computer-based tutorials or simulations of their receivers. Take the time to learn about the particular unit before using it in flight.

In summary, be careful not to rely on GPS to solve all VFR navigational problems. Unless an IFR receiver is installed in accordance with IFR requirements, no standard of accuracy or integrity has been assured. While the practicality of GPS is compelling, the fact remains that only the pilot can navigate the aircraft, and GPS is just one of the pilot's tools to do the job.

Chapter 5 Flight Planning

Appropriate Use

The first question that must be asked when preparing for a flight, is to make sure that the drone is being used for something that is appropriate. An sUAV flight should never be conducted if a law is being broken, and even if there is question of breaking a law, it is best to not fly until you are assured that the flight is lawful.

Similarly, a drone should never be flown near an airport unless you are given permission from that airport's controlling agency. Drone pilots should always check their location with the FAA's B4UFLY App.

Line of Sight

Line of sight can sometimes have two meanings. In a drone's operating manual, line of sight refers to the drone's range of control form the RC controller to the aircraft. This distance of effective control can be as great as one or two kilometers. This is known as

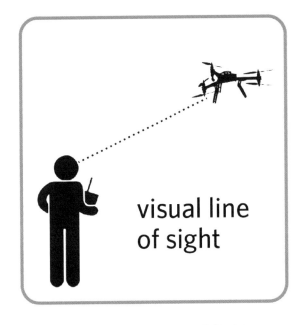

visual line of sight

the Communication Line of Sight (CLOS)

However, the FAA's definition of Line of Sight is more clear. Flying a drone and staying within line of sight means never losing physical sight of your aircraft. Even when you feel that first-person-view (FPV) can be used as a backup in case you lose sight of your drone, FPV is some time unreliable. If you lose sight and control of your drone, it could

cause great damage to person's or property on the ground when it comes back to Earth.

It is important to realize that most sUAS are capable of flying far beyond the VLOS. This is extremely dangerous and illegal.

Night Flight

While somewhat debated still because drone users claim that they can see their drone's LED lights past sunset, this does not mean that the drone should be flown. Whether there is a clear law of not, flying at night clearly means that you cannot see what people, animals, or other objects lay on the ground below the drone while in flight.

When flying manned aircraft, a responsible pilot is constantly saying to themselves "If I lose my engine where is the safest place to land?" This should also always be done by a drone pilot. Therefore, launching up into the darkness of night is simply a foolish endeavor.

Weather

As mentioned previously, the batteries on todays' drone are very sensitive to cold temperatures. When batteries are cold the power, or current, that batteries supply is dependent on chemical reactions and those reactions are slowed by freezing temperatures. Since the reactions are slowed, less energy is produced and the power output is lowered; with a lower output, the battery cannot keep up with the demand and can go dead, producing no current. Even flying at temperature above freezing can still mean that the battery is below freezing because it

lies directly under the cold prop-wash of the spinning blades. Seasoned drone pilots often keep their batteries warm by keeping them in their coat pockets, and even using battery warmers. At a minimum, this will at least extend the useful life of the battery while in flight.

There are other weather conditions that drone pilots must be aware of. Most obvious is flying into conditions when there is no moisture whether it be from mist, rain, or even snow. While the drone's onboard electronics are often housed inside the of the drone's body and protected from the elements, moisture can still find it's way into the aircraft and cause a failure.

Protective coatings are available through various online companies, but be aware that this can add weight and impact the drone's published performance. One piece of trivia I always found interesting was that the paint on a Boeing 747 actually weighs more than a Cessna 172. Therefore, when scaled down, a sprayed on protective coating of just a few grams could still prevent your drone from flying safely, and remember that the added weight will require the motors to work harder and the batteries to drain faster. This is true of any additional equipment you place on your aircraft.

Visibility

The effects of poor visibility can impact the drone and pilot on multiple fronts. Not only is it dangerous to fly during low visibility for reasons already stated, but also because the cause of the low visibility could be dangerous. For emergency workers, flying near smoke means that invisible debris like ask can find its way into the drone's electronics. Even when it seems like the flight is in clear air, small particles might still be present.

The most common cause of low visibility is due to fog. Fog is made up of condensed water droplets which are the result of the air being cooled to the point (actually, the dewpoint) where it can no longer hold all of the water vapor it contains. We often witness fog in the morning, known as radiation fog, because the ground has cooled and causes the air to condense. This can be dangerous for drone pilots because when standing on the ground and looking across a fog mass, it might look uniform, however, thickness of the fog can vary and a flight into a foggy air mass could result in the loss of VLOS. also be aware that the fog of visible moisture, and could damage the onboard electronics.

If there is one positive to flying in conditions of poor visibility, it is that reduced visibility gives the impression that all objects are farther away than they really are. This would mean that the drone would always appear farther away and therefore the operator would actually be closer to the drone then they thought.

Wind

One way to become a proficient pilot of manned aircraft is to fly on windy days. It makes the calm days a whole lot easier. Small single-engine training aircraft are designed with natural stability that allow for the airplane to keeps its normal attitude in flight as long as it's moving forward with enough speed. this means that although wind might make an airplane "bounce

around", it will always return to it original attitude in flight. Technically, this is referred to as Positive Dynamic Stability.

However, copter-type drones must use electronic aides to maintain their stability in flight. This is done by incorporating gyroscopic attitude device known as a flight control board. The flight control board senses changes in attitude and responds by increasing or decrease the power to each motor through and electronic speed controller (ESC).

Prevailing wind

All UAV's (and aircraft) have absolute limits to the maximum wind that they can safely fly. For most small drones the maximum limit for safe flight is around 20 mph (19 m/s, 19 knots). If your drone is flown into wind conditions that are higher, the aircraft may not be able to return home, and the battery life will be shortened (due to increased motor power demand to keep it stable).

For flight planning purposes pilots must always identify where the wind is coming from and at what speed. Airplanes always takeoff into the wind to reduce ground roll and helicopters as well unless there is a reason to do otherwise for safety.

While multi -rotor, copter-type drones are somewhat omni-directional, it is always a wise practice to launch into the wind. Additionally, when flying near buildings, structures or even hilly terrain, the pilot must always be aware of wind direction, speed, and how the wind will impact takeoff and flight. When flying near buildings, the airflow over and around the building will cause turbulence on the sides of the building that are on the downwind side. This turbulence acts like many small tornadoes and will create and unstable flight environment.

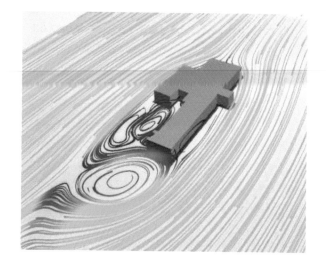

Location

With regard to flight planning, the location of your drone's takeoff point and operator's location are key to a successful flight. If using a copter-type drone, always launch in an area where vertical takeoff of possible without flying upward into overlying tree branches or other obstructions. A seasoned pilot will also establish the "home" position shortly after takeoff in case of an emergency, and the home position should be in an open area where the drone can fly to that is free of obstructions. Remember that when the drone does "Return To Home" (RTH) it will do so autonomously, but it may not have the ability to detect obstacles and avoid them. If available, it is recommended to set the RTH altitude higher than the highest obstacle in the area during preflight preparations.

The position of the drone operator is also important. Most operators are standing next to the drone during takeoff which is a smart practice since takeoff and landing is the most crucial phase of flight. However, sometimes there may be a better vantage point for the operator during the mission phase of the flight. This may be a small hill are larger clearing that allows for the pilot maintain a better line of sight and also provide for a better overall view of the total area during the mission.

Restricted and Prohibited Areas

The FAA has clearly stated that all types of UAV's are not allowed to fly within five miles of any major airport or military airbase. Drones are also not allowed to fly in any U.S. National Park. There are also other instances when the FAA deems it not safe for drone pilots or other folks. These are called Temporary Flight Restrictions (TFR's). One such example would be if the President were on golfing while on vacation. A TFR would be published preventing the drone operating from flying too close. The TFR would be lifted when it was deemed safe to fly.

Congested Areas

While flying over a congested area might seem like an opportunity to get some incredible aerial photos or videos, it is also incredible dangerous. Online searches can show the damage caused by drones when they fall at full speed into a crowd of

people. not to mention the added damage from the spinning propellers.

The FAA has clearly stated that flying over congested areas is not allowed and has fined those operators that have been caught in the act.[1]

Privacy

Historically there have been several legal cases in the 20th century that have defined a person's privacy with regard to overflying aircraft. Most notable is United States vs Causby, in which Causby sued the U.S. for flying military aircraft too low over his property which caused the plaintiff's chickens to jump up against the sides of the chicken house and "burst themselves open and die".[2]

Under Common Law, persons who own real property not only own the ground below their property, but also the air above their property up to the heavens. In terms of manned aircraft, they fly at such altitudes where it is decided that the interference is nil, and the FAA adopted policies to establish minimum altitudes for aircraft in flight. Typically, aircraft can fly no lower than 500 feet over a rural area and no lower than 1500 over a congested area unless for the purposes of landing or taking off. Furthermore, even during the takeoff and landing phase of flight, pilots need to adhere to local departure and landing procedures that are designed to reduce noise and threat to person below. All of this is done citizen's right to privacy.

---

[1] http://www.wsj.com/articles/u-s-federal-aviation-administration-settles-with-videographer-over-drones-1421960972

[2] https://www.oyez.org/cases/1940-1955/328us256

The UAV however, is challenging this premise and causing airspace to be questioned yet again and, while the rulings of the past will likely not change in order to protect privacy, new guidelines and regulations will be adopted by Congress and the FAA. What is clear is that drone operators must always fly way from people on the ground, and never infringe on someone's privacy.

Chapter 6 - Flight Operations

Introduction

One can only imagine that the Wright Brothers probably wrote the very first airplane checklist. It was probably because they quickly saw how many steps were needed to ensure that their Wright Flyer was balanced on the track at Kill Devil's Hill, and because the engine was such a unique design that it too was complicated to start, and of course let's not forget the all-important step of ensuring that the flight controls are "free and correct"

No one in early aviation wrote as much as the Wrights with respect to experimentation, and design. They kept laborious notebooks on their studies, so to think that they did not have such a checklist would be foolish.

It's also comforting to think that aviation started out in this manner with safety being considered as the cornerstone of all air travel.

More than one hundred years later, the checklist has certainly grown, but the key elements for all checklists remains the same; balance verified, controls working properly, systems checked, engine checked, and emergency plans understood.

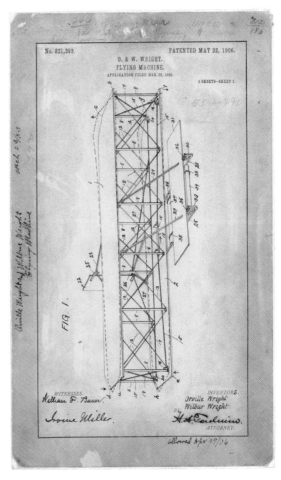

Figure 6-1 *The Wright Brother's patent for their 1903 Wright Flyer which was only accomplished through dedicated note taking, methodology, and checklists.*

For the drone operator, these items are also as critical as they are for manned aircraft. Fortunately, the rigidity of off-the-shelf drones helps ensure that the weight and balance is within limits (known as "the envelope") and flight controls on the RC controller are checked prior to launch. Today's drones have automated systems checks which confirms that such things as compass calibration, GPS signal, SONAR checks, battery temps, gimbal freedom, even motor checks are all working correctly.

A professional drone operator will always examine the flight area and look for safe places to land for each phase of flight

Checklists

The use of checklists is a vital component of Aviation Systems Safety. All humans make mistakes. The use of checklists allows the pilot a methodical, objective method of ensuring that all required tasks are complete.

Whenever possible, both the pilot and observer should complete the checklist together utilizing the "Call and Response" method. Example:

Observer says: "Certificate of Authorization or Waiver." This is the "CALL".
Pilot then "Responds" with, "Current and valid for proposed operation."

For single pilot operations the "Do / Verify" method is preferred. In this method the pilot will read three to five items from the checklist and accomplish those tasks. The pilot then returns to the checklist, reads each of the accomplished items aloud and in order, verifying that each is complete.

The effectiveness of proper checklist use cannot be understated. There is a reason that every major airline, regional airline, and military flight operations spend huge sums of money producing quality checklists and monitor their crews to ensure that they are using them properly. Checklists prevent costly and dangerous mishaps.

An operator who doesn't think they need a checklist is setting themselves up for an accident.

Phases of Flight

Pre-Flight

Proper planning prevents poor performance. A good preflight planning session is an essential part of all professional flight operations. Think of a flight operation as an iceberg. The actual "flight" portion is just the tip of the iceberg. The preflight and post flight operations make up everything that lies beneath the surface.

Preflight Planning should include the following elements:

Identify Type of Operation: Commercial, Public Use, or Recreational

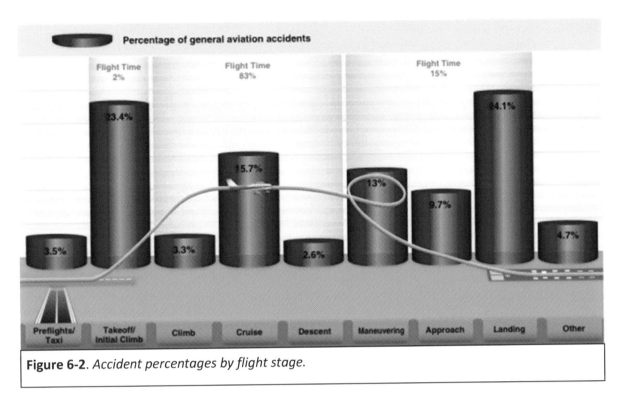

Percentage of general aviation accidents

Flight Time 2%	Flight Time 83%	Flight Time 15%

23.4%

24.1%

15.7%

13%

9.7%

3.5%   3.3%   2.6%   4.7%

| Preflights/ Taxi | Takeoff/ Initial Climb | Climb | Cruise | Descent | Maneuvering | Approach | Landing | Other |

Figure 6-2. *Accident percentages by flight stage.*

Regulatory Compliance Check: Is a 333 Exemption and / or a COA required?

Aircraft Registration Check: Is the aircraft properly registered for the operation? Commercial and Public Use operations require a unique "N" number registration for each aircraft. The FAA's online drone registration does not meet this requirement.

Weather: What is the minimum weather (ceiling and visibility) required for this operation? What is the current weather report? What is the forecast for the flight operation period?

Aircraft Requirements: How long will the aircraft need to be in the air? Will the existing battery charge meet this requirement? Have the effects of cold temperatures on battery life

been considered? Is the aircraft capable of completing the mission?

Pilot / Observer Requirements: Is the pilot / observer qualified IAW all regulations? Does the pilot / observer have any injury or illness that hinder the safety of the operation?

Below is a sample checklist. Pilots may modify this checklist to fit their specific operations / aircraft.

Take-off/Climb

What most professional drone operators will do shortly after takeoff is fly their drone straight up a few feet, establish the "home" position, and perhaps give the flight controls a quick toggle to rotate the drone about all three of it's axis. This is done to verify that the drone is operating correctly. It is much better to have a crash landing from a few feet above the ground instead of from a much higher altitude and far away from the home point.

It's also during this phase of flight that the pilot may then start recording if videography is a part of the mission.

Cruise Flight/Mission

This phase of flight consumes most of the battery power and time. After the drone has launched, the operator will fly it out to the area where the bulk of the flying will take place. For emergency workers, this could be the scene of a fire or car accident. For civil engineers or construction workers, this could be a bridge or building site for inspection.

Prior to this stage (during preflight), the pilot needs to decide where they will stand in order to maximize the signal strength between the RC controller and the aircraft. If the drone's mission is to fly around a building, understand that signal strength could be lost, and the aircraft could crash.

Needless to say, the most common causes of drone accidents during the cruise/mission phase are due to signal loss and loss of orientation.

In order to ensure orientation, spotters should always be used. The typical drone pilot is constantly transferring between First-Person-View (FPV) and then looking up at the aircraft. The back and forth head movements, can sometimes be confusing. Usually, FPV is used to verify aircraft position and orientation, but this does not negate the importance of spotters that can also verify orientation and identify any flight hazards like branches, wire, or ground obstacles.

The pilot and spotters also need to have their communications somewhat rehearsed, meaning they should never be out of ear-shot of each other. Although using radio communications sounds like a good idea, it only adds one more item to the pilot's heavy workload. Pilots and spotters should never be more than 50 yards from each other, and drone flights in which the aircraft is more than 200 yards from the operator should be considered unique special circumstances and not the norm. Beyond two hundred yards, the drone may be within line of sight, but a small drone will certainly be out of visual sight.

On the subject of signal strength, line of sight is even more critical. In this still young industry of drone piloting, there are already countless stories of drone operators that have flown far beyond line of sight and lost their (expensive) drones.

Pilot's of manned aircraft never fly farther then they have too, and likewise, the drone pilot should follow suit.

Return-to-Home/Landing

This phase of flight can sometimes promote a euphoric sense in that there is the pre-mature relief that another successful mission has been completed.

Missions are never completed until the aircraft is safely on the ground and the motors are turned off.

Returning to home, is just as critical as other phases of flight with the added twist that if the drone is oriented toward to pilot, then flight controls will be reversed. If the pilot needs to quickly turn left to avoid a small tree branch, they will need to turn right on their controls. There are flight modes that can keep flight controls always orientated the same way regardless of the drone's direction, but this is not commonly used.

It is also common that the pilot/operator during the course of the flight has also changed

position, and therefore bringing the UAV home will likely be to a new location. This new location will mean a new approach to landing and likely, new obstacles as well.

Landing

Landings themselves are not overly difficult, but they are not without their challenges. Low-level wind can cause a sudden upset of the aircraft, and if the landing position is not flat, that will make is even harder to land and not tumble if there are added wind. Many smaller drones have a narrow footprint on the ground and a high center-of-gravity. These two factors make a landing especially hard.

Fortunately, some drones have downward facing SONAR that help the aircraft slow down its decent in the last few inches, and because the internal flight control board can sense if the drone is level or not, some drones also have a feature that will "shoot" the drone up a few feet in case the landing surface is on a slope of more than 20 degrees. If this occurs, the drone will move over a few feet and land again. This is something that Neil Armstrong probably wishes he had when landing on the moon.

Another item to be aware of while landing is the camera angle. Because most cameras are located directly under the drone and are often facing downward, it can be a very smart idea to rotate the camera direction to level so that upon landing, the loose stones, pebbles or other debris do not get hit surface of the lens.

Post Flight

It is common practice to perform some sort of post flight inspection of the aircraft. This includes examining the aircraft for any damage. Emergency workers, civil engineers, and construction workers for example all fly drones in environments where the airspace can be filled with such things as fire ash, or heavy dust that will cause damage to the drone over time.

Routinely, drones should be cleaned as often as needed. A typically cleaning should include non-toxic baby wipes to wipe down the whole aircraft followed by using a can of compressed air to blow out any dust from inside the drone's body or through the engine areas. Be careful when using compressed air though, because it could blow debris further into the drone.

Other Considerations During Flight Operations

Collisions

Our National Airspace System is filled with more smaller aircraft than larger aircraft. We understand the potentially fatal consequences of a drone colliding with and small airplane. We also hope that everyone follows the rules of the sky and that drones will remain in their airspace while manned aircraft will stay in theirs.

However, there are times when both manned and unmanned aircraft will reside in the same airspace. Most frequently will be when helicopters are landing at locations other than one of our nation's published airports. There will be times when emergency helicopters will land on something like a football field or parking lot to pick up someone severely injured from an accident.

The smartest thing any drone pilot can do, when they hear the blades and motor of an aircraft nearby is to simply land and give them the space the need and deserve.

There will be other collisions that are much less predictable. The ones with our feathered friends. Birds and even insects can collide unexpectedly with drones in flight and cause immediate damage. Because drone flights are often video recorded from the drone's own camera, online searches of these video will reveal spectacular results. So be aware of your surroundings. Conservation land or other wooded areas that are habitats for bird populations might not be the best place to fly your sUAV.

Spinning Propellers

Another hazard to pilots and other folks are the spinning propeller blades from the small drone. The brushless motor, although lightweight, is spinning at speeds of more than 10,000 rpms. Some blades are carbon fiber and can do more damage than a chainsaw. Even the plastic blades that are most common are sharp enough and sturdy enough to cut off a finger.

Fire

Fire is always a risk for drone operators. In spite of today's drones being electrically powered as opposed to the RC helicopters and airplanes that used liquid fuel years ago, most of today's drones use lithium-ion polymer (LiPo) batteries.

LiPo batteries can store great amounts of energy, but it is not without risks, and more commonly, if not handled correctly, these batteries can overheat and cause a fire.

Heat and Cold

While the effects of heat pertain to the battery mostly while it is not being used, the effects of cold are a greater issue when the batteries are in use.

It is a well-documented fact that LiPo batteries perform poorly when they are cold. There are numerous online forums addressing this matter, and recently battery warmers have come on the

LiPo Battery Safety Tips

1. Never purchased used LiPo batteries. You will not know how they were treated.

2. Never use or store damaged or bulging LiPo batteries. If damaged or bulging, contact you local recycling center to dispose of them properly.

3. Never charge LiPo batteries unattended.

4. Because LiPo batteries cause a chemical fire, always have a Class D fire extinguisher nearby.

5. Do not overcharge your LiPo battery. Once charging is complete, safely remove them.

6. Do not use you carrying case for long-term storage. Carrying cases are made with foam and are highly flammable.

7. Do not store LiPo batteries in a hot are such as a car, attic, or garage.

market. Some drone pilots will use small hand warmers sold in sporting good stores, while other pilots will keep their batteries warm by placing them in the pockets of their winter jacket while they fly.

Cold temps slow down the chemical reaction process and thus the effectiveness of the battery.

It is therefore critical to closely monitor flight voltage. When flying your drone in cold temps, be aware that missions will be noticeable shorter. For this reason, it is best to rehearse your mission in advance in order to reduce the time needed in the air to prepare for the next stage of flight.

Even temps as high as 40F or more will still create a cold battery when in flight. Most batteries are uninsulated while on the drone and are located right under to cold prop wash of the blades.

Emergencies

Most advanced drones used for commercial applications have programming built in to return-to-home in the event of some sort of failure. Some examples of these are low battery and loss of signal.

Drones with six blades or more can even lose power to one motor (sometimes more) and the drone will respond by spinning in its own vertical column of air in order to generate its own cushion air. It will then descend down to the ground safely.

Any time there is a failure of the drone during an automated or preprogrammed mission, the first response should always be to take over control of the aircraft and flight it manually home. If upon taking over control manually the threat is eliminated, it can then be safe to resume the mission.

For example, the aircraft may be on a pre-programmed grid mission to survey a property or even look for a missing person. If the pilot notices an obstruction such as a tree branch, he/she should immediately stop the flight, go vertical and then start over perhaps at a higher altitude.

Chapter 7- Aviation Regulations and FAA Compliance

As much as we try to be proactive and create guidelines, rules, and policies to prevent injury and harm. Sometimes, we must accept that we also live in a reactionary society.

Such was the case in 2011 when Raphael Pirker flew a drone recklessly over the University of Virginia. The FAA set out to fine Mr. Pirker $10,000 and he decided to argue in court that he was not flying an aircraft but only a model airplane. The NTSB Safety Board judge initially sided with Mr. Pirker, but eventually the case was overturned and Mr. Pirker's "model airplane" was classified as a drone. Mr. Pirker became the first drone operator to be fined by the FAA, and he will not be the last. His case was settled in early 2015 for $1,100.

Since 2011, the FAA has worked tirelessly to ensure that both drone hobbyists and commercial UAV pilots have the ability to fly in the National Airspace System, without compromising safety.

To that end, the FAA's own Advisory Circular pertaining to model aircraft from 1981 was revised with a new set of guidelines and definitions

Advisory Circular 91-57

In September of 2015, AC 91-57 was updated to (AC 91-57a) and includes statements that relate to today's drone pilots. This includes the basic theoretical operation of UAVs in the National Airspace System (NAS) as well as how to determine if

a remotely piloted aircraft is a model aircraft or a UAV.
See Appendix for the full version of AC-91-57a.

Aircraft Terminology Defined

1. Title 49 U.S. Code § 40102 defines an aircraft as "any contrivance invented, used, or designed to navigate, or fly in, the air." 14 CFR § 1.1 defines an aircraft as "a device that is used or intended to be used for flight in the air."

2. Public Law 112-95 defines unmanned aircraft as an aircraft that is operated without the possibility of direct human intervention from within or on the aircraft.

3. Section 336 of P.L. 112-95 defines a model aircraft as an unmanned aircraft that is capable of sustained flight in the atmosphere, flown within visual line of sight of the person operating the aircraft, and flown only for hobby or recreational purposes.

While aero-modelers generally are concerned about safety and exercise good judgment when flying model aircraft for the hobby and recreational purposes for which they are intended, they may share the airspace in which manned aircraft are operating. Unmanned aircraft, including model aircraft, may pose a hazard to manned aircraft in flight and to persons and property on the surface if not operated safely. Model aircraft operations that endanger the safety of the National Airspace System, particularly careless or reckless operations or those that interfere with or fail to give way to any manned aircraft may be subject to FAA enforcement action.

Model Aircraft

As a recreational user of model aircraft, you are exempt from the some of the FAA's regulations regarding unmanned aircraft. Title 14 Code of Federal Regulations does not apply to the following operations: [3]

- Model aircraft that meet the criteria in 14 CFR part 101.41 (describes circumstances in which model

aircraft can be operated safely in the NAS). For more information, see AC 91-57 (as amended).

- Amateur rockets
- Moored balloons or unmanned free balloons
- Kites
- Operations conducted outside the United States
- Public aircraft operations
- Air carrier operations

Determination of "Model Aircraft" Status

Whether a given unmanned aircraft operation may be considered a "model aircraft operation" is determined with reference to section 336 of Public Law 112-95:

1. The aircraft is flown strictly for hobby or recreational use;
2. The aircraft operates in accordance with a community-based set of safety guidelines and within the programming of a nationwide community-based organization (CBO);
3. The aircraft is limited to not more than 55 pounds, unless otherwise certified through a design, construction, inspection, flight test, and operational safety program administered by a CBO;
4. The aircraft operates in a manner that does not interfere with, and gives way to, any manned aircraft; and
5. When flown within 5 miles of an airport, the operator of the model aircraft

---

[3] 14 CFR parts 101.41 and 107.1; Public law 112-95, FAA Modernization and Reform Act of 2012, Section 336; AC 91-57A, Model Aircraft Operating Standards

provides the airport operator or the airport air traffic control tower (when an air traffic facility is located at the airport) with prior notice of the operation. Model aircraft operators flying from a permanent location within 5 miles of an airport should establish a mutually agreed upon operating procedure with the airport operator and the airport air traffic control tower (when an air traffic facility is located at the airport).

Public Law 112-95 recognizes the authority of the Administrator to pursue enforcement action against persons operating model aircraft who endanger the safety of the National Airspace System. Accordingly, model aircraft operators must comply with any Temporary Flight Restrictions (TFR). TFRs are issued over specific locations due to disasters, or for reasons of national security; or when determined necessary for the management of air traffic in the vicinity of aerial demonstrations or major sporting events. Do not operate model aircraft in designated areas until the TFR is no longer in force.

Model aircraft must not operate in Prohibited Areas, Special Flight Rule Areas or, the Washington National Capital Region Flight Restricted Zone, without specific authorization. Such areas are depicted on charts available at http://www.faa.gov/air_traffic/flight_info/a eronav/.

Additionally, model aircraft operators should be aware of other Notices to Airmen (NOTAMS) which address operations near locations such as military or other federal facilities, certain stadiums, power plants, electric substations, dams, oil refineries, national parks, emergency, services and other industrial complexes. In addition to the previously mentioned link, information regarding published NOTAMS can be found at: https://www.faa.gov/air_traffic/publication s/notices/.

The requirement to not fly within TFRs, or other circumstances where prohibited, would apply to operation of model aircraft that would otherwise comply with section 336 of Public Law 112-95.

Model aircraft operators should follow best practices including limiting operations to 400 feet above ground level (AGL).

All other operators and for additional information on Unmanned Aircraft Systems please visit: http://www.faa.gov/uas/.[4]

Federal Aviation Regulations Applicable to Model Aircraft

When flying a UAV in the National Airspace System, the aircraft is subject to the Federal Aviation Regulations (FARs) that also apply to manned aircraft.[5] Below are some of the key FAR's that UAV operators must be compliance with, unless they receive an

---

[4]
http://www.faa.gov/documentLibrary/media/Adviso ry_Circular/AC_91-57A.pdf

[5] http://www.ecfr.gov/cgi-bin/text-idx?c=ecfr&sid=3efaad1b0a259d4e48f1150a34d1aa 77&rgn=div5&view=text&node=14:2.0.1.3.10&idno= 14

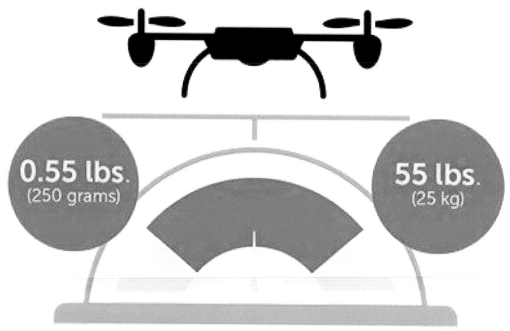

exemption from the FAA. H.R. 658 which is also known as the FAA Modernization Act of 2013 allows for exemptions to be made under Section 333. Simply stated, Section 333 "requires the Secretary to determine if certain drones may operate safely in the national airspace system before completion of the plan".[6]

Small Unmanned Aircraft Systems Defined

14 CFR part 107 applies to the operation of certain civil small unmanned aircraft within the NAS. Except for certain excluded aircraft operations, any aircraft that meets the criteria below is considered a small unmanned aircraft.

Small unmanned aircraft:

- Weigh less than 55 pounds (25 kg), including everything that is onboard or otherwise attached to the aircraft

- Are operated without the possibility of direct human intervention from within or on the aircraft

A small unmanned aircraft system includes the unmanned aircraft itself and its associated elements that are required for safe operation, such as communication links and components that control the aircraft.

Registration

Like other types of civil aircraft, most sUAS must be registered with the FAA prior to operating in the NAS.

Owners must register the sUAS if it is greater than 0.55 lbs and operated under the provisions of 14 CFR part 107. The owner must satisfy the registration requirements described in 14 CFR part 47, *Aircraft Registration,* or part 48, *Registration and Marking Requirements for Small Unmanned Aircraft.* If the owner is

---

[6] https://www.congress.gov/bill/112th-congress/house-bill/658

less than 13 years of age, then the small unmanned aircraft must be registered by a person who is at least 13 years of age.

14 CFR part 48 establishes the streamlined online registration option for sUAS that will be operated only within the territorial limits of the United States.
Visit the Resources page to access:

> FAA guidance on sUAS registration and marking
> FAA's online UAS registration website

An sUAS operation requires a Foreign Aircraft Permit if it involves a civil aircraft that is:

> Registered in a foreign country, or
> Owned, controlled, or operated by someone who is not a U.S. citizen or permanent resident.

If either criteria is met, the Remote PIC should obtain a Foreign Aircraft Permit pursuant to 14 CFR part 375.41 before conducting any operations. Application instructions are specified in 14 CFR part 375.43, *Navigation of Foreign Civil Aircraft within the United States*. Submit the application by electronic mail to the Department of Transportation (DOT) Office of International Aviation, Foreign Air Carrier Licensing Division.
Visit the Resources page to access 14 CFR part 375.43 and additional guidance at the DOT Foreign Air Carrier Economic Licensing website.[7]

Registration number may be enclosed in a compartment ***only*** if you can access the compartment without tools.

Before operation, mark the sUAS to identify that it is registered with the FAA.
The registration marking must be:[8]

- **A unique identifier number.** This is typically the FAA-issued registration number or the serial number, if authorized during registration.

- **Legible and durable.** Sample methods include engraving, permanent marker, or self-adhesive label.

- **Visible or accessible.** The number may be enclosed in a compartment only if you can access the compartment without tools.

---

[7] 14 CFR part 107.13; AC 107, *Small UAS* (as amended)

[8] 14 CFR part 48; AC 107, *Small UAS* (as amended); FAA Small UAS Registration FAQs (https://www.faa.gov/uas/registration/faqs/#mou)

An FAA airworthiness certification is not required for sUAS. However, the Remote PIC must maintain and inspect the sUAS prior to each flight to ensure that it is in a condition for safe operation. For example, inspect the aircraft for equipment damage or malfunctions.

More information about maintenance and preflight inspections is provided later in this course.

The 333 Exemption

With the advent of FAA Part 107, commercial operators who hold a "333 Exemption" are deciding if they should in fact operate under Part 107 or their "333 Exemption".

Companies conducting operations under Section 333 might have more flexibility and be operating under a higher standard which customers may see as better quality and improved safety.

Under Section 333 by law, any aircraft operation in the national airspace system requires a certificated and registered aircraft, a licensed pilot, and operational approval. Section 333 of the FAA Modernization and Reform Act of 2012 grants the Secretary of Transportation the authority to determine whether an airworthiness certificate is required for a UAS to operate safely in the National Airspace System (NAS).

This authority is being leveraged to grant case-by-case authorization for certain unmanned aircraft to perform commercial operations prior to the finalization of the Small UAS Rule, which will be the primary method for authorizing small UAS operations once it is complete.

The Section 333 Exemption process provides operators who wish to pursue safe and legal entry into the NAS a competitive advantage in the UAS marketplace, thus discouraging illegal operations and improving safety. It is anticipated that this activity will result in significant economic benefits, and the FAA Administrator has identified this as a high priority project to address demand for civil operation of UAS for commercial purposes.9

Crew Members

When flying under a 333 Exemption, holders must have the required flight crew as stated in their exemption. When flying under Part 107, this is not required but is encouraged.

9

https://www.faa.gov/uas/legislative_programs/section_333/

Below is a definition of the crew roles:

- **Remote Pilot in Command (PIC):** A person who holds a current remote pilot certificate with an sUAS rating and has the final authority and responsibility for the operation and safety of the sUAS
- **Person manipulating the controls:** A person controlling the sUAS under direct supervision of the Remote PIC
- **Visual observer:** A person acting as a flight crewmember to help see and avoid air traffic or other objects in the sky, overhead, or on the ground

Supporting Crew Roles: Person Manipulating the Controls

A non-certificated person may operate the sUAS under Part 107 **only if:**

- He or she is directly supervised by the
- Remote PIC **and,**

- The Remote PIC has the ability to immediately take direct control of the sUAS

The Remote PIC is ultimately responsible for identifying hazardous conditions. The Remote PIC's ability to regain control of the sUAS is necessary to ensure that he or she can quickly intervene to ensure the safety of the flight and prevent a hazardous situation before an accident or incident occurs.[10]

Supporting Crew Roles: Visual Observer

The role of visual observers (VOs) is to alert the rest of the crew about potential hazards during sUAS operations. The use of VOs is optional. However, the Remote PIC may use one or more VOs to supplement situational awareness and visual-line-of-sight responsibilities while the Remote PIC is conducting other mission-critical duties (such as checking displays).

The Remote PIC must make certain that all VOs:

- Are positioned in a location where they
- are able to see the sUAS continuously
- and sufficiently to maintain visual line of
- sight
- Possess a means to effectively
- communicate the sUAS position and the
- position of other aircraft to the Remote
- PIC and person manipulating the
- controls[11]

---

[10] AC 107, *Small UAS* (as amended)

[11] 14 CFR part 107.3 and 107.33; AC 107, *Small UAS* (as amended)

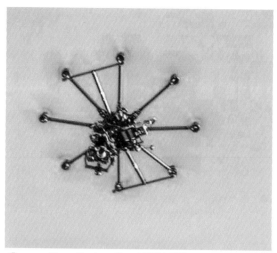

Operating Rules for UAV Pilots

Title 14 CFR Part 107 prohibits operation of a small UAS at night, defined in 14 CFR part 1 as the time between the end of evening civil twilight and the beginning of morning civil twilight, as published in the Federal Air Almanac, and converted to local time.

The Federal Air Almanac provides tables to determine sunrise and sunset at various latitudes. For example:[12]

- In the contiguous United States, evening civil twilight is the period of sunset until 30 minutes after sunset and morning civil twilight is the period of 30 minutes prior to sunrise until sunrise

- In Alaska, the definition of civil twilight differs and is described in the Federal Air Almanac.

Operations in Civil Twilight

When sUAS operations are conducted during civil twilight, the sUAS must be equipped with anti-collision lights that are capable of being visible for at least 3 statute miles.

However, the Remote PIC may reduce the intensity of the lighting if he or she has determined that it would be in the interest of operational safety to do so. For example, the Remote PIC may momentarily reduce the lighting intensity if it impacts his or her night-vision.[13]

Visual Line of Sight

The small unmanned aircraft must remain within visual line-of-sight (VLOS) of flight crewmembers. Visual line of sight means any flight crewmember (i.e. the Remote PIC; person manipulating the controls; and visual observers, if used) is capable of seeing the aircraft with vision unaided by any device other than corrective lenses (spectacles or contact lenses).

Crewmembers must operate within the following limitations.

- Minimum visibility, as observed from the location of the control station, must be no less than 3 statute miles

- Minimum distance from clouds must be no less than 500 feet below a cloud and 2000 feet horizontally from the cloud

Crewmembers must be able to see the small unmanned aircraft at all times during flight.

[12]14 CFR part 107.29; AC 107, *Small UAS* (as amended)
[13]14 CFR part 107.29; AC 107, *Small UAS* (as amended)

Therefore, the small unmanned aircraft must be operated closely enough to the control station to ensure visibility requirements are met during small unmanned aircraft operations.[14]

Restrictions on Vision Aids

Visual line of sight must be accomplished and maintained by unaided vision, except vision that is corrected by the use of eyeglasses (spectacles) or contact lenses.

Vision aids, such as binoculars, may be used only momentarily to enhance situational awareness. For example, the Remote PIC, person manipulating the controls, or visual observer may use vision aids briefly to avoid flying over persons or to avoid conflicting with other aircraft.

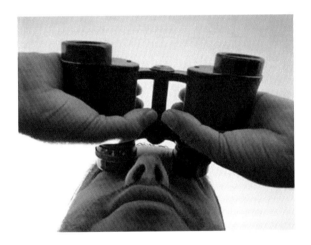

Regaining Visual Line of Sight

The Remote PIC or person manipulating the controls may have brief moments in which he or she is not looking directly at or cannot see the small unmanned aircraft, but still retains the capability to see it or quickly maneuver it back to line of sight.

These moments should be for:

- **The safety of the operation,** such as briefly looking down at the control station or scanning the airspace. To scan for traffic, the crew should systematically

focus on different segments of the sky for short intervals.

- **Operational necessity,** such as intentionally maneuvering the aircraft for a brief period behind an obstruction.

There is no specific time interval for which interruption of visual contact is permissible. Such parameters could potentially allow a hazardous interruption or prohibit a reasonable one.

The Remote PIC or person manipulating the controls must attempt to regain visual line of sight:

- **Immediately,** if he or she unintentionally loses sight of the aircraft
- **As soon as practicable,** if he or she loses sight of the aircraft for operational necessity

Operating Limitations for Small Unmanned Aircraft

The small unmanned aircraft must be operated in accordance with the following limitations:[15]

- Cannot be flown faster than a groundspeed of 87 knots (100 miles per hour)
- Cannot be flown higher than 400 feet above ground level (AGL) unless flown within a 400-foot radius of a structure and is not flown higher than 400 feet above the structure's immediate uppermost limit

Operation in Certain Airspace

Many sUAS operations can be conducted in uncontrolled, Class G airspace without further permission or authorization.

However, operations require prior authorization from Air Traffic Control (ATC) in Class B, C, and D airspace and within the lateral boundaries of

---

[14]14 CFR parts 107.31 and 107.51; AC 107, *Small UAS* (as amended)

[15] 14 CFR part 107.51; AC 107, *Small UAS* (as amended)

the surface area of Class E airspace designated for an airport.

It is incumbent on the Remote PIC to be aware of the type of airspace in which they will be operating their sUAS. As with other flight operations, the Remote PIC should refer to current aeronautical charts and other navigation tools to determine position and related airspace.

Notices to Airmen (NOTAMs)

Temporary Flight Restrictions (TFRs) are inclusive of sUAS operations. For that reason, it is necessary for the Remote PIC to check for Notices to Airmen (NOTAMs) before each flight to determine if there are any applicable airspace restrictions.

Common TFRs that relate to sUAS operations include, but are not limited to:

- Presidential TFRs and NOTAMs

- Emergency response TFRs and NOTAMs

- Standing TFRs that go into and out of effect (e.g., stadiums for sporting events)

Obtaining Airspace Authorizations

ATC has the authority to approve or deny aircraft operations based on traffic density, controller workload, communication issues, or any other type of operations that could potentially impact the safe and expeditious flow of air traffic in that airspace.

When ATC authorization is required, it must be requested and granted before any operation in

that airspace. There is currently no established timeline for approval after ATC permission has been requested because the time required for approval will vary based on the resources available at the ATC facility and the complexity and safety issues raised by each specific request.

For this reason, Remote PICs should contact the appropriate ATC facility as soon as possible prior to any operation in Class B, C and D airspace and within the lateral boundaries of the surface area of Class E airspace designated for an airport.

Frequency Spectrum

Most sUAS use radio frequencies to establish the data link between the control station and the small unmanned aircraft.
Considerations for radio frequencies used in sUAS operations include:

- Frequency interference
- Line of sight/obstructions

Line of Sight and Frequency Obstructions

Both sUAS radio frequency bands (2.4GHz and 5.8GHz) are considered line of sight.
Be aware that the command and control link between the control station and the small unmanned aircraft may not work properly when barriers are between the control station and the unmanned aircraft.

No Operation Over People

You may not operate a small unmanned aircraft directly over another person **unless** that person is:

Directly involved in the operation (such as a visual observer or other crewmember)
OR
Within a safe cover, such as inside a stationary vehicle or a protective structure that would protect a person from harm if the small unmanned aircraft were to crash into that structure.

Protecting Non-Participants

To comply with limitations on sUAS operations near persons not participating in the operation, the Remote PIC should employ the strategies described below.

Select an appropriate operational area for the sUAS flight. Ideally, select an operational area (site) that is sparsely populated. If operating in populated/inhabited areas, make a plan to keep non-participants clear, indoors, or under cover. If operating from a moving vehicle, choose a sparsely populated (or unpopulated) area and make a plan to keep sUAS clear of anyone who may approach

Adopt an appropriate operating distance from non-participants, and take reasonable precautions to keep the operational area free of non-participants

Transporting Another Person's Property

You may also operate an sUAS to transport another person's property (cargo) for compensation or hire provided you comply with the additional requirements described below.

- The total weight of the sUAS (including the cargo) must remain below 55lbs

- The sUAS operation must be within the boundaries of a State (intrastate)
- No items may be dropped from the small unmanned aircraft in a manner that creates an undue hazard to persons or property
- You may not operate the sUAS from a moving land vehicle or water-born vessel

Moving Vehicles: Part 107 Restrictions

Operations from moving vehicles are subject to the same restrictions that apply to all other part 107 sUAS operations.
Examples include:

- **Visual Line of Sight:** The Remote PIC (and the person manipulating the controls, if applicable) operating from a moving vehicle or watercraft is still required to maintain visual line of sight for the sUAS
- **Operations over People:** Operations are still prohibited over persons not directly involved in the operation of the sUAS, unless under safe cover. The Remote PIC is also responsible for ensuring that no person is subject to undue risk as a result of loss of control of the small unmanned aircraft for any reason.

- **Communication:** The visual observer and Remote PIC must still maintain effective communication

- **No Reckless Operation:** Part 107 also prohibits careless or reckless operation of an sUAS. Operating an sUAS while driving a moving vehicle is considered to be careless or reckless because the driver's attention would be hazardously divided. Therefore, the driver of a land vehicle or the operator of a water-borne vehicle must not serve as the Remote PIC, person manipulating the controls, or visual observer.

Moving Vehicles: State and Local Traffic Laws

Other laws, such as State and local traffic laws, may also apply to the conduct of a person driving a vehicle.
Many states currently prohibit distracted driving and state or local laws may also be amended in the future to impose restrictions on how cars and public roads may be used with regard to an sUAS operation. The FAA emphasizes that people involved in an sUAS operation are responsible for complying with all applicable laws and not just the FAA's regulations.

---

[16]14 CFR part 107.17; AC 107, *Small UAS* (as amended)

No Operations While Impaired

Part 107 does not allow operation of an sUAS if the Remote PIC, person manipulating the controls, or visual observer is unable to safely carry out his or her duties and responsibilities.

While drug and alcohol use are known to impair judgment, certain over-the-counter medications and medical conditions could also affect the ability to safely operate a small unmanned aircraft. For example, certain antihistamines and decongestants may cause drowsiness.

You may not directly participate in the operation of an sUAS if you know or have reason to know that you have a physical or mental condition that would interfere with the safe operation of the sUAS.[16]

No Hazardous Operation

No person may operate an sUAS in a careless or reckless manner so as to endanger another person's life or property. Part 107 also prohibits allowing an object to be dropped from an sUAS in a manner that creates an undue hazard to persons or property.[17]

---

[17]14 CFR part 107.23

Examples of hazardous operation include, but are not limited to:

- Operations that interfere with manned aircraft operations
- Operating an sUAS over persons not directly participating in the operation
- Loading the sUAS beyond its capabilities to the point of losing control

Certificates of Waiver

If the Remote PIC determines that the operation cannot be conducted within the regulatory structure of part 107, he or she is responsible for applying for a Certificate of Waiver in accordance with 14 CFR part 107.200 and proposing a safe alternative to the operation.

This Certificate of Waiver will allow an sUAS operation to deviate from certain provisions of part 107 as long as the FAA finds that the proposed operation can be safely conducted under the terms of that Certificate of Waiver.[18]

---

[18]14 CFR part 107.200

Waivable Sections of Part 107

Your request for a waiver may be granted if the FAA finds that the proposed operation can be safely conducted under the terms of that Certificate of Waiver.

A list of the waivable sections of part 107 can be found in 14 CFR part 107.205 and are listed below:

- § 107.25 Operation from a moving vehicle or aircraft. However, no waiver of this provision will be issued to allow the carriage of property of another by aircraft for compensation or hire
- § 107.29 Daylight operation
- § 107.31 Visual line of sight aircraft operation. However, no waiver of this provision will be

issued to allow the carriage of property of another by aircraft for compensation or hire

- § 107.33 Visual observer
- § 107.35 Operation of multiple small unmanned aircraft systems
- § 107.37(a) Yielding the right of way
- § 107.39 Operation over people
- § 107.41 Operation in certain airspace
- § 107.51 Operating limitations for small unmanned aircraft

Emergency Planning and Communication

In case of an in-flight emergency, the Remote _**PIC is permitted to deviate from any rule of part 107 to the extent necessary to meet that emergency**_. Upon FAA request, you must send a written report to the FAA explaining the deviation.

Become familiar with any manufacturer suggested emergency procedures prior to flight. Review emergency actions during preflight planning and inform crew members of their responsibilities.[19]

Common Abnormal and Emergency Situations

The Remote PIC must be prepared to respond to abnormal and emergency situations during sUAS operations.
Refer to the manufacturer's guidance for appropriate procedures in the following situations:

Abnormal situations, such as lost link, alternate landing/recovery sites, and flight termination (controlled flight to the ground)
Emergency situations, such as flyaways, loss of Global Positioning System (GPS), and battery fires.

---

[19]14 CFR part 107.21; AC 107

Lost Link

Without an onboard pilot, sUAS crewmembers rely on the command and control link to operate the aircraft. For example, an uplink transmits command instructions to the aircraft and a downlink transmits the status of the aircraft and provides situational awareness to the Remote PIC or person manipulating the controls.

Lost link is an interruption or loss of the control link between the control station and the unmanned aircraft, preventing control of the aircraft. As a result, the unmanned aircraft performs pre-set lost link procedures. Such procedures ensure that the unmanned aircraft:

- Remains airborne in a predictable or planned maneuver, allowing time to re-establish the communication link
- Autolands, if available, after a predetermined length of time or terminates the flight when the power source is depleted

A lost link is an abnormal situation, but not an emergency. A lost link is not considered a flyaway, which is defined in the next section of this lesson.

Flight Termination

Flight termination is the intentional and deliberate process of performing controlled flight to the ground. Flight termination may be part of lost link procedures, or it may be a contingency that you elect to use if further flight of the aircraft cannot be safely achieved, or if other potential hazards exist that require immediate discontinuation of flight.

Execute flight termination procedures if you have exhausted all other contingencies. Flight termination points (FTPs), if used, or alternative contingency planning measures must:

- Be located within power-off glide distance of the aircraft during all phases of flight
- Be based on the assumption of an unrecoverable system failure
- Take into consideration altitude, winds, and other factors

Flyaways

A **flyaway** begins as a lost link—an interruption or loss of the control link prevents control of the aircraft. As a result, the unmanned aircraft is not operating in a predicable or planned manner. However, in a flyaway, the pre-set lost link procedures are not established or are not being executed by the unmanned aircraft, creating an emergency situation.
If a flyaway occurs while operating in airspace that requires authorization, notify ATC as outlined in the authorization.

Loss of Global Positioning System (GPS)

Global positioning system (GPS) tools can be a valuable resource for flight planning and situational awareness during sUAS operation.

However, as with manned aviation, Remote PICs in sUAS operations must avoid overreliance on automation and must be prepared to operate the unmanned aircraft manually, if necessary.

- Prior to flight, check NOTAMs for any known GPS service disruptions in the planned location of the sUAS operation
- Make a plan of action to prevent or minimize damage in the event of equipment malfunction or failure.

Risk of Battery Fires

Battery fires pose a significant hazard to sUAS.

Both Lithium metal and lithium-ion batteries are:

- Highly flammable

- Capable of self-ignition when a battery short circuits or is overcharged, heated to extreme temperatures, mishandled, or otherwise defective
- Subject to thermal runaway

During thermal runaway, lithium metal batteries generate sufficient heat to cause adjacent cells to go into thermal runaway. As a result, the lithium metal cell releases an explosive combination of a flammable electrolyte and molten lithium metal, accompanied by a large pressure pulse.[20]

---

[20]Safety Alert for Operators (SAFO) 10017, Risks in Transporting Lithium Batteries in Cargo by Aircraft

Preventing Battery Fires: Storage

Ensure careful storage of spare (uninstalled) lithium batteries.
Take the following precautions to prevent a battery fire:[21]

- Prevent short circuits by placing each individual battery in the original retail packaging, a separate plastic bag, or a protective pouch or by insulating exposed terminals with tape.

- Do not allow spare batteries to come in contact with metal objects, such as coins, keys, or jewelry

- Take steps to prevent objects from crushing, puncturing, or applying pressure on the battery

Accident Reporting

The Remote PIC must report any sUAS accident to the FAA, within 10 days of the operation, if any of the following thresholds are met:

- **Serious injury** to any person or any loss of consciousness
- **Damage** to any property, other than the small unmanned aircraft, if the cost is

greater than $500 to repair or replace the property (whichever is lower)

File the report:

> **Electronically,** via the FAA online sUAS accident reporting website
> **By phone** to:
> > The appropriate FAA Regional Operations Center
> > The nearest Flight Standards District Office (FSDO)[22]

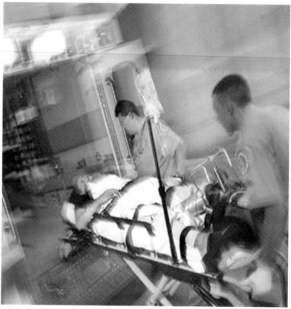

Accident Reporting: Serious Injury Threshold

Under 14 CFR part 107, a serious injury qualifies as Level 3 or higher on the Abbreviated Injury Scale (AIS) of the Association for the Advancement of Automotive Medicine. This scale is an anatomical scoring system that is widely used by emergency medical personnel.

It would be considered a serious injury **if a person requires hospitalization, but the injury is fully reversible** including, but not limited to:[23]

> Head trauma
> Broken bone(s)

---

[21]SAFO 15010, Carriage of Spare Lithium Batteries in Carry-On and Checked Baggage

[22]14 CFR part 107.9; AC 107
[23]14 CFR part 107(III)(I)(2); AC 107

Laceration(s) to the skin that requires suturing

Accident Reporting: Required Information
If the accident meets the previously described thresholds, report the following key information to FAA.

Remote PIC Information
    Name
    Contact Information
    FAA Airman Certificate Number
Aircraft Information
    Registration Number (N-number or unique identifier issued in accordance with 14 CFR part 48)
Accident Information
    Location of the Accident
    Date and Time of the Accident
    Person(s) Injured and Extent of Injury (if any or known)
    Property Damaged and Extent of Damage (if any or known)
    Description of What Happened

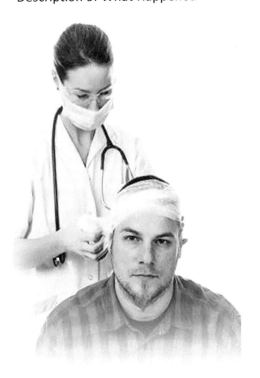

In addition to this FAA report, and in accordance with the criteria established by the National Transportation Safety Board (NTSB), certain sUAS accidents must also be reported to the NTSB.

FAR Part 91: General Operating Rules

In addition to the requirements of FAR Part 107, sUAS operators must also comply with other FAR requirements that are applicable to all aircraft, including but not limited to the following:

91.13 - Careless or reckless operation.

(a) Aircraft operations for the purpose of air navigation. No person may operate an aircraft in a careless or reckless manner so as to endanger the life or property of another.
(b) Aircraft operations other than for the purpose of air navigation. No person may operate an aircraft, other than for the purpose of air navigation, on any part of the surface of an airport used by aircraft for air commerce (including areas used by those aircraft for receiving or discharging persons or cargo), in a careless or reckless manner so as to endanger the life or property of another.

91.15 - Dropping objects.

No pilot in command of a civil aircraft may allow any object to be dropped from that aircraft in flight that creates a hazard to persons or property. However, this section does not prohibit the dropping of any object if reasonable precautions are taken to avoid injury or damage to persons or property.

91.113 - Right-of-way rules: Except water operations.

(a) Inapplicability. This section does not apply to the operation of an aircraft on water.

(b) General. When weather conditions permit, regardless of whether an operation is conducted under instrument flight rules or visual flight rules, vigilance shall be maintained by each person operating an aircraft so as to see and avoid other aircraft. When a rule of this section gives another aircraft the right-of-way, the pilot shall give way to that aircraft and may not pass over, under, or ahead of it unless well clear.

(c) In distress. An aircraft in distress has the right-of-way over all other air traffic.

(d) Converging. When aircraft of the same category are converging at approximately the same altitude (except head-on, or nearly so), the aircraft to the other's right has the right-of-way. If the aircraft are of different categories--

(1) A balloon has the right-of-way over any other category of aircraft;

[(2) A glider has the right-of-way over an airship, powered parachute, weight-shift-control aircraft, airplane, or rotorcraft.

(3) An airship has the right-of-way over a powered parachute, weight-shift-control aircraft, airplane, or rotorcraft.]

However, an aircraft towing or refueling other aircraft has the right-of-way over all other engine-driven aircraft.

(e) Approaching head-on. When aircraft are approaching each other head-on, or nearly so, each pilot of each aircraft shall alter course to the right.

(f) Overtaking. Each aircraft that is being overtaken has the right-of-way and each pilot of an overtaking aircraft shall alter course to the right to pass well clear.

(g) Landing. Aircraft, while on final approach to land or while landing, have the right-of-way over other aircraft in flight or operating on the surface, except that they shall not take advantage of this rule to force an aircraft off the runway surface which has already landed and is attempting to make way for an aircraft on final approach. When two or more aircraft are approaching an airport for the purpose of landing, the aircraft at the lower altitude has the right-of-way, but it shall not take advantage of this rule to cut in front of another which is on final approach to land or to overtake that aircraft.

91.126 - Operating on or in the vicinity of an airport in Class G airspace.

(a) General. Unless otherwise authorized or required, each person operating an aircraft on or in the vicinity of an airport in a Class G airspace area must comply with the requirements of this section.

(b) Direction of turns. When approaching to land at an airport without an operating control tower in Class G airspace--

(1) Each pilot of an airplane must make all turns of that airplane to the left unless the airport displays approved light signals or visual markings indicating that turns should be made to the right, in which case the pilot must make all turns to the right; and

[(2) Each pilot of a helicopter or a powered parachute must avoid the flow of fixed-wing aircraft.]

(c) Flap settings. Except when necessary for training or certification, the pilot in command of a civil turbojet-powered aircraft must use, as a final flap setting, the minimum certificated landing flap setting set forth in the approved performance information in the Airplane Flight Manual for the applicable conditions. However, each pilot in command has the final authority and responsibility for the safe operation of the pilot's airplane, and may use a different flap setting for that airplane if the pilot determines that it is necessary in the interest of safety.

(d) Communications with control towers. Unless otherwise authorized or required by ATC, no person may operate an aircraft to, from, through, or on an airport having an operational control tower unless two-way radio communications are maintained between that aircraft and the control tower. Communications must be established prior to 4 nautical miles from the airport, up to and including 2,500 feet AGL. However, if the aircraft radio fails in flight, the pilot in command may operate that aircraft and land if weather conditions are at or above basic VFR weather minimums, visual contact with the tower is maintained, and a clearance to land is received. If the aircraft radio fails while in flight under IFR, the pilot must comply with Sec. 91.185.

91.127 - Operating on or in the vicinity of an airport in Class E airspace.

(a) Unless otherwise required by part 93 of this chapter or unless otherwise authorized or required by the ATC facility having jurisdiction over the Class E airspace area, each person operating an aircraft on or in the vicinity of an airport in a Class E airspace area must comply with the requirements of Sec. 91.126.

(b) Departures. Each pilot of an aircraft must comply with any traffic patterns established for that airport in part 93 of this chapter.

(c) Communications with control towers. Unless otherwise authorized or required by ATC, no person may operate an aircraft to, from, through, or on an airport having an operational control tower unless two-way radio communications are maintained between that aircraft and the control tower. Communications must be established prior to 4 nautical miles from the airport, up to and including 2,500 feet AGL. However, if the aircraft radio fails in flight, the pilot in command may operate that aircraft and land if weather conditions are at or above basic VFR weather minimums, visual contact with the tower is maintained, and a clearance to land is received. If the aircraft radio fails while in flight under IFR, the pilot must comply with Sec. 91.185.

91.129 - Operations in Class D airspace.

(a) General. Unless otherwise authorized or required by the ATC facility having jurisdiction over the Class D airspace area, each person operating an aircraft in Class D airspace must comply with the applicable provisions of this section. In addition, each person must comply with Secs. 91.126 and 91.127. For the purpose of this section, the primary airport is the airport for which the Class D airspace area is designated. A satellite airport is any other airport within the Class D airspace area.

(b) Deviations. An operator may deviate from any provision of this section under the provisions of an ATC authorization issued by the ATC facility having jurisdiction over the airspace concerned. ATC may authorize a deviation on a continuing basis or for an individual flight, as appropriate.

(c) Communications. Each person operating an aircraft in Class D airspace must meet the following two-way radio communications requirements:

(1) Arrival or through flight. Each person must establish two-way radio communications with the ATC facility (including foreign ATC in the case of foreign airspace designated in the United States) providing air traffic services prior to entering that airspace and thereafter maintain those communications while within that airspace.

(2) Departing flight. Each person--

(i) From the primary airport or satellite airport with an operating control tower must establish and maintain two-way radio communications with the control tower, and thereafter as instructed by ATC while operating in the Class D airspace area; or

(ii) From a satellite airport without an operating control tower, must establish and maintain two-way radio communications with the ATC facility having jurisdiction over the Class D airspace area as soon as practicable after departing.

(d) Communications failure. Each person who operates an aircraft in a Class D airspace area must maintain two-way radio

communications with the ATC facility having jurisdiction over that area.

(1) If the aircraft radio fails in flight under IFR, the pilot must comply with Sec. 91.185 of the part.

(2) If the aircraft radio fails in flight under VFR, the pilot in command may operate that aircraft and land if--

(i) Weather conditions are at or above basic VFR weather minimums;

(ii) Visual contact with the tower is maintained; and

(iii) A clearance to land is received.

[(e) Minimum altitudes when operating to an airport in Class D airspace. (1) Unless required by the applicable distance-from-cloud criteria, each pilot operating a large or turbine-powered airplane must enter the traffic pattern at an altitude of at least 1,500 feet above the elevation of the airport and maintain at least 1,500 feet until further descent is required for a safe landing.

(2) Each pilot operating a large or turbine-powered airplane approaching to land on a runway served by an instrument approach procedure with vertical guidance, if the airplane is so equipped, must:

(i) Operate that airplane at an altitude at or above the glide path between the published final approach fix and the decision altitude (DA), or decision height (DH), as applicable; or

(ii) If compliance with the applicable distance-from-cloud criteria requires glide path interception closer in, operate that airplane at or above the glide path, between the point of interception of glide path and the DA or the DH.

(3) Each pilot operating an airplane approaching to land on a runway served by a visual approach slope indicator must maintain an altitude at or above the glide

path until a lower altitude is necessary for a safe landing.

(4) Paragraphs (e)(2) and (e)(3) of this section do not prohibit normal bracketing maneuvers above or below the glide path that are conducted for the purpose of remaining on the glide path.]

(f) Approaches. Except when conducting a circling approach under Part 97 of this chapter or unless otherwise required by ATC, each pilot must--

(1) Circle the airport to the left, if operating an airplane; or

(2) Avoid the flow of fixed-wing aircraft, if operating a helicopter.

(g) Departures. No person may operate an aircraft departing from an airport except in compliance with the following:

(1) Each pilot must comply with any departure procedures established for that airport by the FAA.

(2) Unless otherwise required by the prescribed departure procedure for that airport or the applicable distance from clouds criteria, each pilot of a turbine-powered airplane and each pilot of a large airplane must climb to an altitude of 1,500 feet above the surface as rapidly as practicable.

(h) Noise abatement. Where a formal runway use program has been established by the FAA, each pilot of a large or turbine-powered airplane assigned a noise abatement runway by ATC must use that runway. However, consistent with the final authority of the pilot in command concerning the safe operation of the aircraft as prescribed in Sec. 91.3(a), ATC may assign a different runway if requested by the pilot in the interest of safety.

(i) Takeoff, landing, taxi clearance. No person may, at any airport with an operating control tower, operate an aircraft on a runway or taxiway, or take off or land an aircraft, unless an appropriate clearance is received from ATC. A clearance to "taxi to" the takeoff runway assigned to the aircraft is not a clearance to cross that assigned takeoff runway, or to taxi on that runway at any point, but is a clearance to cross other runways that intersect the taxi route to that assigned takeoff runway. A clearance to "taxi to" any point other than an assigned takeoff runway is clearance to cross all runways that intersect the taxi route to that point.

91.130 - Operations in Class C airspace.

(a) General. Unless otherwise authorized by ATC, each aircraft operation in Class C airspace must be conducted in compliance with this section and Sec. 91.129. For the purpose of this section, the primary airport is the airport for which the Class C airspace area is designated. A satellite airport is any other airport within the Class C airspace area.

(b) Traffic patterns. No person may take off or land an aircraft at a satellite airport within a Class C airspace area except in compliance with FAA arrival and departure traffic patterns.

(c) Communications. Each person operating an aircraft in Class C airspace must meet the following two-way radio communications requirements:

(1) Arrival or through flight. Each person must establish two-way radio communications with the ATC facility (including foreign ATC in the case of foreign airspace designated in the United States) providing air traffic services prior to entering that airspace and thereafter maintain those

communications while within that airspace.

(2) Departing flight. Each person--

(i) From the primary airport or satellite airport with an operating control tower must establish and maintain two-way radio communications with the control tower, and thereafter as instructed by ATC while operating in the Class C airspace area; or

(ii) From a satellite airport without an operating control tower, must establish and maintain two-way radio communications with the ATC facility having jurisdiction over the Class C airspace area as soon as practicable after departing.

(d) Equipment requirements. Unless otherwise authorized by the ATC having jurisdiction over the Class C airspace area, no person may operate an aircraft within a Class C airspace area designated for an airport unless that aircraft is equipped with the applicable equipment specified in Sec. 91.215.

(e) Deviations. An operator may deviate from any provision of this section under the provisions of an ATC authorization issued by the ATC facility having jurisdiction over the airspace concerned. ATC may authorize a deviation on a continuing basis or for an individual flight, as appropriate.

91.131 - Operations in Class B airspace.

(a)   Operating rules. No person may operate an aircraft within a Class B airspace area except in compliance with Sec. 91.129 and the following rules:

(1) The operator must receive an ATC clearance from the ATC facility having jurisdiction for that area before operating an aircraft in that area.

(2) Unless otherwise authorized by ATC, each person operating a large turbine engine-powered airplane to or from a primary airport for which a Class B airspace area is designated must operate at or above the designated floors of the Class B airspace area while within the lateral limits of that area.

(3) Any person conducting pilot training operations at an airport within a Class B airspace area must comply with any procedures established by ATC for such operations in that area.

(b) Pilot requirements.

(1) No person may take off or land a civil aircraft at an airport within a Class B airspace area or operate a civil aircraft within a Class B airspace area unless--

(i) The pilot in command holds at least a private pilot certificate;

(ii) The pilot in command holds a recreational pilot certificate and has met--

(A) The requirements of Sec. 61.101(d) of this chapter; or

(B) The requirements for a student pilot seeking a recreational pilot certificate in Sec. 61.94 of this chapter;

(iii) The pilot in command holds a sport pilot certificate and has met--

(A) The requirements of Sec. 61.325 of this chapter; or

(B) The requirements for a student pilot seeking a recreational pilot certificate in Sec. 61.94 of this chapter; or

(iv) The aircraft is operated by a student pilot who has met the requirements of Sec. 61.94 or Sec. 61.95 of this chapter, as applicable.

(2) Notwithstanding the provisions of paragraphs (b)(1)(ii), (b)(1)(iii) and (b)(1)(iv) of this section, no person may take off or land a civil aircraft at those airports listed in section 4 of appendix D to this part unless

the pilot in command holds at least a private pilot certificate.

(c) Communications and navigation equipment requirements. Unless otherwise authorized by ATC, no person may operate an aircraft within a Class B airspace area unless that aircraft is equipped with--

(1) For IFR operation. An operable VOR or TACAN receiver or an operable and suitable RNAV system; and

(2) For all operations. An operable two-way radio capable of communications with ATC on appropriate frequencies for that Class B airspace area.

[(d) Other equipment requirements. No person may operate an aircraft in a Class B airspace area unless the aircraft is equipped with--

(1) The applicable operating transponder and automatic altitude reporting equipment specified in Sec. 91.215 (a), except as provided in Sec. 91.215 (e), and

(2) After January 1, 2020, the applicable Automatic Dependent Surveillance-Broadcast Out equipment specified in Sec. 91.225.]

91.133 - Restricted and prohibited areas.

(a) No person may operate an aircraft within a restricted area (designated in part 73) contrary to the restrictions imposed, or within a prohibited area, unless that person has the permission of the using or controlling agency, as appropriate.

(b) Each person conducting, within a restricted area, an aircraft operation (approved by the using agency) that creates the same hazards as the operations for which the restricted area was designated may deviate from the rules of this subpart that are not compatible with the operation of the aircraft.

91.135 - Operations in Class A airspace.

Except as provided in paragraph (d) of this section, each person operating an aircraft in Class A airspace must conduct that operation under instrument flight rules (IFR) and in compliance with the following:

(a) Clearance. Operations may be conducted only under an ATC clearance received prior to entering the airspace.

(b) Communications. Unless otherwise authorized by ATC, each aircraft operating in Class A airspace must be equipped with a two-way radio capable of communicating with ATC on a frequency assigned by ATC. Each pilot must maintain two-way radio communications with ATC while operating in Class A airspace.

[(c) Equipment requirements. Unless otherwise authorized by ATC, no person may operate an aircraft within Class A airspace unless that aircraft is equipped with the applicable equipment specified in Sec. 91.215, and after January 1, 2020, Sec. 91.225.]

(d) ATC authorizations. An operator may deviate from any provision of this section under the provisions of an ATC authorization issued by the ATC facility having jurisdiction of the airspace concerned. In the case of an inoperative transponder, ATC may immediately approve an operation within a Class A airspace area allowing flight to continue, if desired, to the airport of ultimate destination, including any intermediate stops, or to proceed to a place where suitable repairs can be made, or both. Requests for deviation from any provision of this section must be submitted in writing, at least 4 days before the proposed operation. ATC may authorize a deviation on a continuing basis or for an individual flight.

91.137 - Temporary flight restrictions in the vicinity of disaster/hazard areas.

(a) The Administrator will issue a Notice to Airmen (NOTAM) designating an area within which temporary flight restrictions apply and specifying the hazard or condition requiring their imposition, whenever he determines it is necessary in order to--
(1) Protect persons and property on the surface or in the air from a hazard associated with an incident on the surface;
(2) Provide a safe environment for the operation of disaster relief aircraft; or
(3) Prevent an unsafe congestion of sightseeing and other aircraft above an incident or event which may generate a high degree of public interest. The Notice to Airmen will specify the hazard or condition that requires the imposition of temporary flight restrictions.
(b) When a NOTAM has been issued under paragraph (a)(1) of this section, no person may operate an aircraft within the designated area unless that aircraft is participating in the hazard relief activities and is being operated under the direction of the official in charge of on scene emergency response activities.
(c) When a NOTAM has been issued under paragraph (a)(2) of this section, no person may operate an aircraft within the designated area unless at least one of the following conditions are met:

(1) The aircraft is participating in hazard relief activities and is being operated under the direction of the official in charge of on scene emergency response activities.

(2) The aircraft is carrying law enforcement officials.
(3) The aircraft is operating under the ATC approved IFR flight plan.
(4) The operation is conducted directly to or from an airport within the area, or is necessitated by the impracticability of VFR flight above or around the area due to weather, or terrain; notification is given to the Flight Service Station (FSS) or ATC facility specified in the NOTAM to receive advisories concerning disaster relief aircraft operations; and the operation does not hamper or endanger relief activities and is not conducted for the purpose of observing the disaster
(5) The aircraft is carrying properly accredited news representatives, and, prior to entering the area, a flight plan is filed with the appropriate FAA or ATC facility specified in the Notice to Airmen and the operation is conducted above the altitude used by the disaster relief aircraft, unless otherwise authorized by the official in charge of on scene emergency response activities.
(d) When a NOTAM has been issued under paragraph (a)(3) of this section, no person may operate an aircraft within the designated area unless at least one of the following conditions is met:

(1) The operation is conducted directly to or from an airport within the area, or is necessitated by the impracticability of VFR flight above or around the area due to weather or terrain, and the operation is not conducted for the purpose of observing the incident or event.
(2) The aircraft is operating under an ATC approved IFR flight plan.
(3) The aircraft is carrying incident or event personnel, or law enforcement officials.

(4) The aircraft is carrying properly accredited news representatives and, prior to entering that area, a flight plan is filed with the appropriate FSS or ATC facility specified in the NOTAM.

(e) Flight plans filed and notifications made with an FSS or ATC facility under this section shall include the following information:

(1) Aircraft identification, type and color.

(2) Radio communications frequencies to be used.

(3) Proposed times of entry of, and exit from, the designated area.

(4) Name of news media or organization and purpose of flight.

(5) Any other information requested by ATC.

91.138 - Temporary flight restrictions in national disaster areas in the State of Hawaii.

(a) When the Administrator has determined, pursuant to a request and justification provided by the Governor of the State of Hawaii, or the Governor's designee, that an inhabited area within a declared national disaster area in the State of Hawaii is in need of protection for humanitarian reasons, the Administrator will issue a Notice to Airmen (NOTAM) designating an area within which temporary flight restrictions apply. The Administrator will designate the extent and duration of the temporary flight restrictions necessary to provide for the protection of persons and property
on the surface.

(b) When a NOTAM has been issued in accordance with this section, no person may operate an aircraft within the designated airspace unless:

(1) That person has obtained authorization from the official in charge of associated emergency or disaster relief response activities, and is operating the aircraft under the conditions of that authorization;

(2) The aircraft is carrying law enforcement officials;

(3) The aircraft is carrying persons involved in an emergency or a legitimate scientific purpose;

(4) The aircraft is carrying properly accredited news persons, and that prior to entering the area, a flight plan is filed with the appropriate FAA or ATC facility specified in the NOTAM and the operation is conducted in compliance with the conditions and restrictions established by the official in charge of on-scene emergency response activities; or,

(5) The aircraft is operating in accordance with an ATC clearance or instruction.

(c) A NOTAM issued under this section is effective for 90 days or until the national disaster area designation is terminated, whichever comes first, unless terminated by notice or extended by the Administrator at the request of the Governor of the State of Hawaii or the Governor's designee.

91.139 - Emergency air traffic rules.

(a) This section prescribes a process for utilizing Notices to Airmen (NOTAMs) to advise of the issuance and operations under emergency air traffic rules and regulations and designates the official who is authorized to issue NOTAMs on behalf of the Administrator in certain matters under this section.

(b) Whenever the Administrator determines that an emergency condition exists, or will exist, relating to the FAA's ability to operate the air traffic control system and during which normal flight operations under this chapter cannot be conducted consistent with the required levels of safety and efficiency—

(1) The Administrator issues an immediately effective air traffic rule or regulation in response to that emergency condition; and

(2) The Administrator or the Associate Administrator for Air Traffic may utilize the NOTAM system to provide notification of the issuance of the rule or regulation. Those NOTAMs communicate information concerning the rules and regulations that govern flight operations, the use of navigation facilities, and designation of that airspace in which the rules and regulations apply.

(c) When a NOTAM has been issued under this section, no person may operate an aircraft, or other device governed by the regulation concerned, within the designated airspace except in accordance with the authorizations, terms, and conditions prescribed in the regulation covered by the NOTAM.

91,141 - Flight restrictions in the proximity of the Presidential and other parties.

No person may operate an aircraft over or in the vicinity of any area to be visited or traveled by the President, the Vice President, or other public figures contrary to the restrictions established by the Administrator and published in a Notice to Airmen (NOTAM).

91.143 - Flight limitation in the proximity of space flight operations.

[When a Notice to Airmen (NOTAM) is issued in accordance with this section, no person may operate any aircraft of U.S. registry, or pilot any aircraft under the authority of an airman certificate issued by the Federal Aviation Administration, within areas designated in a NOTAM for space flight operation except when authorized by ATC.]

91.144 - Temporary restriction on flight operations during abnormally high barometric pressure conditions.

(a) Special flight restrictions. When any information indicates that barometric pressure on the route of flight currently exceeds or will exceed 31 inches of mercury, no person may operate an aircraft or initiate a flight contrary to the requirements established by the Administrator and published in a Notice to Airmen issued under this section.

(b) Waivers. The Administrator is authorized to waive any restriction issued under paragraph (a) of this section to permit emergency supply, transport, or medical services to be delivered to isolated communities, where the operation can be conducted with an acceptable level of safety.

91.145 - Management of aircraft operations in the vicinity of aerial demonstrations and major sporting events.

(a)   The FAA will issue a Notice to Airmen (NOTAM) designating an area of airspace in which a temporary flight restriction applies when it determines that a temporary flight restriction is necessary to protect persons or property on the surface or in the air, to maintain air safety and efficiency, or to prevent the unsafe congestion of aircraft in the vicinity of an aerial demonstration or major sporting event. These demonstrations and events may include:

(1) United States Naval Flight Demonstration Team (Blue Angels);
(2) United States Air Force Air Demonstration Squadron (Thunderbirds);
(3) United States Army Parachute Team (Golden Knights);
(4) Summer/Winter Olympic Games;
(5) Annual Tournament of Roses Football Game;
(6) World Cup Soccer;
(7) Major League Baseball All-Star Game;
(8) World Series;
(9) Kodak Albuquerque International Balloon Fiesta;
(10) Sandia Classic Hang Gliding Competition;
(11) Indianapolis 500 Mile Race;
(12) Any other aerial demonstration or sporting event the FAA determines to need a temporary flight restriction in accordance with paragraph (b) of this section.
(b) In deciding whether a temporary flight restriction is necessary for an aerial demonstration or major sporting event not listed in paragraph (a) of this section, the FAA considers the following factors:
(1) Area where the event will be held.
(2) Effect flight restrictions will have on known aircraft operations.
(3) Any existing ATC airspace traffic management restrictions.
(4) Estimated duration of the event.
(5) Degree of public interest.
(6) Number of spectators.
(7) Provisions for spectator safety.
(8) Number and types of participating aircraft.
(9) Use of mixed high and low performance aircraft.
(10) Impact on non-participating aircraft.
(11) Weather minimums.
(12) Emergency procedures that will be in effect.
(c) A NOTAM issued under this section will state the name of the aerial demonstration or sporting event and specify the effective dates and times, the geographic features or coordinates, and any other restrictions or procedures governing flight operations in the designated airspace.
(d) When a NOTAM has been issued in accordance with this section, no person may operate an aircraft or device, or engage in any activity within the designated airspace area, except in accordance with the authorizations, terms, and conditions of the temporary flight restriction published in the NOTAM, unless otherwise authorized by:
(1) Air traffic control; or
(2) A Flight Standards Certificate of Waiver or Authorization issued for the demonstration or event.
(e) For the purpose of this section:
(1) Flight restricted airspace area for an aerial demonstration--The amount of airspace needed to protect persons and property on the surface or in the air, to maintain air safety and efficiency, or to prevent the unsafe congestion of aircraft will vary depending on the aerial demonstration and the factors listed in paragraph (b) of this section. The restricted airspace area will normally be limited to a 5 nautical mile radius from the center of the demonstration and an altitude 17000 mean

sea level (for high performance aircraft) or 13000 feet above the surface (for certain parachute operations), but will be no greater than the minimum airspace necessary for the management of aircraft operations in the vicinity of the specified area.

(2) Flight restricted area for a major sporting event--The amount of airspace needed to protect persons and property on the surface or in the air, to maintain air safety and efficiency, or to prevent the unsafe congestion of aircraft will vary depending on the size of the event and the factors listed in paragraph (b) of this section. The

restricted airspace will normally be limited to a 3 nautical mile radius from the center of the event and 2500 feet above the surface but will not be greater than the minimum airspace necessary for the management of aircraft operations in the vicinity of the specified area.

(f) A NOTAM issued under this section will be issued at least 30 days in advance of an aerial demonstration or a major sporting event, unless the FAA finds good cause for a shorter period and explains this in the NOTAM.

(g) When warranted, the FAA Administrator may exclude the following flights from the provisions of this section:

(1) Essential military.

(2) Medical and rescue.

(3) Presidential and Vice Presidential.

(4) Visiting heads of state.

(5) Law enforcement and security.

(6) Public health and welfare.

Below is a general rule of thumb to differentiate between the UAV hobbyist and the commercial operator:

Hobby or Recreation (Section 336)

1. Flying a model aircraft at the local model aircraft club.
2. Taking photographs with a model aircraft for personal use.
3. Using a model aircraft to move a box from point to point without any kind of compensation.
4. Viewing a field to determine whether crops need water when they are grown for personal enjoyment.

Not Hobby or Recreation (Part 107)

1. Receiving money for demonstrating aerobatics with a model aircraft.
2. A realtor using a model aircraft to photograph a property that he is trying to sell and using the photos in the property's real estate listing.
3. A person photographing a property or event and selling the photos to someone else.
4. Delivering packages to people for a fee.
5. Determining whether crops need to be watered that are grown as part of commercial farming operation.

The Certificate of Authorization or Waiver (COA)

The FAA realizes that the restrictions of the FAR's may not be appropriate or make sense for all operators. For example, an engineering firm using a drone to survey and airport and the surrounding property could not possibly comply with restrictions that prohibit this type of operation. Therefore, the FAA provides operators with a method to seek a special authorization or waiver from the existing regulations. This process is known as the Certificate of Waiver or Authorization (COA).

In the COA application, the operator must specify which regulations from which they are requesting relief, the reason for the request, and demonstrate an "equivalent level of safety" to what is provided by the regulations. The COA process is open to both Civil and Public Aircraft operators.

Government entities (Federal, State, and political subdivisions of the State) are also able to apply for Public Aircraft status. Doing so allows the government entity to self-certify its pilots and provides waivers from many of the restrictions that civil operators must comply with. This is accomplished by way of a "Public Use COA" application.

The Public Use COA is an authorization issued by the Air Traffic Organization to a public operator for a specific UA activity. After a complete application is submitted, FAA conducts a comprehensive operational and technical review. If necessary, provisions or limitations may be imposed as part of the approval to ensure the UA can operate safely with other airspace users. In most cases, FAA will provide a formal response within 60 days from the time a completed application is submitted.

To better support the needs of its customers, FAA deployed a web-based application system. The UAS COA Online System provides applicants with an electronic method of requesting a COA.

Applicants will need to obtain an account in order to access the online system.[24]

Other Requirements for Operators of UAV's

When the President signed into law the FAA Modernization and Reform Act of 2012 (P.L. 112-95) (the Act), which established, in Section 336, a "special rule for model aircraft." Below are a few of the key elements. See the Appendix for the full report.

"By definition, a model aircraft must be "flown within visual line of sight of the person operating the aircraft." P.L. 112-95, section 336(c)(2).1 Based on the plain language of the statute, the FAA interprets this requirement to mean that: (1) the aircraft must be visible at all times to the operator; (2) that the operator must use his or her own natural vision (which includes vision corrected by standard eyeglasses or contact lenses) to observe the aircraft; and (3) people other than the operator may not be used in lieu of the operator for maintaining visual line of sight. Under the criteria above, visual line of sight would mean that the operator has an unobstructed view of the model aircraft. To ensure that the operator has the best view of the aircraft, the statutory requirement would preclude the use of vision-enhancing devices, such as binoculars, night vision goggles, powered vision magnifying devices, and goggles designed to provide a "first-person view" from the model. Such devices would limit the operator's field of view thereby:

24

https://www.faa.gov/about/office_org/headquarter

s_offices/ato/service_units/systemops/aaim/organiz ations/uas/coa/

1 For purposes of the visual line of sight requirement, "Operator" means the person manipulating the model aircraft's controls.

2 The FAA is aware that at least one community-based organization permits "first person view" (FPV) operations during which the hobbyist controls the aircraft while wearing goggles that display images transmitted from a camera mounted in the front of the model aircraft. While the intent of FPV is to provide reducing his or her ability to see-and-avoid other aircraft in the area. Additionally, some of these devices could dramatically increase the distance at which an operator could see the aircraft, rendering the statutory visual-line-of-sight requirements meaningless. Finally, based on the plain language of the statute, which says that aircraft must be "flown within the visual line of sight of the person operating the aircraft," an operator could not rely on another person to satisfy the visual line of sight requirement. See id. (emphasis added). While the statute would not preclude using an observer to augment the safety of the operation, the operator must be able to view the aircraft at all times."[25]

It must be clearly understood by all UAV pilots that if a drone operation is in ANY way connected to your employment either directly or indirectly, then you are NOT considered a hobbyist. Realtors are perhaps the most common violators of this interpretation. While drone videography is not required for their business (it is incidental), it is a part of the business.

Scope of FAA's Enforcement Authority

As previously stated, if a model aircraft is operated consistently with the terms of section 336(a) and (c), then it would not be subject to future FAA regulations regarding model aircraft. However, Congress also recognized the potential for such operations to endanger other aircraft and systems of the NAS. Therefore, it specifically stated that "[n]othing in this section shall be construed to limit the authority of the Administrator to pursue enforcement action against persons operating model aircraft who endanger the safety of the national airspace system." P.L. 112-95, section 336(b).

Through this language, Congress specifically recognized the FAA's existing authority to take enforcement action to protect the safety of the NAS. Moreover, it did not limit the FAA's authority to take enforcement action where a violation of a regulation results in the endangerment of the NAS. As demonstrated by the FAA's statutory and regulatory authorities, their charge to protect the safety of the NAS[26] is not only intended to protect users of the airspace, but is also intended to protect persons and property on the ground.

25

https://www.faa.gov/uas/media/model_aircraft_spe c_rule.pdf

26

https://www.faa.gov/uas/media/model_aircraft_spe c_rule.pdf

Examples of Regulations That Apply to Model Aircraft

The FAA could apply several regulations in part 91 when determining whether to take enforcement action against a model aircraft operator for endangering the NAS. The FAA's general operating and flight rules are housed in part 91 of the FAA's regulations. These rules are the baseline rules that apply to all aircraft operated in the United States with limited exceptions,14 and are the appropriate rules to apply when evaluating model aircraft operations. See 14 CFR 91.1.

Rules relevant to these operations fall generally into three categories: (1) how the aircraft is operated; (2) operating rules for designated airspace; and, (3) special restrictions such as temporary flight restrictions (TFRs) and notices to airmen (NOTAMs). These rules are discussed in greater detail below.

Rules addressing operation of the aircraft may include prohibitions on careless or reckless operation and dropping objects so as to create a hazard to persons or property. See 14 CFR 91.13 through 91.15. Additionally, § 91.113 establishes right-of-way rules for converging aircraft.15 Model aircraft that do not comply with those rules could be subject to FAA enforcement action.

Rules governing operations in designated airspace are found in §§ 91.126 through 91.135. In general, those rules establish requirements for operating in the various classes. Part 91 does not apply to moored balloons, kites, unmanned rockets, and unmanned free balloons, and ultralights vehicles operated under14 CFR parts 101 and 103.

Additionally, model aircraft must not interfere with and must always give way to any manned aircraft. Section 336(a)(4).

The third category of rules relevant to model aircraft operations are rules relating to operations in areas covered by temporary flight restrictions and NOTAMs found in §§ 91.137 through 91.145. The FAA would expect that model aircraft operations comply with restrictions on airspace when established under these rules.

Other rules in part 91, or other parts of the regulations, may apply to model aircraft operations, depending on the particular circumstances of the operation. The regulations cited above are not intended to be an exhaustive list of rules that could apply to model aircraft operations. The FAA anticipates that the cited regulations are the ones that would most commonly apply to model aircraft operations.

Chapter 8 - The Flight Environment

Types of Airspace

Within the National Airspace System (NAS) there are four types of airspace:

1. Controlled
2. Uncontrolled
3. Special Use
4. Other Airspace

Controlled Airspace

Controlled Airspace is a generic term that covers the different classification of airspace (Class A, Class B, Class C, Class D, and Class E airspace) and defined dimensions within which air traffic control service is provided to IFR flights and to VFR flights in accordance with the airspace classification.

Class A Airspace

Class A airspace is generally the airspace from 18,000 feet mean sea level (MSL) up to and including flight level (FL) 600, including the airspace overlying the waters within 12 nautical miles (NM) of the coast of the 48 contiguous states and Alaska. Unless otherwise authorized, all operation in Class A airspace is conducted under instrument flight rules (IFR).

Class B Airspace

Class B airspace is generally airspace from the surface to 10,000 feet MSL surrounding the nation's busiest airports in terms of airport operations or passenger enplanements. The

configuration of each Class B airspace area is individually tailored, consists of a surface area and two or more layers (some Class B airspace areas resemble
upside-down wedding cakes), and is designed to contain all published instrument procedures once an aircraft enters the airspace. An ATC clearance is required for all aircraft to operate in the area, and all aircraft that are so cleared receive separation services within the airspace.

Class C Airspace

Class C airspace is generally airspace from the surface to 4,000 feet above the airport elevation (charted in MSL) surrounding those airports that have an

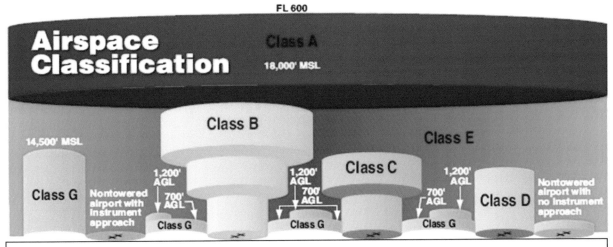

Figure 9-1 *Airspace Classifications*

operational control tower, are serviced by a radar approach control, and have a certain number of IFR operations or passenger enplanements. Although the configuration of each Class C area is individually tailored, the airspace usually consists of a surface area with a five NM radius, an outer circle with a ten NM radius that extends from 1,200 feet to 4,000 feet above the airport elevation, and an outer area. Each aircraft must establish two-way radio communications with the ATC facility providing air traffic services prior to entering the airspace and thereafter maintain those communications while within the airspace.

Class D Airspace

Class D airspace is generally airspace from the surface to 2,500 feet above the airport elevation (charted in MSL) surrounding those airports that have an operational control tower. The configuration of each Class D airspace area is individually tailored and when instrument procedures are published, the airspace is normally designed to contain the procedures. Arrival extensions for instrument approach procedures (IAPs) may be Class D or Class E airspace. Unless otherwise authorized, each aircraft must establish two-way radio communications with the ATC facility providing air traffic services prior to entering the airspace and thereafter maintain those communications while in the airspace.

Class E Airspace

If the airspace is not Class A, B, C, or D, and is controlled airspace, then it is Class E airspace. Class E airspace extends upward from either the surface or a design overlying or adjacent

Airspace			Flight Visibility	Distance from Clouds
Class A			Not applicable	Not applicable
Class B			3 statute miles	Clear of clouds
Class C			3 statute miles	1,000 feet above 500 feet below 2,000 feet horizontal
Class D			3 statute miles	1,000 feet above 500 feet below 2,000 feet horizontal
Class E	At or above 10,000 feet MSL		5 statute miles	1,000 feet above 1,000 feet below 1 statute mile horizontal
	Less than 10,000 feet MSL		3 statute miles	1,000 feet above 500 feet below 2,000 feet horizontal
Class G	1,200 feet or less above the surface (regardless of MSL altitude).	Day, except as provided in section 91.155(b)	1 statute mile	Clear of clouds
		Night, except as provided in section 91.155(b)	3 statute miles	1,000 feet above 500 feet below 2,000 feet horizontal
	More than 1,200 feet above the surface but less than 10,000 feet MSL.	Day	1 statute mile	1,000 feet above 500 feet below 2,000 feet horizontal
		Night	3 statute miles	1,000 feet above 500 feet below 2,000 feet horizontal
	More than 1,200 feet above the surface and at or above 10,000 feet MSL.		5 statute miles	1,000 feet above 1,000 feet below 1 statute mile horizontal

Figure 9-2 *Airspace weather requirements*

controlled airspace. When designated as a surface area, the airspace is configured to contain all instrument procedures. Also in this class are federal airways, airspace beginning at either 700 or 1,200 feet above ground level (AGL) used to transition to and from the terminal or en route environment, and en route domestic and offshore airspace areas designated below 18,000 feet MSL. Unless designated at a lower altitude, Class E airspace begins at 14,500 MSL over the United States, including that airspace overlying the waters within 12 NM of the coast of the 48 contiguous states and Alaska, up to but not including 18,000 feet MSL, and the airspace above FL 600.

Uncontrolled Airspace

Class G Airspace

Uncontrolled airspace or Class G airspace is the portion of the airspace that has not been designated as Class A, B, C, D, or E. It is therefore designated uncontrolled airspace. Class G airspace extends from the surface to the base of the overlying Class E airspace. Although ATC has no authority or responsibility to control air traffic, pilots should remember there are visual flight rules (VFR) minimums which apply to Class G airspace.

Special Use Airspace

Special use airspace or special area of operation (SAO) is the designation for airspace in which certain activities must be confined, or where limitations may be imposed on aircraft operations that are not part of those activities. Certain special use airspace areas can create limitations on the mixed use of airspace. The special use airspace depicted on instrument charts includes the area name or number, effective altitude, time and weather conditions of operation, the controlling agency, and the chart panel location. On National Aeronautical Charting Group (NACG) en route charts, this information is available on one of the end panels. Special use airspace usually consists of:

- Prohibited areas
- Restricted areas
- Warning areas
- Military operation areas (MOAs)
- Alert areas
- Controlled firing areas (CFAs)

Prohibited Areas

Prohibited areas contain airspace of defined dimensions within which the flight of aircraft is prohibited. Such areas are established for security or other reasons associated with the national welfare. These areas are published in

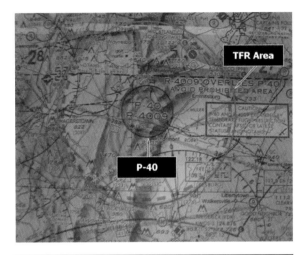

Figure 9-3 A Prohibited Area in marked by a blue circle with hash marks on its interior. The controlling agency of each prohibited area can be found at the bottom of the VFR sectional.

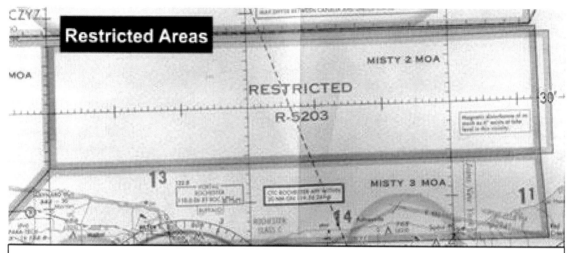

Figure 9-4 *A restricted area is airspace within which the operation of aircraft is subject to restriction. Restricted areas are established to separate activities considered to be hazardous to other aircraft, such as artillery firing or aerial gunnery.*

the Federal Register and are depicted on aeronautical charts. The area is charted as a "P" followed by a number (e.g., P-40). Examples of prohibited areas include Camp David and the National Mall in Washington, D.C., where the White House and the Congressional buildings are located.

Restricted Areas

Restricted areas are areas where operations are hazardous to nonparticipating aircraft and contain airspace within which the flight of aircraft, while not wholly prohibited, is subject to restrictions. Activities within these areas must be confined because of their nature, or limitations may be imposed upon aircraft operations that are not a part of those activities, or both. Restricted areas denote the existence of unusual, often invisible, hazards to aircraft (e.g., artillery firing, aerial gunnery, or guided missiles). IFR flights may be authorized to transit the airspace and are routed accordingly. Penetration of restricted areas without authorization from the using or controlling agency may be extremely hazardous to the aircraft and its occupants.

ATC facilities apply the following procedures when aircraft are operating on an IFR clearance

(including those cleared by A TC to maintain VFR on top) via a route which lies within joint-use restricted airspace:

6. If the restricted area is not active and has been released to the Federal Aviation Administration (FAA), the ATC facility allows the aircraft to operate in the restricted airspace without issuing specific clearance for it to do so.
7. If the restricted area is active and has not been released to the FAA, the ATC facility issues a clearance which ensures the aircraft avoids the restricted airspace.

Restricted areas are charted with an "R" followed by a number (e.g., R-4401) and are depicted on the en route chart appropriate for use at the altitude or FL being flown. [Figure 9-4] Restricted area information can be obtained on the back of the chart.

Warning Areas

Warning areas are similar in nature to restricted areas; however, the United States government does not have sole jurisdiction over the airspace. A warning area is airspace of defined dimensions, extending from 12 NM outward from the coast of the United States, containing activity that may be hazardous to nonparticipating aircraft. The purpose of such areas is to warn nonparticipating pilots of the potential danger. A warning area may be located over domestic or international waters or both. The airspace is designated with a "W" followed by a number (e.g., W-237).

Military Operation Areas (MOAs)

MOAs consist of airspace with defined vertical and lateral limits established for the purpose of separating certain military training activities from IFR traffic. Whenever an MOA is being used, nonparticipating IFR traffic may be cleared through an MOA if IFR separation can be provided by ATC. Otherwise, ATC reroutes or restricts nonparticipating IFR traffic. MOAs are depicted on sectional, VFR terminal area, and en route low altitude charts and are not numbered (e.g., "Camden Ridge MOA"). However, the MOA is also further defined on the back of the sectional charts with times of operation, altitudes affected, and the controlling agency.

Alert Areas

Alert areas are depicted on aeronautical charts with an "A" followed by a number (e.g., A-211) to inform nonparticipating pilots of areas that may contain a high volume of pilot training or an unusual type of aerial activity. Pilots should exercise caution in alert areas. All activity within an alert area shall be conducted in accordance with regulations, without waiver, and pilots of participating aircraft, as well as pilots transiting the area, shall be equally responsible for collision avoidance. [Figure 14-6]

Controlled Firing Areas (CFAs)

CFAs contain activities, which, if not conducted in a controlled environment, could be hazardous to nonparticipating aircraft. The difference between CFAs and other special use airspace is that activities must be suspended when a spotter aircraft, radar, or ground lookout position indicates an aircraft might be approaching the area. There is no need to chart CFAs since they do not cause a nonparticipating aircraft to change its flightpath.

"Other" Airspace

Military Training Routes (MTRs)

Generally, MTRs are established below 10,000 feet MSL for operations at speeds in excess of 250 knots. However, route segments may be defined at higher altitudes for purposes of route continuity. For example, route segments may be defined for descent, climbout, and mountainous terrain.

Temporary Flight Restrictions

A temporary flight restriction (TFR) is a regulatory action that temporarily restricts certain aircraft from operating within a defined area in order to protect persons or property in the air or on the ground. TFRs are issued in a NOTAM. You must obtain the NOTAM that establishes a TFR and understand what is and isn't allowed. To obtain the most current information it is necessary to contact a FSS. There are several types of TFRs defined in the regulations. Since TFRs are, by definition, "temporary" in nature, it is extremely important to check the FDC NOTAMs before every flight you make.
TFRs are not depicted on any navigational charts. Size, shape, altitudes, and other details vary. Resources are available to help you visualize and understand restrictions.

TFR Format

FDC NOTAMs that establish TFRs follow a very specific format. All begin with the phrase, "FLIGHT RESTRICTIONS" and include the following information:
1   Location of the TFR area
2   Effective period

3   Defined area
4   Altitudes affected
5   FAA coordination facility and telephone number
6   Reason for the TFR
7   Agency directing relief activities (if applicable) and telephone number
8   Any other information considered appropriate.

Types of TFR's

Presidential TFRs

No matter where you live, chances are good that you will at some point be affected by TFRs issued under 14 CFR 91.141, "Flight restrictions in the proximity of the Presidential and other parties." This rule states that:

No person may operate an aircraft over or in the vicinity of any area to be visited or traveled by the President, the Vice President, or other public figures contrary to the restrictions established by the Administrator and published in a Notice to Airmen (NOTAM).

Violation of a TFR issued under this regulation could lead to very adverse consequences, since security of the President and Vice President is taken very seriously. This rule is also used to establish TFRs for the protection of presidential candidates. Because "presidential TFRs" are often established on very short notice, it is

extremely important to check FDC NOTAMS before every flight – even routine flights in the vicinity of your home airport.

Air Shows and Sporting Events

For aircraft operations in the vicinity of aerial demonstrations and major sporting events, 14 CFR 91.145 gives the FAA authority to establish TFRs to protect persons or property on the ground or in the air, to maintain air safety and

For more information on TFR's goto the FAA's TFR website:

http://tfr.faa.gov/tfr2/list.html

efficiency, or to prevent the unsafe congestion of aircraft in the vicinity of an aerial demonstration or sporting event. In practice, TFRs issued under 14 CFR 91.145 are issued primarily for air shows. The FAA determines when a 14 CFR 91.145 TFR should be issued for a sporting event on a case-by-case basis.

Stadiums

FDC 9/5151, issued under 14 CFR 99.7 on "Special Security Instructions," restricts flight over stadiums during major league baseball, National Football League, NCAA, and motor speedway events. The so-called "stadium TFR" prohibits all aircraft and parachute operations at or below 3,000 AGL within a 3 nm radius of any stadium with a seating capacity of 30,000 or more people when there is a major league baseball game, NFL game, NCAA division one football game, or major motor speedway event occurring. This TFR applies to the entire US domestic national airspace system, and takes effect from one hour before the scheduled event time until one hour after the event concludes.

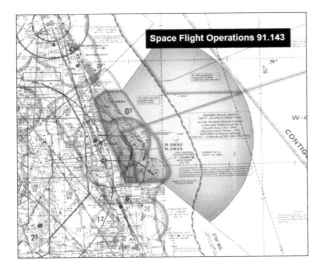

Disaster/Hazard Areas

The FAA has the authority under 14 CFR 91.137 to restrict aircraft operation in designated areas unless they are participating in disaster/hazard relief efforts. The three types of TFRs issued under this regulation are to:

1   ***Protect persons or property*** on the surface or in the air from a hazard associated

with an incident on the surface (14 CFR 91.137(a)(1)). Fire fighting activities involving the use of aircraft are normally protected by a TFR.

2   ***Provide a safe environment*** for the operation of disaster relief aircraft (14 CFR 91.137(a)(2)).

3   ***Prevent unsafe congestion*** of sightseeing or other aircraft above an incident or event which may generate a high degree of public interest (14 CFR 91.137(a)(3)). Aircraft accident sites or similar activities may be issued a TFR.

Space Flight

The FAA has the authority under 14 CFR 91.143 to issue FDC NOTAMs restricting flight in areas designated for space flight operations.

For detailed information on each type of regulatory TFR, please review FAA Advisory Circular AC 91-63C, which includes recent changes to 14 CFR Part 91.

As is the case for any kind of TFR, it is imperative that you carefully review and fully understand the NOTAM that establishes a TFR before attempting to fly in, or in the vicinity of, such restrictions.

Altitudes: AGL vs MSL

When flying your drone, you are given the option between metric and imperial systems. This is simply a matter of your own personal preference. However, do bear in mind that when using items such as VFR Sectionals or other U.S. Gov't printed material, measurements will be in imperial form (feet, miles, lbs, etc.)

The drone is not concerned with its height about sea level which in aviation is known as True Altitude. More often, the drone is using its onboard SONAR pointed toward the ground as well as the GPS system to determine the exact height above the ground. In aviation, this is known as Absolute Altitude.

Two Types of Altitude

True Altitude—the vertical distance of the aircraft above sea level—the actual altitude. It is often expressed as feet above mean sea level (MSL). Airport, terrain, and obstacle elevations on aeronautical charts are true altitudes.

Absolute Altitude—the vertical distance of an aircraft above the terrain, or above ground level (AGL).

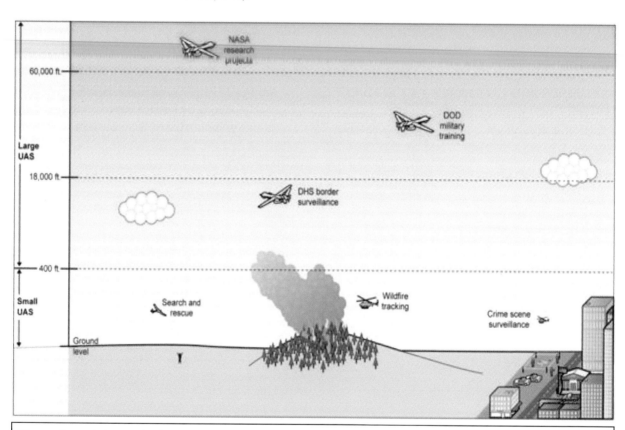

Figure 9-5 *While much of aviation focuses on altitude based on MSL in order to ensure proper separation of aircraft. Civilian drone operations are commonly based on AGL.*

Chapter 9 - Equipment Inspection

One of the first things that any pilot learns about when flying manned aircraft is the importance of the preflight inspection. The purpose of the preflight inspection is to identify any items on the aircraft that could cause the flight to be unsafe. Whether you are flying a full-scale airplane or a drone, each can cause severe damage if there is a sudden loss of power and they are forced to land without control.

Launching your drone is not nearly as simple as turning it and launching into the heavens. Fortunately, many of today's drones have numerous built in features that conduct preflight inspections automatically. However, as you gain more and more experience and prepare for more flights, you will develop your own checklist that will likely exceed any published checklist. Your UAV preflight inspection should include at least the following:

Overall Drone Inspection

1. Check for crack in joints and structural members
2. Check for loose or damaged screws, ties, fasteners, straps
3. Check for loose or damaged wiring
4. Check for loose or damaged connections (solder, plugs, etc.)
5. Inspect prop mounts and screws and apply slight counter pressure on arms to check for loosened components
6. If flying FPV, inspect / clean FPV (Camera) Lens and insure it is secured and connections are firmly attached
7. Check that camera settings are correct (still images, video, framerate)

8. Inspect that batteries are fully charged, properly seated and secured
9. Check that fail-safe equipment functioning
10. Verify that RTH (return to home) is working properly
11. Inspect recovery chute (if installed)
12. Verify that Firmware Airport Proximity Detection Functioning
13. Check to ensure that props are smooth and free of damage / defect (check blade, surface and hub)
14. Check that prop adapters are tight / secure
15. Ensure voltage alarm is connected
16. Ensure arming / idle timeout is properly configured
17. Correct model is selected in transmitter (if applicable)
18. Check RC transmitter shows the right range and centering for all sticks
19. Perform range test if possible

The safe inspection does not end there. Prior to launch these additional items should be checked:

1. Verifying all transmitter, on-board aircraft and camera batteries are fully charged; (confirm voltages)
2. Ensure no frequency conflicts with both video and transmitter / receiver
3. Checking all control surfaces for signs of damage, loose hinges, and overall condition; Looking over the wing/rotors to ensure they are in good structural condition and properly secured;
4. Check motor/engine and mounting attached to the airframe;
5. Study propellers / mounting hardware (tight) / rotor blades for chips and deformation;

6. Check the landing gear for damage and function
7. Test electrical connections, plugged in and secure
8. Ensure photo / video equipment mounting system is secure and operational.
9. Check location of GPS equipment controlling the autopilot.
10. Check the IMU movements in the ground control software.
11. UAV in stabilization mode, ensure control surfaces move towards the correct positions
12. UAV / Drone is in a level location safe for takeoff
13. FPV / Power up ground station
14. FPV / Power up Video receiver / goggles
15. If using Video recorder turn on camera system
16. Camera settings are correct (still images, video, framerate)
17. SD camera memory clear and inserted into the camera
18. Action / Start filming
19. Confirm that all transmitter controls move freely in all directions
20. Confirm that all transmitter trims in neutral position
21. Confirm that all transmitter switches in correct position (typically away)
22. Set transmitter throttle to zero
23. Radio transmitter on
24. Connect / power on battery to airframe
25. Ensure led indicators and audible tones are correct
26. Timer on (if applicable)
27. FPV, confirm video is in monitor / goggles
28. Scan for nearby cars / people / animals

29. Say "CLEAR!"
30. Arm flight controller
31. Increase throttle slightly listening for any abnormalities
32. Short 20-30 second hover at 3-5 feet (listen for vibrations / loose items)
33. Confirm Voltage levels are correct

Spotter/Observer

One thing to note is the significant difference between the drone hobbyist and the professional drone operator. The difference is the importance of having safety spotters when flying.

Safety spotters or observers are needed to act as an additional set of eyes while flying. Observers can look for nearby aircraft or other safety hazards that you may not notice because your attention is on the drone's position or because you are looking at the display screen. Observers can also be on the lookout for any issues on the ground such as curious onlookers that may get too close the pilot and cause a distraction. Sometimes, curious folks may even get too close to the subject of the drone's mission such as a bridge or building, and the observer can step in and let them know what is happening. Needless to say, having observers can be critical to and successful mission and they should always be within earshot of the pilot in order to communicate any hazards.

Chapter 10 - Pre-Flight Considerations

Rules for Safe Operation of UAS: Pre-Flight Considerations

Maintenance Requirements

Maintenance for sUAS includes scheduled and unscheduled overhaul, repair, inspection, modification, replacement, and system software upgrades for the unmanned aircraft itself and all components necessary for flight. This first section of the lesson examines maintenance requirements and best practices.

Scheduled Maintenance

Manufacturers may recommend a maintenance or replacement schedule for the unmanned aircraft and system components based on time-in-service limits and other factors. Follow all manufacturer maintenance recommendations to achieve the longest and safest service life of the sUAS.
If the sUAS or component manufacturer does not provide scheduled maintenance instructions, it is recommended that you establish your own scheduled maintenance protocol. For example:

• Document any repair, modification, overhaul, or replacement of a system component resulting from normal flight operations

• Record the time-in-service for that component at the time of the maintenance procedure

• Assess these records over time to establish a reliable maintenance schedule for the sUAS and components.

Unscheduled Maintenance

During the course of a preflight inspection, you may discover that an sUAS component requires some form of maintenance outside of the scheduled maintenance period.
For example, an sUAS component may require servicing (such as lubrication), repair, modification, overhaul, or replacement as a result of normal or abnormal flight operations. Or, the sUAS manufacturer or component manufacturer may require an unscheduled system software update to correct a problem.
In the event such a condition is found, do not conduct flight operations until the discrepancy is corrected.

Performing Maintenance

In some instances, the sUAS or component manufacturer may require certain maintenance tasks be performed by the manufacturer or by a person or facility (personnel) specified by the manufacturer.

It is highly recommended that the maintenance be performed in accordance with the manufacturer's instructions. However, if you decide not to use the manufacturer or the personnel recommended by the manufacturer and you are unable to perform the required maintenance yourself, you should:

Solicit the expertise of maintenance personnel familiar with the specific sUAS and its components

Consider using certificated maintenance providers, such as repair stations, holders of mechanic and repairman certificates, and persons working under the supervision of a mechanic or repairman

If you or the maintenance personnel are unable to repair, modify, or overhaul an sUAS or component back to its safe operational specification, then it is advisable to replace the sUAS or component with one that is in a condition for safe operation.

Complete all required maintenance before each flight—preferably in accordance with the manufacturer's instructions or, in lieu of that, within known industry best practices.[27]

Preflight Inspection

Before beginning any sUAS flight operation:

- Assess the operating environment
- Inform any supporting crewmembers about the operation and their roles
- Inspect the sUAS to ensure that it is in a condition for safe operation
- Maintain documents required in the event of an on-site FAA inspection[28]

Operating Environment

Before an sUAS operation, assess the operating environment.
The assessment must include, but is not limited to:

- Local weather conditions
- Local airspace and any flight restrictions
- The location of persons and property on the surface
- Other ground hazards

Information for the Crew

Before any sUAS operation, at a minimum, ensure that all persons directly participating in the sUAS operation are informed about:

- Operating conditions
- Emergency procedures
- Contingency procedures
- Roles and responsibilities of each person involved in the operation
- Potential hazards

Condition of Aircraft

Before any sUAS operation, inspect the aircraft for equipment damage or malfunctions.[29]
For example, ensure that:

- All control links between the control station and the small unmanned aircraft are working properly
- There is sufficient power to continue controlled flight operations to a normal landing
- Any object attached or carried by the small unmanned aircraft

[27] AC 107, *Small UAS* (as amended)
[28] 14 CFR parts 107.15 and 107.49; AC 107, *Small UAS* (as amended)

[29] 14 CFR parts 107.15 and 107.49; AC 107, *Small UAS* (as amended)

is secure and does not adversely affect the flight characteristics or controllability of the aircraft

• The unique identifier is readily accessible and visible upon inspection of the small unmanned aircraft

Benefits of Recordkeeping

Careful recordkeeping can be highly beneficial for sUAS owners and operators. For example, recordkeeping provides essential safety support for commercial operators who may experience rapidly accumulated flight operational hours/cycles.
Consider maintaining a hardcopy and/or electronic logbook of all periodic inspections, maintenance, preventative maintenance, repairs, and alterations performed on the sUAS.
Such records should include all components of the sUAS, including the:

• Small unmanned aircraft itself

• Control station
• Launch and recovery equipment
• Data link equipment
• Payload
• Any other components required to safely operate the sUAS

FAA Inspections

You must make available to the FAA, upon request, the sUAS for inspection or testing.
In addition, you must verify before flight that all required documentation is physically or electronically available in the event of an on-site FAA inspection. Such documentation may include:

• Pilot certificate
• Aircraft registration
• Any necessary waiver or exemption
• Other documentation related to the operation

Loading and Performance

Prior to each flight, the Remote PIC must ensure that any object attached to or carried by the small unmanned aircraft is secure and does not adversely affect the flight characteristics or controllability of the aircraft.[30]

Loading Considerations: General Weight and Balance

As with any aircraft, compliance with weight and balance limits is critical to the safety of flight for sUAS. An

---

[30] 14 CFR part 107.49; AC 107, *Small UAS* (as amended)

unmanned aircraft that is loaded out of balance may exhibit unexpected and unsafe flight characteristics.
Before any flight, verify that the unmanned aircraft is correctly loaded by determining the weight and balance condition.

Review any available manufacturer weight and balance data and follow all restrictions and limitations.

If the manufacturer does not provide specific weight and balance data, apply general weight and balance principals to determine limits for a given flight. For example, add weight to the unmanned aircraft in a manner that does not adversely affect the aircraft's center of gravity (CG) location—a point at which the unmanned aircraft would balance if it were suspended at that point.

Factors that Affect Maximum Gross Takeoff Weight

Although a maximum gross takeoff weight is normally specified for a given unmanned aircraft, the aircraft may not be able to launch with this load under all conditions. Or if it does become airborne, the unmanned aircraft may exhibit unexpected and unusually poor flight characteristics.

Factors that may require a reduction in weight prior to flight include:

• High density altitude conditions
• High elevations
• High air temperatures
• High humidity
• Runway/launch area length

• Surface
• Slope
• Surface wind
• Presence of obstacles

Common Performance Deficiencies of Overloaded Aircraft

Excessive weight reduces the flight performance in almost every respect. In addition, operating above the maximum weight limitation can compromise the structural integrity of an unmanned aircraft.

The most common performance deficiencies of an overloaded aircraft are:

• Reduced rate of climb
• Lower maximum altitude
• Shorter endurance
• Reduced maneuverability

Loading Considerations: Effects of Weight Changes

Weight changes have a direct effect on aircraft performance.

Fuel burn is the most common weight change that takes place during flight. For battery-powered unmanned aircraft, weight change during flight may occur when expendable items are used on board (e.g., agricultural use). Changes of mounted equipment between flights, such as the installation of cameras, battery packs, or other instruments, may also affect the weight and balance and performance of an sUAS.

Loading Considerations: Effects of Load Factor

Unmanned airplane performance can be decreased due to an increase in load factor when the airplane is operated in maneuvers other than straight and level flight.
The load factor increases at a terrific rate after a bank has reached 45° or 50°. The load factor for any aircraft in a coordinated level turn at 60° bank is 2 Gs. The load factor in an 80° bank is 5.76 Gs. The wing must produce lift equal to these load factors if altitude is to be maintained. The Remote PIC should be mindful of the increased load factor and its possible effects on the aircraft's structural integrity and the results of an increase in stall speed. As with manned aircraft, an unmanned airplane will stall when critical angle of attack is exceeded. Due to the low altitude operating environment, consideration should be given to ensure aircraft control is maintained and the aircraft isn't operated outside its performance limits.

Carriage of Hazardous Material

A small unmanned aircraft may not carry hazardous material as defined in 49 CFR part 171.8:

"Hazardous material means a substance or material that the Secretary of Transportation has determined is capable of posing an unreasonable risk to health, safety, and property when

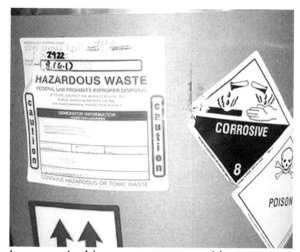

transported in commerce, and has designated as hazardous under section 5103 of Federal hazardous materials transportation law (49 U.S.C. 5103). The term includes hazardous substances, hazardous wastes, marine pollutants, elevated temperature materials, materials designated as hazardous in the Hazardous Materials Table (see 49 CFR 172.101), and materials that meet the defining criteria for hazard classes and divisions in part 173 of subchapter C of this chapter."[31]

Carriage of Lithium Batteries

Lithium batteries that are installed in an sUAS for power during the operation are not considered a hazardous material under part 107.
However, spare (uninstalled) lithium batteries would meet the definition of hazardous material and may not be carried on the sUAS.

Determining Performance: Sources of Performance Data

Performance or operational information may be provided by the manufacturer in the form of an Aircraft Flight Manual, Pilot's Operating Handbook, or owner's manual. Follow all manufacturer recommendations for evaluating performance to ensure safe and efficient operation.

Even when specific performance data is not provided, the Remote PIC should be familiar with:

- The operating environment
- All available information regarding the safe and recommended operation of the sUAS

Remote PIC Responsibilities for Determining Performance

The Remote PIC is responsible for ensuring that every flight can be accomplished safely, does not pose an undue hazard, and does not increase the likelihood of a loss of positive control.
Consider how your decisions affect the safety of flight. For example:

---
[31] 14 CFR part 107.36; 49 CFR part 171.8

- If you attempt flight in windy conditions, the unmanned aircraft may require an unusually high power setting to ascend. This action may cause a rapid depletion of battery power and result in a failure mode.

- If you attempt flight in wintery weather conditions, ice may accumulate on the unmanned aircraft's surface. Ice increases the weight and adversely affects performance characteristics of the small unmanned aircraft.

Due to the diversity and rapidly-evolving nature of sUAS operations, individual Remote PICs have flexibility to determine what equipage methods, if any, mitigate risk sufficiently to meet performance-based requirements, such as the prohibition on creating an undue hazard if there is a loss of aircraft control.

Determining Performance: Operational Data

The FAA acknowledges that some manufacturers provide comprehensive operational data and manuals, such as Aircraft Flight Manuals or Pilot's Operating Handbooks, and others do not. When operational data is provided, follow the manufacturer's instructions

and recommendations.
Even when operational data is not supplied by the manufacturer, the Remote PIC can better understand the unmanned aircraft's capabilities and limitations by establishing a process for tracking malfunctions, defects, and flight characteristics in various environments and conditions. Use this operational data to establish a baseline for determining performance, reliability, and risk assessment for your particular system.

Effects of Weather on Performance

Even though sUAS operations are often conducted at very low altitudes, weather factors can greatly influence performance and safety of flight.

Specifically, factors that affect sUAS performance and risk management include.

> Atmospheric pressure and stability
> Wind and currents
> Uneven surface heating
> Visibility and cloud clearance

As with any flight, the Remote PIC should check and consider the weather conditions prior to and during every sUAS flight.

This section of the lesson describes the effects of weather on aircraft performance.

Wind

Wind and currents can affect sUAS performance and maneuverability during all phases of flight. Be vigilant when operating sUAS at low altitudes, in confined areas, near buildings or other manmade structures, and near natural obstructions (such as mountains, bluffs, or canyons).

Consider the following effects of wind on performance:

• Obstructions on the ground affect the flow of wind, may create rapidly changing wind gusts, and can be an unseen danger

• The intensity of the turbulence associated with ground obstructions depends on the size of the obstacle and the primary velocity of the win

• Even when operating in an open field, wind blowing against surrounding trees can create significant low level turbulence

• High winds may make it difficult to maintain a geographical position in flight and may consume more battery power

Operations Near Buildings

Flying UAV's near structures is perhaps the most dangerous type of flight operation and demands special consideration. Even when there is no apparent wind, the uneven heating of the structures materials can cause unforeseen wind currents.

Remember that local conditions, geological features, and other anomalies can change the wind direction and speed close to the Earth's surface.

For example, when operating close to a building, winds blowing against the building could cause strong updrafts that can result in ballooning or a loss of positive control. On the other hand, winds blowing over the building from the opposite side can cause significant downdrafts that can have a dramatic sinking effect on the unmanned aircraft.

Currents

Different surfaces radiate heat in varying amounts.

The resulting uneven heating of the air creates small areas of local circulation called convective currents. Convective currents can cause bumpy, turbulent air that can dramatically affect the Remote PIC's ability to control unmanned aircraft at lower altitudes.
For example:

- Plowed ground, rocks, sand, and barren land give off a large amount of heat and are likely to result in updrafts

- Water, trees, and other areas of vegetation tend to absorb and retain heat and are likely to result in downdrafts

Visibility and Clouds

As in manned aircraft operations, good visibility and safe distance from clouds enhances the Remote PIC's ability to see and avoid other aircraft. Similarly, good visibility and cloud clearance may be the only means for other aircraft to see and avoid the unmanned aircraft. The regulatory requirements for visibility and cloud clearance are discussed in a later module. But it should be noted here that adherence to the regulatory requirements in conjunction with good airmanship and effective scanning techniques can preclude in-flight collisions. And collision avoidance is an essential aspect to the safe integration of sUAS into the NAS.

Chapter 11 - Communication and Flight Information

Filing A Flight Plan

Filing a flight plan with the FAA is the first step in notifying Air Traffic Control (ATC) of a proposed flight. When a flight plan is filed correctly, effected ATC facilities will receive the flight plan approximately 30 minutes prior to the proposed departure time. Filing a flight plan will decrease the amount of time an sUAS Pilot will spend speaking with ATC on the phone. They will already know the location, aircraft type, altitude, airspeeds, etc.; thereby reducing Pre Flight preparation times.

The following paragraphs are an excerpt from the Aeronautical Information Manual concerning flight plans. It has been edited to remove any material not applicable to sUAS operations.

Flight Plan – VFR Flights

a. Except for operations in or penetrating a Coastal or Domestic ADIZ or DEWIZ a flight plan is not required for VFR flight.

REFERENCE–
AIM, Paragraph 5–6–1 , National Security

b. It is strongly recommended that a flight plan (for a VFR flight) be filed with an FAA FSS. This will ensure that you receive VFR Search and Rescue Protection.

REFERENCE–
AIM, Paragraph 6–2–6 , Search and Rescue, gives the proper method of
filing a VFR flight plan.

c. To obtain maximum benefits from the flight plan program, flight plans should be filed directly with the nearest FSS. For your convenience, FSSs provide aeronautical and

meteorological briefings while accepting flight plans. Radio may be used to file if no other means are available.

NOTE–
Some states operate aeronautical communications facilities which will accept and forward flight plans to the FSS for further handling.

d. When a "stopover" flight is anticipated, it is recommended that a separate flight plan be filed for each "leg" when the stop is expected to be more than 1 hour duration.

e. Pilots are encouraged to give their departure times directly to the FSS serving the departure airport or as otherwise indicated by the FSS when the flight plan is filed. This will ensure more efficient flight plan service and permit the FSS to advise you of significant changes in aeronautical facilities or meteorological conditions. When a VFR flight plan is filed, it will be held by the FSS until 1 hour after the proposed departure time unless:

1. The actual departure time is received.
2. A revised proposed departure time is received.
3. At a time of filing, the FSS is informed that the proposed departure time will be met, but actual time cannot be given because of inadequate communications (assumed departures).

FLIGHT PLAN FORM

U.S. DEPARTMENT OF TRANSPORTATION FEDERAL AVIATION ADMINISTRATION **FLIGHT PLAN**	(FAA USE ONLY) ☐ PILOT BRIEFING ☐ VNR ☐ STOPOVER		TIME STARTED	SPECIALIST INITIALS

1. TYPE VFR IFR DVFR	2. AIRCRAFT IDENTIFICATION	3. AIRCRAFT TYPE/ SPECIAL EQUIPMENT	4. TRUE AIRSPEED KTS	5. DEPARTURE POINT	6. DEPARTURE TIME PROPOSED (Z) / ACTUAL (Z)	7. CRUISING ALTITUDE

8. ROUTE OF FLIGHT

9. DESTINATION (Name of airport and city)	10. EST. TIME ENROUTE HOURS / MINUTES	11. REMARKS

12. FUEL ON BOARD HOURS / MINUTES	13. ALTERNATE AIRPORT(S)	14. PILOT'S NAME, ADDRESS & TELEPHONE NUMBER & AIRCRAFT HOME BASE	15. NUMBER ABOARD
		17. DESTINATION CONTACT/TELEPHONE (OPTIONAL)	

16. COLOR OF AIRCRAFT	CIVIL AIRCRAFT PILOTS, FAR 91 requires you file an IFR flight plan to operate under instrument flight rules in controlled airspace. Failure to file could result in a civil penalty not to exceed $1,000 for each violation (Section 901 of the Federal Aviation Act of 1958, as amended). Filing of a VFR flight plan is recommended as a good operating practice. See also Part 99 for requirements concerning DVFR flight plans.

FAA Form 7233-1 (8-82)   CLOSE VFR FLIGHT PLAN WITH _____ FSS ON ARRIVAL

---

i. When filing VFR flight plans, indicate aircraft equipment capabilities by appending the appropriate suffix to aircraft type in the same manner as that prescribed for IFR flight.

REFERENCE–
AIM, Paragraph 5–1–8 , Flight Plan– Domestic IFR Flights

Explanation of VFR Flight Plan Items.

Block 1. Check the type flight plan. (sUAS must operate VFR)

Block 2. Enter your complete aircraft identification including the prefix "N" if applicable.

Block 3. Enter the designator for the aircraft, or if unknown, consult an FSS briefer.

Block 4. Enter your true airspeed (TAS)

Block 5. Enter the departure airport identifier. (For "off airport" locations, used radial and distance from nearest airport, example 030 degrees at 3.5NM)

Block 6. Enter the proposed departure time in Coordinated Universal Time (UTC) (Z). (Editor's note: Most FSS Briefers and online services will convert this for you.)

Block 7. Enter the appropriate VFR altitude (to assist the briefer in providing weather and wind information).

Block 8. Enter "LOCAL" if returning to original departure point. If not, define the route of flight by using NAVAID identifier codes and airways. (This would be rare for sUAS operations)

Block 9. Enter the destination airport identifier code, or if unknown, the airport name. (For "off airport" locations, used radial and distance from nearest airport, example 030 degrees at 3.5NM)

NOTE– Include the city name (or even the state name) if needed for clarity.

Block 10. Enter your estimated time en route in hours and minutes.

Block 11. Enter only those remarks pertinent to the clarification of other flight plan information, such as the radiotelephony (call sign) associated with a designator filed in Block 2, if the radiotelephony is new, has changed within the last 60 days, or is a special FAA-assigned temporary radiotelephony. Items of a personal nature are not accepted.

Block 12. Specify the fuel on board in hours and minutes.

Block 13. Specify an alternate airport (N/A)

Block 14. Enter your complete name, address, and telephone number. Enter sufficient information to identify home base, airport, or operator.

Block 15. Enter total number of persons on board (POB) including crew. (N/A)

Block 16. Enter the predominant colors.

Block 17. Record the FSS name for closing the flight plan. If the flight plan is closed with a different FSS or facility, state the recorded FSS name that would normally have closed your flight plan or cancel your flight plan within 1/2 hour after your estimated time of arrival (ETA).

Airport Operations

Radio Communications

Operating in and out of a towered airport, as well as in a good portion of the airspace system, requires that an aircraft have two-way radio communication capability. For this reason, a pilot should be knowledgeable of radio station license requirements and radio communications equipment and procedures.

Radio License

There is no license requirement for a pilot operating in the United States; however, a pilot who operates internationally is required to hold a restricted radiotelephone permit issued by the Federal Communications Commission (FCC). There is also no station license requirement for most general aviation aircraft operating in the United States. A station license is required however for an aircraft which is operating internationally, which uses other than a VHF radio, and which meets other criteria.

Radio Equipment

In general aviation, the most common types of radios are VHF. A VHF radio operates on frequencies between 118.0 and 136.975 and is classified as 720 or 760 depending on the number of channels it can accommodate. The 720 and 760 use .025 spacing (118.025, 118.050) with the 720 having a frequency range up to 135.975 and the 760 going up to 136.975. VHF radios are limited to line of sight transmissions; therefore, aircraft at higher altitudes are able to transmit and receive at greater distances.
In March of 1997, the International Civil Aviation Organization (ICAO) amended its International Standards and Recommended Practices to incorporate a channel plan specifying 8.33 kHz channel spacings in the Aeronautical Mobile Service. The 8.33 kHz channel plan was adopted to alleviate the

Character	Morse Code	Telephony	Phonic Pronunciation
A	• —	Alfa	(AL-FAH)
B	— • • •	Bravo	(BRAH-VOH)
C	— • — •	Charlie	(CHAR-LEE) or (SHAR-LEE)
D	— • •	Delta	(DELL-TAH)
E	•	Echo	(ECK-OH)
F	• • — •	Foxtrot	(FOKS-TROT)
G	— — •	Golf	(GOLF)
H	• • • •	Hotel	(HOH-TEL)
I	• •	India	(IN-DEE-AH)
J	• — — —	Juliett	(JEW-LEE-ETT)
K	— • —	Kilo	(KEY-LOH)
L	• — • •	Lima	(LEE-MAH)
M	— —	Mike	(MIKE)
N	— •	November	(NO-VEM-BER)
O	— — —	Oscar	(OSS-CAH)
P	• — — •	Papa	(PAH-PAH)
Q	— — • —	Quebec	(KEH-BECK)
R	• — •	Romeo	(ROW-ME-OH)
S	• • •	Sierra	(SEE-AIR-RAH)
T	—	Tango	(TANG-GO)
U	• • —	Uniform	(YOU-NEE-FORM) or (OO-NEE-FORM)
V	• • • —	Victor	(VIK-TAH)
W	• — —	Whiskey	(WISS-KEY)
X	— • • —	Xray	(ECKS-RAY)
Y	— • — —	Yankee	(YANG-KEY)
Z	— — • •	Zulu	(ZOO-LOO)
1	• — — — —	One	(WUN)
2	• • — — —	Two	(TOO)
3	• • • — —	Three	(TREE)
4	• • • • —	Four	(FOW-ER)
5	• • • • •	Five	(FIFE)
6	— • • • •	Six	(SIX)
7	— — • • •	Seven	(SEV-EN)
8	— — — • •	Eight	(AIT)
9	— — — — •	Nine	(NIN-ER)
0	— — — — —	Zero	(ZEE-RO)

Figure 11-2 *Phonetic Alphabet*

shortage of VHF ATC channels experienced in western Europe and in the United Kingdom. Seven western European countries and the United Kingdom implemented the 8.33 kHz channel plan on January 1, 1999. Accordingly, aircraft operating in the airspace of these countries must have the capability of transmitting and receiving on the 8.33 kHz spaced channels.

Using proper radio phraseology and procedures contribute to a pilot's ability to operate safely and efficiently in the airspace system. A review of the Pilot/Controller Glossary contained in the AIM assists a pilot in the use and understanding of standard terminology. The AIM also contains many examples of radio communications.

ICAO has adopted a phonetic alphabet, which should be used in radio communications. When communicating with ATC, pilots should use this alphabet to identify their aircraft.

Sources of Information (Charts, NOAA Publications, Digital TPP)

Aeronautical Charts

An aeronautical chart is the road map for a pilot flying under VFR. The chart provides information which allows pilots to track their position and provides available information which enhances safety. The three aeronautical charts used by VFR pilots are:

• Sectional
• VFR Terminal Area
• World Aeronautical (For long range flights, therefore not discussed in this text)

A free catalog listing aeronautical charts and related publications including prices and instructions for ordering is available at the National Aeronautical Charting Group (NACG) web site: www.naco.faa.gov.

Sectional Charts

Sectional charts are the most common charts used by pilots today. The charts have a scale of 1:500,000 (1 inch = 6.86 nautical miles (NM) or approximately 8 statute miles (SM)) which allows for more detailed information to be included on the chart.

The charts provide an abundance of information, including airport data, navigational aids, airspace, and topography. Figure 11-3 is an excerpt from the legend of a sectional chart. By referring to the chart legend, a pilot can interpret most of the information on the chart. A pilot should also check the chart for other legend information, which includes air traffic control (ATC) frequencies and information on airspace. These charts are revised semiannually except for some areas outside the

conterminous United States where they are revised annually.

VFR Terminal Area Charts

VFR terminal area charts are helpful when flying in or near Class B airspace. They have a scale of 1:250,000 (1 inch = 3.43 NM or approximately 4 SM). These charts provide a more detailed display of topographical information and are revised semiannually, except for several Alaskan and Caribbean charts. [Figure 11-4]

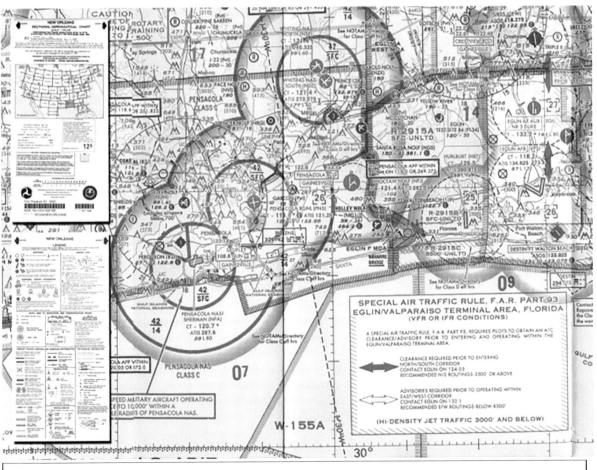

Figure 11-3 *VFR Sectional Chart*

160

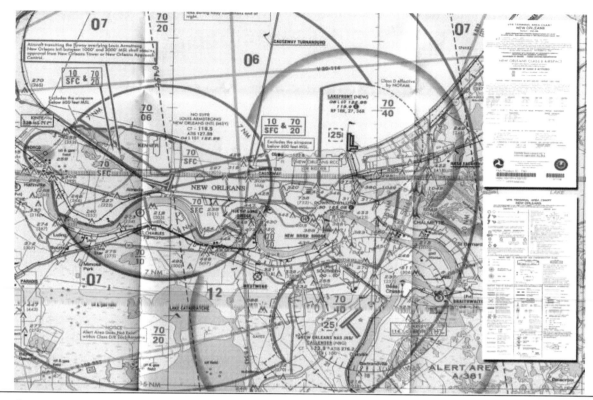

Figure 11-4 *VFR Terminal Area Chart (TAC)*

Airport/Facility Directory (A/FD)

The A/FD provides the most comprehensive information on a given airport. It contains information on airports, heliports, and seaplane bases that are open to the public. The A/FD is published in seven books, which are organized by regions and are revised every 56 days. The A/FD is also available digitally at www.naco.faa.gov. Figure **11-5** contains an excerpt from a directory. For a complete listing of information provided in an A/FD and how the information may be decoded, refer to the "Directory Legend Sample" located in the front of each A/FD.

In addition to airport information, each A/FD contains information such as special notices, Federal Aviation Administration (FAA) and National Weather Service (NWS) telephone numbers, preferred instrument flight rules (IFR) routing, visual flight rules (VFR) waypoints, a listing of very high frequency (VHF)

omnidirectional range (VOR) receiver checkpoints, aeronautical chart bulletins, land and hold short operations (LAHSO) for selected airports, airport diagrams for selected towered airports, en route flight advisory service (EFAS) outlets, parachute jumping areas, and facility telephone numbers. It would be helpful to review an A/FD to become familiar with the information it contains.

Notices to Airmen (NOTAMs)

NOTAMs provide the most current information available. They provide time-critical information on airports and changes that affect the national airspace system (NAS) and are of concern to IFR operations. NOTAM information is classified into three categories. These are NOTAM-D or distant, NOTAM-L or local, and flight data center (FDC) NOTAMs. NOTAM-Ds are attached to hourly weather reports and are available at automated flight service stations (AFSS) or FSS.

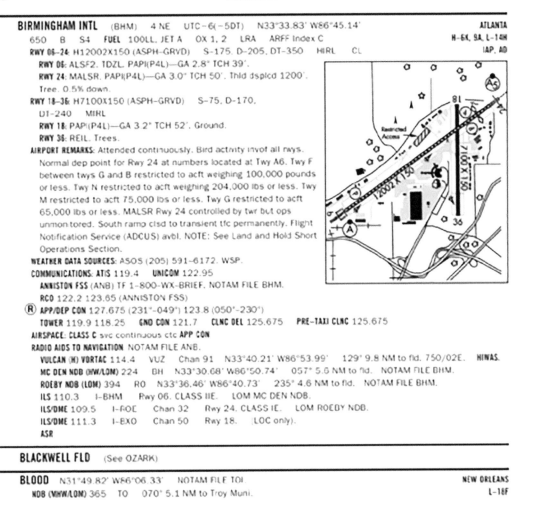

BIRMINGHAM INTL (BHM)   4 NE   UTC−6(−5DT)   N33°33.83' W86°45.14'   ATLANTA
650   B   S4   FUEL 100LL, JET A   OX 1, 2   LRA   ARFF Index C   H−6K, 9A, L−14H
RWY 06−24: H12002X150 (ASPH−GRVD)   S−175, D−205, DT−350   HIRL   CL   IAP, AD
RWY 06: ALSF2. TDZL. PAPI(P4L)—GA 2.8° TCH 39'.
RWY 24: MALSR. PAPI(P4L)—GA 3.0° TCH 50'. Thld dsplcd 1200'.
Tree. 0.5% down.
RWY 18−36: H7100X150 (ASPH−GRVD)   S−75, D−170,
DT−240   MIRL
RWY 18: PAPI(P4L)—GA 3.2° TCH 52'. Ground.
RWY 36: REIL. Trees.
AIRPORT REMARKS: Attended continuously. Bird activity invof all rwys.
Normal dep point for Rwy 24 at numbers located at Twy A6. Twy F
between twys G and B restricted to acft weighing 100,000 pounds
or less. Twy N restricted to acft weighing 204,000 lbs or less. Twy
M restricted to acft 75,000 lbs or less. Twy G restricted to acft
65,000 lbs or less. MALSR Rwy 24 controlled by twr but ops
unmonitored. South ramp clsd to transient tfc permanently. Flight
Notification Service (ADCUS) avbl. NOTE: See Land and Hold Short
Operations Section.
WEATHER DATA SOURCES: ASOS (205) 591−6172. WSP.
COMMUNICATIONS: ATIS 119.4   UNICOM 122.95
ANNISTON FSS (ANB) TF 1−800−WX−BRIEF. NOTAM FILE BHM.
RCO 122.2 123.65 (ANNISTON FSS)
Ⓡ APP/DEP CON 127.675 (231°−049°) 123.8 (050°−230°)
TOWER 119.9 118.25   GND CON 121.7   CLNC DEL 125.675   PRE−TAXI CLNC 125.675
AIRSPACE: CLASS C svc continuous ctc APP CON
RADIO AIDS TO NAVIGATION: NOTAM FILE ANB.
VULCAN (H) VORTAC 114.4   VUZ   Chan 91   N33°40.21' W86°53.99'   129° 9.8 NM to fld. 750/02E.   HIWAS.
MC DEN NDB (HW/LOM) 224   BH   N33°30.68' W86°50.74'   057° 5.6 NM to fld.   NOTAM FILE BHM.
ROEBY NDB (LOM) 394   RO   N33°36.46' W86°40.73'   235° 4.6 NM to fld.   NOTAM FILE BHM.
ILS 110.3   I−BHM   Rwy 06. CLASS IIE.   LOM MC DEN NDB.
ILS/DME 109.5   I−ROE   Chan 32   Rwy 24. CLASS IE.   LOM ROEBY NDB.
ILS/DME 111.3   I−BXO   Chan 50   Rwy 18.   (LOC only).
ASR

BLACKWELL FLD   (See OZARK)

BLOOD   N31°49.82' W86°06.33'   NOTAM FILE TOI   NEW ORLEANS
NDB (MHW/LOM) 365   TO   070° 5.1 NM to Troy Muni.   L−18F

Figure 11-5 *Airport / Facility Directory*

FDC NOTAMs are issued by the National Flight Data Center and contain regulatory information, such as temporary flight restrictions or an amendment to instrument approach procedures. The NOTAM-Ds and FDC NOTAMs are contained in the NOTAM publication, which is issued every 28 days. Prior to any flight, pilots should check for any NOTAMs that could affect their intended flight.

NOTAM-D information includes such data as taxiway closures, personnel and equipment near or crossing runways, and airport lighting aids that do not affect instrument approach criteria, such as visual approach slope indicator (VASI). NOTAM-D information is distributed locally only and is not attached to the hourly weather reports. A separate file of local NOTAMs is maintained at each FSS for facilities in their area only. NOTAM-D information for other FSS areas must be specifically requested directly from the FSS that has responsibility for the airport concerned.

Chapter 12 - Aviation Meteorology

The Atmosphere

The atmosphere is a blanket of air made up of a mixture of gases that surrounds the Earth and reaches almost 350 miles from the surface of the Earth. This mixture is in constant motion. If the atmosphere were visible, it might look like an ocean with swirls and eddies, rising and falling air, and waves that travel for great distances.

Life on Earth is supported by the atmosphere, solar energy, and the planet's magnetic fields. The atmosphere absorbs energy from the Sun, recycles water and other chemicals, and works with the electrical and magnetic forces to provide a moderate climate. The atmosphere also protects life on Earth from high energy radiation and the frigid vacuum of space.

Composition of the Atmosphere

In any given volume of air, nitrogen accounts for 78 percent of the gases that comprise the atmosphere, while oxygen makes up 21 percent. Argon, carbon dioxide, and traces of other gases make up the remaining one percent. This cubic foot also contains some water vapor, varying from zero to about five percent by volume. This small amount of water vapor is responsible for major changes in the weather.

The envelope of gases surrounding the Earth changes from the ground up. Four distinct layers or spheres of the atmosphere

Figure 12-1. *Composition of the atmosphere*

have been identified using thermal characteristics (temperature changes), chemical composition, movement, and density.

The first layer, known as the troposphere, extends from sea level up to 20,000 feet (8 kilometers (km)) over the northern and southern poles and up to 48,000 feet (14.5 km) over the equatorial regions. The vast majority of weather, clouds, storms, and temperature variances occur within this first layer of the atmosphere. Inside the troposphere, the temperature decreases at a rate of about 2 °Celsius (C) every 1,000 feet of altitude gain, and the pressure decreases at a rate of about one inch per 1,000 feet of altitude gain.

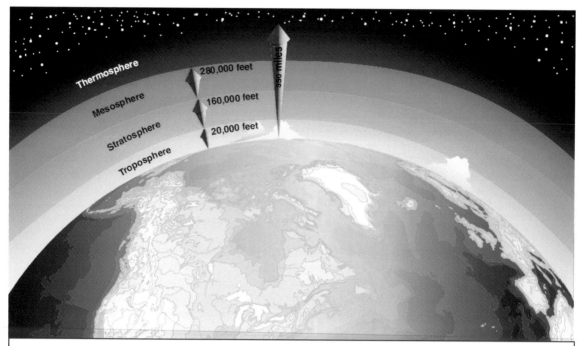

Figure 12-2. *The Troposphere is where most aircraft fly, including UAV's. Above the Troposphere (18,000 mean sea level) is the start of Class A airspace where most airliners will fly. Of course, all civilian drones are limited to just 400 feet unless specific permission is received from the FAA.*

At the top of the troposphere is a boundary known as the tropopause, which traps moisture and the associated weather in the troposphere. The altitude of the tropopause varies with latitude and with the season of the year; therefore, it takes on an elliptical shape, as opposed to round. Location of the tropopause is important because it is commonly associated with the location of the jet stream and possible clear air turbulence.

Above the tropopause are three more atmospheric levels. The first is the stratosphere, which extends from the tropopause to a height of about 160,000 feet (50 km). Little weather exists in this layer and the air remains stable although certain types of clouds occasionally extend in it. Above the stratosphere are the mesosphere and thermosphere which have little influence over weather.

Atmospheric Circulation

Figure 12-3. *Atmospheric circulation, single-cell model.*

As noted earlier, the atmosphere is in constant motion. Certain factors combine to set the atmosphere in motion, but a major factor is the uneven heating of the Earth's surface. This heating upsets the equilibrium of the atmosphere, creating changes in air movement and atmospheric pressure. The movement of air around the surface of the Earth is called atmospheric circulation.

Heating of the Earth's surface is accomplished by several processes, but in the simple convection-only model used for this discussion, the Earth is warmed by energy radiating from the sun. The process causes a circular motion that results when warm air rises and is replaced by cooler air.

Warm air rises because heat causes air molecules to spread apart. As the air expands, it becomes less dense and lighter than the surrounding air. As air cools, the molecules pack together more closely, becoming denser and heavier than warm air. As a result, cool, heavy air tends to sink and replace warmer, rising air.

Because the Earth has a curved surface that rotates on a tilted axis while orbiting the sun, the equatorial regions of the Earth receive a greater amount of heat from the sun than the polar regions. The amount of sun that heats the Earth depends on the time of year and the latitude of the specific region. All of these factors affect the length of time and the angle at which sunlight strikes the surface.

Solar heating causes higher temperatures in equatorial areas which causes the air to be less dense and rise. As the warm air flows toward the poles, it cools, becoming denser, and sinks back toward the surface. [Figure 11-3]

Atmospheric Pressure

The unequal heating of the Earth's surface not only modifies air density and creates circulation patterns; it also causes changes in air pressure or the force exerted by the weight of air molecules. Although air molecules are invisible, they still have weight and take up space.

Imagine a sealed column of air that has a footprint of one square inch and is 350 miles high. It would take 14.7 pounds of effort to lift that column. This represents the air's weight; if the column is shortened, the pressure exerted at the bottom (and its weight) would be less.

The weight of the shortened column of air at 18,000 feet is approximately 7.4 pounds; almost 50 percent that at sea level. For instance, if a bathroom scale (calibrated for sea level) were raised to 18,000 feet, the column of air weighing 14.7 pounds at sea level would be 18,000 feet shorter, and would weigh approximately 7.3 pounds (50 percent) less than at sea level. [Figure 12-4]

The actual pressure at a given place and time differs with altitude, temperature, and density of the air. These conditions also affect aircraft performance, especially with regard to takeoff, rate of climb, and landings.

Measurement of Atmosphere Pressure

Atmospheric pressure is typically measured in inches of mercury ("Hg) by a mercurial barometer. [Figure 12-5] The barometer measures the height of a column of

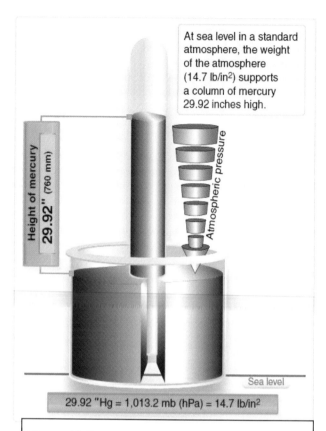

At sea level in a standard atmosphere, the weight of the atmosphere (14.7 lb/in²) supports a column of mercury 29.92 inches high.

Height of mercury 29.92" (760 mm)

Atmospheric pressure

Sea level

29.92 "Hg = 1,013.2 mb (hPa) = 14.7 lb/in²

Figure 12-5. *Mercury Barometer measuring Atmospheric Pressure*

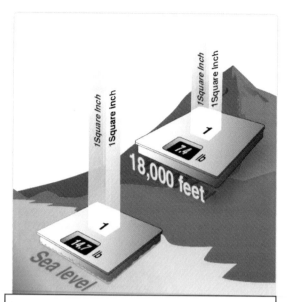

1Square Inch 1Square Inch

1Square Inch 1Square Inch

7.4 lb

18,000 feet

1

1

14.7 lb

Sea level

Figure 12-4. Atmospheric Pressure

mercury inside a glass tube. A section of the mercury is exposed to the pressure of the atmosphere, which exerts a force on the mercury. An increase in pressure forces the mercury to rise inside the tube. When the pressure drops, mercury drains out of the tube, decreasing the height of the column. This type of barometer is typically used in a laboratory or weather observation station, is not easily transported, and difficult to read.

Coriolis Effect

In general atmospheric circulation theory, areas of low pressure exist over the equatorial regions and areas of high pressure exist over the polar regions due to a difference in temperature. The resulting

low pressure allows the high- pressure air at the poles to flow along the planet's surface toward the equator. While this pattern of air circulation is correct in theory, the circulation of air is modified by several forces, the most important of which is the rotation of the Earth.

The force created by the rotation of the Earth is known as the Coriolis Effect (or force). This force is not perceptible to humans as they walk around because humans move slowly and travel relatively short distances compared to the size and rotation rate of the Earth. However, the Coriolis force significantly affects bodies that move over great distances, such as an air mass or body of water.

The Coriolis force deflects air to the right in the Northern Hemisphere, causing it to follow a curved path instead of a straight line. The amount of deflection differs depending on the latitude. It is greatest at the poles, and diminishes to zero at the equator. The magnitude of Coriolis force also differs with the speed of the moving body—the greater the speed, the greater the deviation. In the Northern Hemisphere, the rotation of the Earth deflects moving air to the right and changes the general circulation pattern of the air.

The speed of the Earth's rotation causes the general flow to break up into three distinct cells in each hemisphere. In the Northern Hemisphere, the warm air at the equator rises upward from the surface, travels northward, and is deflected eastward by the rotation of the Earth. By the time it has traveled one-third of the distance from the equator to the North Pole, it is no longer moving northward, but eastward. This air cools and sinks in a belt-like area at about 30° latitude, creating an area of high pressure as it sinks toward the surface. Then, it flows southward along the surface back toward the equator. Coriolis force bends the flow to the right, thus creating the northeasterly trade winds that prevail from 30° latitude to the equator. Similar forces create circulation cells that encircle the Earth between 30° and 60° latitude, and between 60° and the poles. This circulation pattern results in the prevailing westerly winds in the conterminous United States.

Circulation patterns are further complicated by seasonal changes, differences between the surfaces of continents and oceans, and other factors such as frictional forces caused by the topography of the Earth's surface which modify the movement of the air in the atmosphere. For example, within 2,000 feet of the ground, the friction between the surface and the atmosphere slows the moving air. The wind is diverted from its path because the frictional force reduces the Coriolis force. Thus, the wind direction at the surface varies somewhat from the wind direction just a few thousand feet above the Earth.

Weather Hazards

Knowledge of thunderstorms and the associated hazards with thunderstorms is critical to the safety of flight. For a thunderstorm to form, the air must have sufficient water vapor, an unstable lapse rate, and an initial upward boost (lifting). A thunderstorm lifecycle progresses through three stages: the cumulus, the mature, and the dissipating. Figure 1, Mature Stage of Thunderstorm, is an example of a mature thunderstorm and the updrafts and downdrafts contained within them. Weather recognizable as a thunderstorm should be considered hazardous, as penetration of any thunderstorm can lead to an aircraft accident and fatalities to those on board.

THUNDERSTORM TYPES

Thunderstorms pack just about every weather hazard known to aviation. Pilots may encounter thunderstorms of different size and types. Thunderstorm types may be classified as:

1. Single Cell. A single cell (or common) thunderstorm cell often develops on warm and humid summer days. These cells may be severe and produce hail and microburst winds.

2. Thunderstorm Cluster (Multi Cell). Thunderstorms often develop in clusters with numerous cells. These can cover large areas. Individual cells within the cluster may

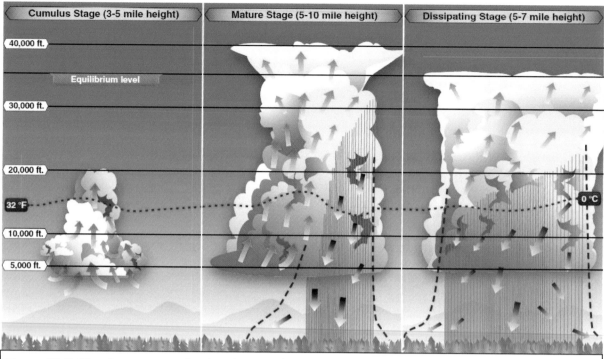

Figure 12-6. *The three stages of a thunderstorm's life cycle.*

move in one direction while the whole system moves in another.

3. Squall Line. A squall line is a narrow band of active thunderstorms. Often it develops on or ahead of a cold front in moist, unstable air, but it may develop in unstable air far removed from any front. The line may be too long to detour easily around and too wide and severe to penetrate.

4. Supercell. A supercell is a single long-lived thunderstorm which is responsible for nearly all of the significant tornadoes produced in the United States and for most of the hailstones larger than golf ball-size.

Turbulence

Potentially hazardous turbulence is present in all thunderstorms, and a severe thunderstorm can destroy an aircraft. Strongest turbulence within the cloud occurs between updrafts and downdrafts. Outside the cloud, shear turbulence is encountered several thousand feet above and up to 20 miles laterally from a severe storm. Additionally, clear air turbulence

may be encountered 20 or more miles from the anvil cloud edge.

It is almost impossible to hold a constant altitude in a thunderstorm, and maneuvering in an attempt to do so greatly increases stress on the aircraft. Stresses are least if the aircraft is held in a constant attitude.

A low-level turbulent area is associated with the gust front. Often, a "roll cloud" or "shelf cloud" on the leading edge of the storm marks the top of the extreme turbulence zone. Gust fronts often move far ahead (up to 15 miles) of associated precipitation. The gust front causes a rapid and sometimes drastic change in surface wind ahead of an approaching storm.

The downward moving column of air in a typical thunderstorm is large. The resultant outflow may produce wind shear, and in some cases the most severe type of wind shear, the microburst.

Other Hazards During Flight

Microbursts

A microburst is a small-scale, intense downdraft that when reaching the surface, spreads outward in all directions from the downdraft center. Virga, streaks of precipitation falling from a thunderstorm cloud but not reaching the ground, may precede a microburst. The current edition of AC 00-54, Pilot Windshear Guide, explains in greater detail the hazards associated with gust fronts, wind shear, and microbursts.

Icing

Updrafts in a thunderstorm support abundant liquid water with relatively large droplet sizes and when carried above the freezing level, the water may become supercooled. As the upward current of air cools to a temperature of about -15°C, the remaining water vapor sublimates as ice crystals. Above this level, at lower temperatures, the amount of supercooled water decreases.
Supercooled water freezes on impact with an aircraft. Clear icing can occur at any altitude above the freezing level but at high levels, icing from smaller droplets may be rime or mixed rime and clear. The abundance of large, supercooled water droplets makes clear icing very rapid between 0°C and -15°C, and encounters can be frequent in a cluster of cells. Thunderstorm icing can be extremely hazardous.

Hail

Hail competes with turbulence as the greatest thunderstorm hazard to aircraft. Supercooled drops above the freezing level begin to freeze. Once a drop has frozen, other drops latch on and freeze to it, so the hailstone grows—sometimes into a huge iceball. Large hail occurs with severe thunderstorms with strong updrafts that have built to great heights. Eventually, the hailstones fall, possibly some distance from the storm core. Hail may be encountered in clear air several miles from the thunderstorm.
As hailstones fall through air with temperatures above 0°C, they begin to melt and precipitation may reach the ground as either hail or rain. Rain at the surface does not mean the absence of hail aloft. Pilots should anticipate possible hail with any thunderstorm, especially beneath the anvil of a large cumulonimbus. Hailstones larger than one-half inch in diameter can significantly damage an aircraft in a few seconds.

Visibility

Low Ceiling and Visibility. Generally, visibility is near zero within a thunderstorm cloud. Ceiling and visibility also may be restricted in precipitation and dust between the cloud base and the ground. The restrictions create the same problem as all ceiling and visibility restrictions, but the hazards are increased when associated with the other thunderstorm hazards of turbulence, hail, and lightning that make precision instrument flying virtually impossible.

Effect on Altimeters

Pressure usually falls rapidly with the approach of a thunderstorm. Pressure then usually rises sharply with the onset of the first gust, and arrival of the cold downdraft and heavy rain, falling back to normal as the thunderstorm passes. This cycle of pressure change may occur in 15 minutes. If the pilot does not receive a corrected altimeter setting, the altimeter may be more than 100 feet in error.

Lightning

A lightning strike can puncture the skin of an aircraft and can damage communications and electronic navigational equipment. Lightning has been suspected of igniting fuel vapors causing an explosion; however, serious accidents due to lightning strikes are extremely rare. Nearby lightning can blind the pilot, rendering the pilot momentarily unable to navigate either by instrument or by visual reference. Nearby lightning can also induce permanent errors in the magnetic compass. Lightning discharges, even distant ones, can disrupt radio communications on low and medium frequencies. Though lightning intensity and frequency have no simple relationship to other storm parameters, severe storms, as a rule, have a high frequency of lightning.

Aviation Weather Services

In aviation, weather service is a combined effort of the National Weather Service (NWS), Federal Aviation Administration (FAA), Department of Defense (DOD), other aviation groups, and individuals. Because of the increasing need for worldwide weather services, foreign weather organizations also provide vital input. While weather forecasts are not 100 percent accurate, meteorologists, through careful scientific study and computer modeling, have the ability to predict weather patterns, trends, and characteristics with increasing accuracy. Through a complex system of weather services, government agencies, and independent weather observers, pilots and other aviation professionals receive the benefit of this vast knowledge base in the form of up-to-date weather reports and forecasts. These reports and forecasts enable pilots to make informed decisions regarding weather and flight safety before and during a flight.

Observations

The data gathered from surface and upper altitude observations form the basis of all weather forecasts, advisories, and briefings. There are four types of weather observations: surface, upper air, radar, and satellite. Surface Aviation Weather Observations Surface aviation weather observations (METARs) are a compilation of elements of the current weather at individual ground stations across the United States. The network is made up of government and privately contracted facilities that provide continuous up-to-date weather information. Automated weather sources, such as the Automated Weather Observing Systems (AWOS), Automated Surface Observing Systems (ASOS), Air Route Traffic Control Center (ARTCC) facilities, as well as other automated facilities, also play a major role in the gathering of surface observations. Surface observations provide local weather conditions and other relevant information for a radius of five miles of a specific airport. This information includes the type of report, station identifier, date and time, modifier (as required), wind, visibility, runway visual range (RVR), weather phenomena, sky condition, temperature/dew point, altimeter reading, and applicable remarks. The information gathered for the surface observation may be from a person, an automated station, or an automated station that is updated or enhanced by a weather observer. In any form, the surface observation provides valuable information about individual airports around the country. Although the reports cover only a small radius, the pilot can generate a good picture of the weather over a wide area when many reporting stations are looked at together.

Upper Air Observations

Observations of upper air weather are more challenging than surface observations. There are only two methods by which upper air weather phenomena can be observed: radiosonde observations and pilot weather reports (PIREPs). A radiosonde is a small cubic instrumentation package which is suspended below a six foot hydrogen or helium filled balloon. Once released, the balloon rises at a rate of approximately 1,000 feet per minute (fpm). As it ascends, the instrumentation gathers various pieces of data such as air temperature and pressure, as well as wind speed and direction. Once the information is gathered, it is relayed to ground stations via a 300 milliwatt radio transmitter.
The balloon flight can last as long as 2 hours or more and can ascend to altitudes as high as 115,000 feet and drift as far as 125 miles. The temperatures and pressures

experienced during the flight can be as low as -130 °F and pressures as low as a few thousandths of what is experienced at sea level.

Since the pressure decreases as the balloon rises in the atmosphere, the balloon expands until it reaches the limits of its elasticity. This point is reached when the diameter has increased to over 20 feet. At this point, the balloon pops and the radiosonde falls back to Earth. The descent is slowed by means of a parachute. The parachute aids in protecting people and objects on the ground. Each year over 75,000 balloons are launched. Of that number, 20 percent are recovered and returned for reconditioning. Return instructions are printed on the side of each radiosonde.

Pilots also provide vital information regarding upper air weather observations and remain the only real-time source of information regarding turbulence, icing, and cloud heights. This information is gathered and filed by pilots in flight. Together, PIREPs and radiosonde observations provide information on upper air conditions important for flight planning. Many domestic and international airlines have equipped their aircraft with instrumentation that automatically transmits inflight weather observations through the DataLink system to the airline dispatcher who disseminates the data to appropriate weather forecasting authorities.
Satellite

Aviation Weather Reports

Aviation weather reports are designed to give accurate depictions of current weather conditions. Each report provides current information that is updated at different times. Some typical reports are METAR, PIREPs, and radar weather reports (SDs).

Aviation Routine Weather Report (METAR)

A METAR is an observation of current surface weather reported in a standard international format. While the METAR code has been adopted worldwide, each country is allowed to make modifications to the code. Normally, these differences are minor but necessary to accommodate local procedures or particular units of measure. This discussion of METAR will cover elements used in the United States.

Metars are issued hourly unless significant weather changes have occurred. A special METAR (SPECI) can be issued at any interval between routine METAR reports.

Example: METAR KGGG 161753Z AUTO 14021G26 3/4SM +TSRA BR BKN008 OVC012CB 18/17 A2970 RMK PRESFR

A typical METAR report contains the following information in sequential order:

1. Type of report—there are two types of METAR reports. The first is the routine METAR report that is transmitted every hour. The second is the aviation selected SPECI. This is a special report that can be given at any time to update the METAR for rapidly changing weather conditions, aircraft mishaps, or other critical information.

2. Station identifier—a four-letter code as established by the International Civil Aviation Organization (ICAO). In the 48 contiguous states, a unique threeletter identifier is preceded by the letter "K." For example, Gregg County Airport in Longview, Texas, is identified by the letters "KGGG," K being the country designation and GGG being the airport identifier. In other regions of the world, including Alaska and Hawaii, the first two letters of the four-letter ICAO identifier indicate the region, country, or state. Alaska identifiers always begin with the letters "PA" and Hawaii identifiers always begin with the letters "PH." A list of station identifiers can be found at an FSS or NWS office. 12-7 27A WSA 20K+ RWY 250 20 27D WSA 20K+ RWY 250 20 2MD 1MD 9 RWY 27 1MF 2MF 3MF Figure 12-7. Example of what the controller sees on the ribbon display in the tower cab.

3. Date and time of report—depicted in a six-digit group (161753Z). The first two digits are the date. The last four digits are the time of the METAR, which is always given in coordinated universal time (UTC). A "Z" is appended to the end of the time to denote the time is given in Zulu time (UTC) as opposed to local time.

4. Modifier—denotes that the METAR came from an automated source or that the report was corrected. If the notation "AUTO" is listed in the METAR, the report came from an automated source. It also lists "AO1" or "AO2" in the remarks section to indicate the type of precipitation sensors employed at the automated station. When the modifier "COR" is used, it identifies a corrected report sent out to replace an earlier

report that contained an error (for example: METAR KGGG 161753Z COR).

5. Wind—reported with five digits (14021) unless the speed is greater than 99 knots, in which case the wind is reported with six digits. The first three digits indicate the direction the true wind is blowing in tens of degrees. If the wind is variable, it is reported as "VRB." The last two digits indicate the speed of the wind in knots unless the wind is greater than 99 knots, in which case it is indicated by three digits. If the winds are gusting, the letter "G" follows the wind speed (G26). After the letter "G," the peak gust recorded is provided. If the wind varies more than 60° and the wind speed is greater than six knots, a separate group of numbers, separated by a "V," will indicate the extremes of the wind directions.

6. Visibility—the prevailing visibility (¾ SM) is reported in statute miles as denoted by the letters "SM." It is reported in both miles and fractions of miles. At times, runway visual range (RVR) is reported following the prevailing visibility. RVR is the distance a pilot can see down the runway in a moving aircraft. When RVR is reported, it is shown with an R, then the runway number followed by a slant, then the visual range in feet. For example, when the RVR is reported as R17L/1400FT, it translates to a visual range of 1,400 feet on runway 17 left.

7. Weather—can be broken down into two different categories: qualifiers and weather phenomenon (+TSRA BR). First, the qualifiers of intensity, proximity, and the descriptor of the weather will be given. The intensity may be light (-),

moderate ( ), or heavy (+). Proximity only depicts weather phenomena that are in the airport vicinity. The notation "VC" indicates a specific weather phenomenon is in the vicinity of five to ten miles from the airport. Descriptors are used to describe certain types of precipitation and obscurations. Weather phenomena may be reported as being precipitation, obscurations, and other phenomena such as squalls or funnel clouds. Descriptions of weather phenomena as they begin or end, and hailstone size are also listed in the remarks sections of the report. [Figure 12-8]

8. Sky condition—always reported in the sequence of amount, height, and type or indefinite ceiling/ height (vertical visibility) (BKN008 OVC012CB). The heights of the cloud bases are reported with a three-digit number in hundreds of feet AGL. Clouds above 12,000 feet are not detected or reported by an automated station. The types of clouds, specifically towering cumulus (TCU) or cumulonimbus (CB) clouds, are reported with their height. Contractions are used to describe the amount of cloud coverage and obscuring phenomena. The amount of sky coverage is reported in eighths of the sky from horizon to horizon. [Figure 12-9]

9. Temperature and dew point—the air temperature and dew point are always given in degrees Celsius (C) or (°C 18/17). Temperatures below 0 °C are preceded by the letter "M" to indicate minus.

10. Altimeter setting—reported as inches of mercury ("Hg) in a four-digit number group (A2970). It is always preceded by

the letter "A." Rising or falling pressure may also be denoted in the remarks sections as "PRESRR" or "PRESFR" respectively.

11. Zulu time—a term used in aviation for UTC which places the entire world on one time standard.

12. Remarks—the remarks section always begins with the letters "RMK." Comments may or may not appear in this section of the METAR. The information contained in this section may include wind data, variable visibility, beginning and ending times of particular phenomenon, pressure information, and various other information deemed necessary. An example of a remark regarding weather phenomenon that does not fit in any other category would be: OCNL LTGICCG. This translates as occasional lightning in the clouds and from cloud to ground. Automated stations also use the remarks section to indicate the equipment needs maintenance.

Example:
METAR KGGG 161753Z AUTO 14021G26 3/4SM +TSRA BR BKN008 OVC012CB 18/17 A2970 RMK PRESFR

Explanation: Routine METAR for Gregg County Airport for the 16th day of the month at 1753Z automated source. Winds are 140 at 21 knots gusting to 26. Visibility is ¾ statute mile. Thunderstorms with heavy rain and mist. Ceiling is broken at 800 feet, overcast at 1,200 feet with cumulonimbus clouds. Temperature 18 °C and dew point 17 °C. Barometric pressure is 29.70 "Hg and falling rapidly.

Qualifier		Weather Phenomena		
Intensity or Proximity 1	Descriptor 2	Precipitation 3	Obscuration 4	Other 5
- Light	**MI** Shallow	**DZ** Drizzle	**BR** Mist	**PO** Dust/sand whirls
Moderate (no qualifier)	**BC** Patches	**RA** Rain	**FG** Fog	**SQ** Squalls
+ Heavy	**DR** Low drifting	**SN** Snow	**FU** Smoke	**FC** Funnel cloud
VC in the vicinity	**BL** Blowing	**SG** Snow grains	**DU** Dust	**+FC** Tornado or waterspout
	SH Showers	**IC** Ice crystals (diamond dust)	**SA** Sand	**SS** Sandstorm
	TS Thunderstorms	**PL** Ice pellets	**HZ** Haze	**DS** Dust storm
	FZ Freezing	**GR** Hail	**PY** Spray	
	PR Partial	**GS** Small hail or snow pellets	**VA** Volcanic ash	
		UP *Unknown precipitation		

The weather groups are constructed by considering columns 1–5 in this table in sequence:
intensity, followed by descriptor, followed by weather phenomena (e.g., heavy rain showers(s) is coded as +SHRA).
* Automated stations only

Sky Cover	Contraction
Less than 1/8 (Clear)	SKC, CLR, FEW
1/8-2/8 (Few)	FEW
3/8-4/8 (Scattered)	SCT
5/8-7/8 (Broken)	BKN
8/8 or (Overcast)	OVC

Aviation Forecasts

Observed weather condition reports are often used in the creation of forecasts for the same area. A variety of different forecast products are produced and designed to be used in the preflight planning stage. The printed forecasts that pilots need to be familiar with are the terminal aerodrome forecast (TAF), aviation area forecast (FA), inflight weather advisories (SIGMET, AIRMET), and the winds and temperatures aloft forecast (FD).

Terminal Aerodrome Forecasts (TAF)

A TAF is a report established for the five statute mile radius around an airport. TAF reports are usually given for larger airports. Each TAF is valid for a 30-hour time period, and is updated four times a day at 0000Z, 0600Z, 1200Z, and 1800Z. The TAF utilizes the same descriptors and abbreviations as used in the METAR report. The TAF includes the following information in sequential order:

1. Type of report—a TAF can be either a routine forecast (TAF) or an amended forecast (TAF AMD).

2. ICAO station identifier—the station identifier is the same as that used in a METAR.

3. Date and time of origin—time and date of TAF origination is given in the six-number code with the first two being the date, the last four being the time. Time is always given in UTC as denoted by the Z following the number group.

4. Valid period date and time—the valid forecast time period is given by a six-digit number group. The first two numbers indicate the date, followed by the twodigit beginning time for the valid period, and the last two digits are the ending time.

5. Forecast wind—the wind direction and speed forecast are given in a five-digit number group. The first three indicate the direction of the wind in reference to true north. The last two digits state the windspeed in knots as denoted by the letters "KT." Like the METAR, winds greater than 99 knots are given in three digits.

6. Forecast visibility—given in statute miles and may be in whole numbers or fractions. If the forecast is greater than six miles, it will be coded as "P6SM."

7. Forecast significant weather—weather phenomena are coded in the TAF reports in the same format as the METAR. If no significant weather is expected during the forecast time period, the denotation "NSW" is included in the "becoming" or "temporary" weather groups.

8. Forecast sky condition—given in the same manner as the METAR. Only cumulonimbus (CB) clouds are forecast in this portion of the TAF report as opposed to CBs and towering cumulus in the METAR.

9. Forecast change group—for any significant weather change forecast to occur during the TAF time period, the expected conditions and time period are included in this group. This information may be shown as from (FM), becoming

(BECMG), and temporary (TEMPO). "FM" is used when a rapid and significant change, usually within an hour, is expected. "BECMG" is used when a gradual change in the weather is expected over a period of no more than 2 hours. "TEMPO" is used for temporary fluctuations of weather, expected to last less than one hour.

10. Probability forecast—a given percentage that describes the probability of thunderstorms and precipitation occurring in the coming hours. This forecast is not used for the first 6 hours of the 24-hour forecast.

Example: TAF KPIR 111130Z 111212 15012KT P6SM BKN090 TEMPO 1214 5SM BR FM1500 16015G25KT P6SM SCT040 BKN250 FM0000 14012KT P6SM BKN080 OVC150 PROB40 0004 3SM TSRA BKN030CB FM0400 1408KT P6SM SCT040 OVC080 TEMPO 0408 3SM TSRA OVC030CB BECMG 0810 32007KT=

Explanation: Routine TAF for Pierre, South Dakota…on the 11th day of the month, at 1130Z…valid for 24 hours from 1200Z on the 11th to 1200Z on the 12th…wind from 150° at 12 knots…visibility greater than 6 sm…broken clouds at 9,000 feet…temporarily, between 1200Z and 1400Z, visibility 5 sm in mist…from 1500Z winds from 160° at 15 knots, gusting to 25 knots visibility greater than 6 sm…clouds scattered at 4,000 feet and broken at 25,000 feet…from 0000Z wind from 140° at 12 knots…visibility greater than 6 sm…clouds broken at 8,000 feet, overcast at 15,000 feet…between 0000Z and 0400Z, there is 40 percent probability of visibility 3 sm…thunderstorm with moderate rain showers…clouds broken at 3,000 feet with

cumulonimbus clouds…from 0400Z…winds from 140° at 8 knots…visibility greater than 6 miles…clouds at 4,000 scattered and overcast at 8,000…temporarily between 0400Z and 0800Z…visibility 3 miles…thunderstorms with moderate rain showers…clouds overcast at 3,000 feet with cumulonimbus clouds…becoming between 0800Z and 1000Z…wind from 320° at 7 knots…end of report (=).

Area Forecasts (FA)

The FA gives a picture of clouds, general weather conditions, and visual meteorological conditions (VMC) expected over a large area encompassing several states. There are six areas for which area forecasts are published in the contiguous 48 states. Area forecasts are issued three times a day and are valid for 18 hours. This type of forecast gives information vital to en route operations, as well as forecast information for smaller airports that do not have terminal forecasts.

Area forecasts are typically disseminated in four sections and include the following information:

1. Header—gives the location identifier of the source of the FA, the date and time of issuance, the valid forecast time, and the area of coverage.

Example: DFWC FA 120945 SYNOPSIS AND VFR CLDS/WX SYNOPSIS VALID UNTIL 130400 CLDS/WX VALID UNTIL 122200…OTLK VALID 122200-130400 OK TX AR LA MS AL AND CSTL WTRS

Explanation: The area forecast shows information given by Dallas Fort Worth, for the region of Oklahoma, Texas, Arkansas,

Louisiana, Mississippi, and Alabama, as well as a portion of the Gulf coastal waters. It was issued on the 12th day of the month at 0945. The synopsis is valid from the time of issuance until 0400 hours on the 13th. VFR clouds and weather information on this area forecast are valid until 2200 hours on the 12th and the outlook is valid until 0400 hours on the 13th.

2. Precautionary statements—IFR conditions, mountain obscurations, and thunderstorm hazards are described in this section. Statements made here regarding height are given in MSL, and if given otherwise, AGL or ceiling (CIG) will be noted.

Example:
SEE AIRMET SIERRA FOR IFR CONDS AND MTN OBSCN. TS IMPLY SEV OR GTR TURB SEV ICE LLWS AND IFR CONDS. NON MSL HGTS DENOTED BYAGL OR CIG.

Explanation:
The area forecast covers VFR clouds and weather, so the precautionary statement warns that AIRMET Sierra should be referenced for IFR conditions and mountain obscuration. The code TS indicates the possibility of thunderstorms and implies there may be occurrences of severe or greater turbulence, severe icing, low-level wind shear, and IFR conditions. The final line of the precautionary statement alerts the user that heights, for the most part, are MSL. Those that are not MSL will be AGL or CIG.

3. Synopsis—gives a brief summary identifying the location and movement of pressure systems, fronts, and circulation patterns.

Example:
SYNOPSIS...LOW PRES TROF 10Z OK/TX PNHDL AREA FCST MOV EWD INTO CNTRL-SWRN OK BY 04Z. WRMFNT 10Z CNTRL OK-SRN AR-NRN MS FCST LIFT NWD INTO NERN OK-NRN AR EXTRM NRN MS BY 04Z.

Explanation:
As of 1000Z, there is a low pressure trough over the Oklahoma and Texas panhandle area, which is forecast to move eastward into central southwestern Oklahoma by 0400Z. A warm front located over central Oklahoma, southern Arkansas, and northern Mississippi at 1000Z is forecast to lift northwestward into northeastern Oklahoma, northern Arkansas, and extreme northern Mississippi by 0400Z.

4. VFR Clouds and Weather—This section lists expected sky conditions, visibility, and weather for the next 12 hours and an outlook for the following 6 hours.

Example: S CNTRL AND SERN TX AGL SCT-BKN010. TOPS 030. VIS 3-5SM BR. 14-16Z BECMG AGL SCT030. 19Z AGL SCT050. OTLK...VFR OK PNDLAND NW...AGL SCT030 SCT-BKN100. TOPS FL200. 15Z AGL SCT040 SCT100. AFT 20Z SCT TSRA DVLPG.. FEW POSS SEV. CB TOPS FL450. OTLK...VFR

Explanation:
In south central and southeastern Texas, there is a scattered to broken layer of clouds from 1,000 feet AGL with tops at 3,000 feet, visibility is 3 to 5 sm in mist. Between 1400Z and 1600Z, the cloud bases are expected to increase to 3,000 feet AGL. After 1900Z, the cloud bases are expected to continue to increase to 5,000 feet AGL and the outlook is VFR.

In northwestern Oklahoma and panhandle, the clouds are scattered at 3,000 feet with another scattered to broken layer at 10,000 feet AGL, with the tops at 20,000 feet. At 1500 Z, the lowest cloud base is expected to increase to 4,000 feet AGL with a scattered layer at 10,000 feet AGL. After 2000Z, the forecast calls for scattered thunderstorms with rain developing and a few becoming severe; the CB clouds will have tops at flight level 450 or 45,000 feet MSL.

It should be noted that when information is given in the area forecast, locations may be given by states, regions, or specific geological features such as mountain ranges. Figure 12-12 shows an area forecast chart with six regions of forecast, states, regional areas, and common geographical features.

Appenix A

CHECKLIST &

FIELD MANUAL

NOTICE: The rules and regulations pertaining to the operation of Unmanned Aerial Systems (UAS) are changing rapidly as the industry continues to grow at record pace. This Checklist is intended only as guide. It is the individual UAS Operator's responsibility to be familiar with and comply with all Federal, State, and Local laws. UAS Operators should consult www.faa.gov/uas for current regulations, interpretations of rules, and guidance.

Operation Classification

A. **Commercial:** Is this flight for profit, in support of a business, or government entity regardless of whether or not you are paid or a volunteer? If No, proceed to **Recreational Operation**. If Yes, continue.

B. **Civil or Public Aircraft:**

    a. Is aircraft owned or leased (exclusive, 90-day min.) by local, state, or federal gov't?

    b. Is crew qualified under approved standards of said government?

If No to either a or b above, Proceed to **Commercial Flight**.

If yes to both a and b above, Proceed to **Public Use Fight**.

Commercial Operation

Regulatory Compliance Check:

A. Part 333 Exemption: Check current and valid for proposed operation. (If Applicable

B. Operator is in possession of 333 Exemption (paper or digital)

C. Operator in possession of all applicable Certificate of Waiver or Authorization (COA)

D. Aircraft Registered and marked with valid N- Number

E. Operator is in possession of aircraft registration (paper)

F. Operator possesses valid Remote Pilot Certificate.

G. Operator in possession of current and valid Driver's License or FAA Airman's Medical Certificate.

Location:

A. More than 5 Nautical Miles from an Airport? Or 2NM from Heliport with an Instrument Approach Procedure IAW FAR Part 97?

No: Ensure approved COA's permit operation.

If NO: File COA for proposed operation.

If YES: Contact Air Traffic Control Tower (or Airport Manager, if non-towered), coordinate operation.

Yes: Proceed with Checklist

Resouces: www.Skyvector.com www.faa.gov/air_traffic/flight_info/aeronav/digital_products/dtpp/

B. Check Special Use Airspace Restrictions

C. Check Notice To Airmen https://pilotweb.nas.faa.gov/PilotWeb/

D. Check Temporary Flight Restrictions (TFR) http://tfr.faa.gov/tfr2/list.html

Altitude:

A. Remain less than 400' Above Ground Level (AGL). If planned flight requires operation above 400' AGL ensure COA permits operation. If not, file COA for operation.

Endurance:

A. Estimate Flight Time

B. Check battery quantity and charge level

C. Ensure batteries adequate for Estimated Flight Time plus reserve of _____ Minutes

Proceed to **Controller Checklist**

Public Use Operation

Regulatory Compliance Check:

A. Certificate of Authorization or Waiver: Check current and valid for proposed operation.

B. Operator is in possession of COA (paper or digital)

C. Aircraft Registered and marked IAW FAR's.

D. Operator is in possession of aircraft registration (paper)

E. Operator in possession of valid Airmen's Certificate or as required by COA.

F. Operator in possession of current and valid Driver's License or FAA Airman's Medical Certificate.

Location:

A. More than 5 Nautical Miles from an Airport? Or 2NM from Heliport with an Instrument Approach Procedure IAW FAR Part 97?

B. No: Ensure approved COA's permit operation.

C. If NO: File COA for proposed operation.

D. If YES: Contact Air Traffic Control Tower (or Airport Manager, if non-towered), coordinate operation.

E. Yes: Proceed with Checklist

Resouces: www.Skyvector.com www.faa.gov/air_traffic/flight_info/aeronav/digital_products/dtpp/

F. Check Special Use Airspace Restrictions

G. Check Notice To Airmen https://pilotweb.nas.faa.gov/PilotWeb/

H. Check Temporary Flight Restrictions (TFR) http://tfr.faa.gov/tfr2/list.html

Altitude:

I. A. Remain less than 400' Above Ground Level (AGL). If planned flight requires operation above 400' AGL ensure COA permits operation. If not, file COA for operation.

J. Endurance:

K. Estimate Flight Time

L. Check battery quantity and charge level

M. Ensure batteries adequate for Estimated Flight Time plus reserve of _____ Minutes

N. Proceed to Controller Checklist

Recreational Operation:

Location:

A. More than 5 Nautical Miles from an Airport? Or 2NM from Heliport with an

Instrument Approach Procedure IAW FAR Part 97?

No: Contact Air Traffic Control Tower (or Airport Manager, if non-towered), notify of operation.

Resouces: www.Skyvector.com www.faa.gov/air_traffic/flight_info/aeronav/digital_products/dtpp/

Yes: Proceed with Checklist

B. Check Notice To Airmen https://pilotweb.nas.faa.gov/PilotWeb/

C. Check Temporary Flight Restrictions (TFR) http://tfr.faa.gov/tfr2/list.html

Altitude:

A. Remain less than 400' Above Ground Level (AGL)

Endurance:

A. Estimate Flight Time

B. Check battery quantity and charge level

C. Ensure batteries adequate for Estimated Flight Time plus reserve of _____Minutes

Regulatory Compliance Check:

A. Aircraft and Pilot Registered IAW FAA requirements.

B. Aircraft Marked with Registration Number

C. Operator's Registration Card in possession (paper or digital)

Proceed to **Controller Checklist**

CONTROLLER CHECKLIST

A. Tablet / Phone: Mounted & Connected

B. Sun Shield: Mounted & Adjusted

C. Antennas: Positioned

D. Flight Mode SW: Desired Position

E. Battery: Fully Charged

AIRCRAFT CHECKLIST

A. Micro SD Card: Install

B. Gimbal Clamp: Removed, Stowed

C. Format SD Card: As Necessary

D. Battery: Check Fully Charged, Off, Installed

E. Propellers   Check Condition

ENGINE START / RUNUP

A. Controller Power: ON

B. Battery Status: Confirm

C. Controller Status: Check, No Errors

D. Tablet/Phone/Laptop   ON

E. Unnecessary Apps & Features   OFF

F. Firmware / APP (ex DJI GO)   OPEN

G. Camera Icon   SELECT

H. Camera Options   CHECK & SET

I. Compass Calibration   AS
    REQUIRED

J. Return to Home   Check
    Settings

K. Aircraft   On
    Level Ground

L. Propellers   Check
    Secure

M. Aircraft Power   ON

N. Battery Status   Check,
    No Errors

O. Compass Calibration   As
    Required

P. Aircraft Status Indicator   No
    Errors

TAKEOFF CHECKLIST

A. Launch Site   Clear

B. GPS / VPS   Confirm

C. Motors   Start

D. Takeoff   Low Hover

E. Flight Controls   Check

F. Landing Gear   Raise

LANDING CHECKLIST

A. Camera   Full Up

B. Video Recorder   Stop

C. Landing Gear   Lower

D. Landing Area   Clear

E. Landing Gear   Confirm Down

F. Approach   To
    Hover

G. Land   Auto or Manual

POST FLIGHT

A. Aircraft Power   OFF

B. Battery   Remove

C. Controller Power   OFF

D. Propellers   Check
    Condition

E. Accessories   Secure

F. Tower / Apt. Manager   Notify End of
    Ops

EMERGENCY PROCEDURES

Loss of GPS Signal:

Loss of adequate GPS Signal will cause most sUAS to revert to ATTI or Manual Control Modes

 a. Manually Control Aircraft

 b. Assess Flight Conditions, If safe to fly:

Continue Mission

Be prepared for Loss of Comm Sig

If Unsafe to fly:

Land as soon as practicable

Loss of Communication Signal (Comm.Sig.):

A Loss of Comm. condition will usually result in either the activation of an immediate "Auto Land" function or a "Return to Home" Function

"Auto Land": Aircraft begins uncommanded descent while maintaining lateral positioning.

Thrust lever – Full up and hold (Nobody ever crashed into the sky)

Flight Mode Switch - ATTI

Operator- Move away from potential interference (Metal Structures, Bldgs, etc.)

Regain Comm. Sig - Attempt

If Comm. Sig. Returns – Land as soon as practicable. Evaluate cause.

If unable to regain Comm. Sig. – Recover Aircraft. Evaluate Cause.

"Return To Home" RTH: Aircraft will begin with an uncommanded climb to preselected attitude then proceed GPS Direct to Home Waypoint.

Aircraft: Maintain in view

Controller: Check for inadvertent RTH activation.

RTH Function: Cancel if Active

Flight Mode Switch: ATTI

Aircraft: Attempt Manual Control

Battery: Low Temp

Land as soon as practicable

Replace Battery

Battery: Overheat

Electrical Load: Reduce

Land as soon as practicable

Be prepared for **Electrical Fire**

Electrical Fire

All personnel: Clear of smoke

Land Immediately

Aircraft Power: OFF, if safe to do so

Battery: Remove if safe

Fire: Extinguish

Airspace Incursion

Land Immediately

Unstable Flight

INDICATIONS: AIRCRAFT turns in a spiral

MEANING: The Compass is not calibrated. AV cannot maintain its location

ACTIONS

1.   Flight Mode   Set to "ATTI"

2.   Flight   Verify Steady at ATTI

3.   LAND AS SOON AS POSSIBLE

NOTE After Landing perform Compass Calibration. Refer to Maintenance Manual.

Additional Resources

Using Google Earth:

1.   Download and Install Google Earth Pro for fee at http://www.google.com/earth

2.   To start, click the Show Ruler icon. In the pop-up dialog box, click to select the Circle tab. Next, choose the units of measure for the Radius field.

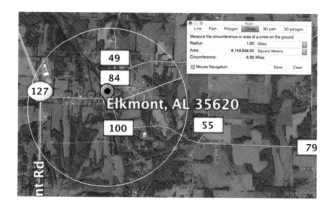

2. Select the airport name hyperlink to bring up airport information.

3. Scroll down the page to "Ownership Information" for contact info.

3. With the Radius set, click the Google Earth Pro cursor on the imagery and release the mouse button.

4. Now move the cursor away from the point you just clicked. Watch the Radius field read-out of radius length as you move. Simply click again when desired radius interval is reached. In the Ruler dialog box, click Save to save the radius ring.

5. When saving the radius ring, the New Path dialog box pops up. Ignore naming the radius ring, or instead give it a name that will later serve as the label for that ring (if you choose to label the rings).

Using Skyvector.com

1. Right click on airport symbol

Using: FAA Digital - Terminal Procedures Publication (d-TPP)/Airport Diagrams

https://www.faa.gov/air_traffic/flight_info/aer
onav/digital_products/dtpp/

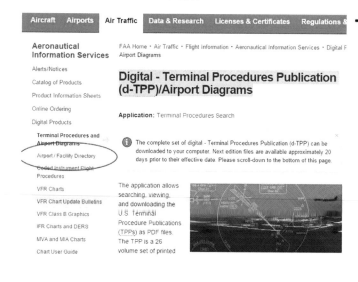

Digital - Terminal Procedures Publication (d-TPP)/Airport Diagrams

Application: Terminal Procedures Search

The complete set of digital - Terminal Procedures Publication (d-TPP) can be downloaded to your computer. Next edition files are available approximately 20 days prior to their effective date. Please scroll-down to the bottom of this page.

The application allows searching, viewing, and downloading the U.S. Terminal Procedure Publications (TPPs) as PDF files. The TPP is a 26 volume set of printed

Aeronautical Information Services

FAA Home · Air Traffic · Flight Information · Aeronautical Information Services · Digital P
Airport Diagrams

Alerts/Notices

Catalog of Products

Product Information Sheets

Online Ordering

Digital Products

Terminal Procedures and Airport Diagrams

Airport / Facility Directory

Coded Instrument Flight Procedures

VFR Charts

VFR Chart Update Bulletins

VFR Class B Graphics

IFR Charts and DERS

MVA and MIA Charts

Chart User Guide

Browse Airports/NAVAIDs By:

State   Volume

```
NORWOOD MEM  (OWD)(KOWD)    2 E   UTC-5(-4DT)
  49   B  S4  FUEL 100LL, JET A  OX 4    NOTAM FILE
  RWY 17-35: H4008X100 (ASPH)  S-58, D-69, 2S-88  MI
    RWY 17: PAPI(P4R)—GA 3.0° TCH 40´. Trees.
    RWY 35: MALSF. PAPI(P4L)—GA 3.0° TCH 40´. Rgt tfc.
  RWY 10-28: H3995X75 (ASPH)  S-58, D-69, 2S-88
    RWY 10: PAPI(P4R)—GA 4.0° TCH 25´. Thld dsplcd 987
    RWY 28: Thld dsplcd 213´. Trees. Rgt tfc.
  LAND AND HOLD-SHORT OPERATIONS
    LDG RWY        HOLD-SHORT POINT        AVBL LD
    RWY 35          10-28                   3320
  RUNWAY DECLARED DISTANCE INFORMATION
    RWY 10: TORA-3995  TODA-3995  ASDA-3782  LDA
    RWY 28: TORA-3995  TODA-3995  ASDA-3808  LDA
  AIRPORT REMARKS: Attended Mon-Fri 1300-2200Z‡. Bird ac
    wildlife hivof arpt. 1049(1199) and 1310(1210) TV twr
    north-northwest. 125´ flagpole 1 mile northwest of Rwy
    1184(1063.5) twr 8.5 NM north-northwest. Rwy 28 and
    touch and go ldg only. All acft exceeding 87 effective per
    level in decibels or 75 decibels, as measured in Part 36 pr
    using arpt. Gate 2 taxilane limited to acft with wingspans c
    Gate 3 taxilane limited to acft with wingspans of 45´ or le
    clsd ACTIVATE MIRL Rwy 17-35, MALSF Rwy 35 and P
    Rwy 17, Rwy 35—CTAF. Ldg fee for transient acft with n
  AIRPORT MANAGER: 781-255-5616
  WEATHER DATA SOURCES: ASOS (781) 762-4314 LAWRS.
  COMMUNICATIONS: CTAF 126.0
    ATIS 119.95 (781-769-3825)
  Ⓡ BOSTON APP/DEP CON 124.1
```

2B2	NEWBURYPORT	MA	PLUM ISLAND		NEW YORK	NE (PDF)	ne_121_04FEB2016 (PDF)
AQW (KAQW)	NORTH ADAMS	MA	HARRIMAN-AND-WEST		NEW YORK	NE (PDF)	ne_122_04FEB2016 (PDF)
7B2	NORTHAMPTON	MA	NORTHAMPTON		NEW YORK	NE (PDF)	ne_122_04FEB2016 (PDF)
OWD (KOWD)	NORWOOD	MA	NORWOOD MEM		NEW YORK	NE (PDF)	ne_123_04FEB2016 (PDF)
ORE (KORE)	ORANGE	MA	ORANGE MUNI		NEW YORK	NE (PDF)	ne_123_04FEB2016 (PDF)

Appendix B
METAR / TAF DECODER

Key to Aerodrome Forecast (TAF) and Aviation Routine Weather Report (METAR) (Front)

TAF	KPIT 091730Z 0918/1024 15005KT 5SM HZ FEW020 WS010/31022KT
	FM091930 30015G25KT 3SM SHRA OVC015
	TEMPO 0920/0922 1/2SM +TSRA OVC008CB
	FM100100 27008KT 5SM SHRA BKN020 OVC040
	PROB30 1004/1007 1SM -RA BR
	FM101015 18005KT 6SM -SHRA OVC020
	BECMG 1013/1015 P6SM NSW SKC

NOTE: Users are cautioned to confirm **DATE** and **TIME** of the TAF. For example FM**100000** is 0000Z on the **10th**. Do not confuse with *1000Z!*

METAR KPIT 091955Z COR 22015G25KT 3/4SM R28L/2600FT TSRA OVC010CB 18/16 A2992 RMK SLP045 T01820159

Forecast	Explanation	Report
TAF	Message type: <u>TAF</u>-routine or <u>TAF AMD</u>-amended forecast, <u>METAR</u>-hourly, <u>SPECI</u>-special or <u>TESTM</u>-non-commissioned ASOS report	METAR
KPIT	ICAO location indicator	KPIT
091730Z	Issuance time: ALL times in UTC "<u>Z</u>", 2-digit date, 4-digit time	091955Z
0918/1024	Valid period, either 24 hours or 30 hours. The first two digits of EACH four digit number indicate the date of the valid period, the final two digits indicate the time (valid from 18Z on the 9th to 24Z on the 10th).	
	In U.S. METAR: <u>COR</u>rected of; or <u>AUTO</u>mated ob for automated report with no human intervention; omitted when observer logs on.	COR
15005KT	Wind: 3 digit true-north direction, nearest 10 degrees (or <u>VaRiaBle</u>); next 2-3 digits for speed and unit, <u>KT</u> (KMH or MPS); as needed, <u>G</u>ust and maximum speed; 00000KT for calm; for METAR, if direction varies 60 degrees or more, <u>V</u>ariability appended, e.g., 180<u>V</u>260	22015G25KT
5SM	Prevailing visibility; in U.S., <u>S</u>tatute <u>M</u>iles & fractions; above 6 miles in TAF <u>Plus6SM</u>. (Or, 4-digit minimum visibility in meters and as required, lowest value with direction)	3/4SM
	Runway Visual Range: <u>R</u>; 2-digit runway designator <u>L</u>eft, <u>C</u>enter, or <u>R</u>ight as needed; "<u>/</u>", Minus or Plus in U.S., 4-digit value, <u>Fee</u>T in U.S., (usually meters elsewhere); 4-digit value <u>V</u>ariability 4-digit value (and tendency <u>D</u>own, <u>U</u>p or <u>N</u>o change)	R28L/2600FT
HZ	Significant present, forecast and recent weather: see table (on back)	TSRA
FEW020	Cloud amount, height and type: <u>SK</u>y <u>C</u>lear 0/8, <u>FEW</u> >0/8-2/8, <u>SCaT</u>tered 3/8-4/8, <u>BroKeN</u> 5/8-7/8, <u>OV</u>er<u>C</u>ast 8/8; 3-digit height in hundreds of ft; <u>T</u>owering <u>CU</u>mulus or <u>C</u>umulonim<u>B</u>us in **METAR**; in TAF, only <u>CB</u>. <u>V</u>ertical <u>V</u>isibility for obscured sky and height "VV004". More than 1 layer may be reported or forecast. In automated **METAR** reports only, <u>CLeaR</u> for "clear below 12,000 feet"	OVC 010CB
	Temperature: degrees Celsius; first 2 digits, temperature "<u>/</u>" last 2 digits, dew-point temperature; <u>M</u>inus for below zero, e.g., M06	18/16
	Altimeter setting: indicator and 4 digits; in U.S., <u>A</u>-inches and hundredths; (<u>Q</u>-hectoPascals, e.g., Q1013)	A2992
WS010/31022KT	In U.S. **TAF**, non-convective low-level (≤2,000 ft) <u>W</u>ind <u>S</u>hear; 3-digit height (hundreds of ft); "<u>/</u>"; 3-digit wind direction and 2-3 digit wind speed above the indicated height, and unit, <u>KT</u>	

Key to Aerodrome Forecast (TAF) and Aviation Routine Weather Report (METAR) (Back)

	In **METAR**, ReMarK indicator & remarks. For example: Sea- Level Pressure in hectoPascals & tenths, as shown: 1004.5 hPa; Temp/dew-point in tenths _C, as shown: temp. 18.2_C, dew-point 15.9_C	**RMK SLP045 T01820159**
FM091930	FroM: changes are expected at: 2-digit date, 2-digit hour, and 2-digit minute beginning time: indicates significant change. Each FM starts on a new line, indented 5 spaces	
TEMPO 0920/0922	TEMPOrary: changes expected for <1 hour and in total, < half of the period between the 2-digit date and 2-digit hour beginning, and 2-digit date and 2-digit hour ending time	
PROB30 1004/1007	PROBability and 2-digit percent (30 or 40): probable condition in the period between the 2-digit date & 2-digit hour beginning time, and the 2-digit date and 2-digit hour ending time	
BECMG 1013/1015	BECoMinG: change expected in the period between the 2-digit date and 2-digit hour beginning time, and the 2-digit date and 2-digit hour ending time	

Table of Significant Present, Forecast and Recent Weather - Grouped in categories and used in the order listed below; or as needed in TAF, No Significant Weather.

Qualifiers

Intensity or Proximity

"-" = Light	**No sign** = Moderate	"+" = Heavy

"**VC**" = Vicinity, but not at aerodrome. In the US METAR, 5 to 10 SM from the point of observation. In the US TAF, 5 to 10 SM from the center of the runway complex. Elsewhere, within 8000m.

Descriptor

BC – Patches	**BL** – Blowing	**DR** – Drifting	**FZ** – Freezing
MI – Shallow	**PR** – Partial	**SH** – Showers	**TS** – Thunderstorm

Weather Phenomena

Precipitation

DZ – Drizzle	**GR** – Hail	**GS** – Small Hail/Snow Pellets	
IC – Ice Crystals	**PL** – Ice Pellets	**RA** – Rain	**SG** – Snow Grains
SN – Snow	**UP** – Unknown Precipitation in automated observations		

Obscuration

BR – Mist (≥5/8SM)	**DU** – Widespread Dust	**FG** – Fog (<5/8SM)	**FU** – Smoke
HZ – Haze	**PY** – Spray	**SA** – Sand	**VA** – Volcanic Ash

Other

DS – Dust Storm	**FC** – Funnel Cloud	**+FC** – Tornado or Waterspout	
PO – Well developed dust or sand whirls	**SQ** – Squall	**SS** – Sandstorm	

- Explanations in parentheses "()" indicate different worldwide practices.
- Ceiling is not specified; defined as the lowest broken or overcast layer, or the vertical visibility.
- NWS TAFs exclude BECMG groups and temperature forecasts, NWS TAFS do not use PROB in the first 9 hours of a TAF; NWS METARs exclude trend forecasts. US Military TAFs include Turbulence and Icing groups.

A Terminal Aerodrome Forecast (TAF) is a concise statement of the expected meteorological conditions at an airport during a specified period (usually 24 hours). Each ICAO state may modify the code as needed. The TAF code, as described here, is the one used in the United States. TAFs use the same weather code found in METAR weather reports.

TAF Report Elements

TAF

KOKC 051130Z 051212 14008KT 5SM BR BKN030 TEMPO 1316 1 1/2SM BR

FM1600 16010KT P6SM SKC

BECMG 2224 20013G20KT 4SM SHRA OVC020 PROB40 0006 2SM TSRA OVC008CB

BECMG 0608 21015KT P6SM NSW SCT040 =

A TAF report contains the following sequence of elements in the following order:
- 1. Type of Report
- 2. ICAO Station Identifier
- 3. Date and Time of Origin
- 4. Valid Period Date and Time
- 5. Forecast Meteorological Conditions

  The international TAF also contains forecast temperature, icing, and turbulence. These three elements are not included in National Weather Service (NWS) prepared TAFs. The U.S. has no requirement to forecast temperatures in an aerodrome forecast and the NWS will continue to forecast icing and turbulence in AIRMETs and SIGMETs.

Type of Report: ie. (TAF)

The report type header will always appear as the first element in the TAF forecast. There are two types of TAF reports, a routine forecast, TAF, and an amended forecast, TAF AMD. An amended TAF is issued when the current TAF no longer adequately describes the ongoing weather or the forecasterfeels the TAF is not representative of the current or expected weather.

Corrected (COR) or delayed (RTD) TAFs are identified only in the communications header which precedes the forecast text.

ICAO Station Identifier: ie. (KOKC)

The TAF code uses the ICAO four-letter location identifiers. In the conterminous United States, the three-letter identifier is prefixed with a K. For example SEA (Seattle) becomes KSEA. Elsewhere, the first one or two letters of the ICAO identifier indicate in which region of the world and country (or state) the station is. Pacific locations such as Alaska, Hawaii, and the Marianas islands start with P followed by an A, H, or G respectively. The last two letters reflect the specific station identification. If the location's three-letter identification begins with an A, H, or G, the P is just added to the beginning. If the location's three-letter identification does not begin with an A, H, or G, the last letter is dropped and the P is added to the beginning.

Examples:

- ANC (Anchorage, AK) becomes PANC
- OME (Nome, AK) becomes PAOM
- HNL (Honolulu, HI) becomes PHNL
- KOA (Keahole Point, HI) becomes PHKO
- GRO (Rota Becomesland) becomes PGRO
- UAM (Anderson AFB) becomes PGUA

Canadian station identifiers start with C. Mexican and western Caribbean station identifiers start with M. The identifier for the eastern Caribbean is T, followed by the individual country's letter.

Date and Time of Origin: ie. (051130Z)

This element is the UTC date and time the forecast is actually prepared. The format is a two-digit date and four-digit time followed, without a space, by the letter Z. Routine TAFs are prepared and filed approximately one-half hour prior to scheduled issuance times. TAFs are scheduled for issuance foure times daily at 0000Z, 0600Z, 1200Z, and 1800Z.

Example:

091050Z - Forecast prepared on the ninth day of the month at 1050Z.

Valid Period Date and Time: ie. (051212)

The UTC valid period of the forecast is a two-digit date followed by the two-digit beginning hour and two-digit ending hour. Routine TAFs are valid for 24-hours. Valid periods beginning at 0000Z shall be indicated as 00. Valid periods ending at 0000Z shall be indicated as 24. The 24 indication applies to all time group ending times.

In the case of an amended forecast, or a forecast which is corrected or delayed, the valid period may be for less than 24 hours. Where an airport or terminal operates on a part-time basis (less than 24 hours/day) the TAFs issued for those locations will have the abbreviated statement NIL AMD SKED AFT (closing time) Z, added to the end of the forecast. For the TAFS issued while these locations are closed, the word NIL will appear in place of the forecast text. A delayed (RTD) forecast will then be issued for these locations after two complete observations are received.

Examples:

- 091212 - Forecast valid from the ninth at 1200Z til the tenth at 1200Z.
- 110024 - Forecast valid from the eleventh at 0000Z till the twelfth at 0000Z.
- 010524 - Amended forecast valid from the first at 0500Z till the second at 0000Z.

Forecast Meteorological Conditions

This is the body of the TAF. The basic format is:

Wind - Visibility - Weather - Sky Condition - Optional Data (Wind Shear)

The wind, visibility, and sky condition elements are always included in the initial time group of the forecast. Weather is included in the initial time group only if significant to aviation. If a significant, lasting change in any of the elements is expected during the valid period, a new time period with changes is included. It should be noted that, with the exception of a FM group, the new time period will include only those elements which are expected to change; i.e., if a lowering of the visibility is expected but the wind is expected to remain the same, the new time period reflecting the lower visibility would not include a forecast wind. The forecast wind would remain the same as in the previous time period.

Any temporary conditions expected during a specific time period are included with that time period.

Wind: ie. (14008KT)

The wind group includes forecast surface winds. The surface wind is the expected wind direction (first three digits) and speed (last two or three digits if 100 knots or greater). The contraction KT follows to denote the units of wind speed in knots. Wind gusts are noted by the letter G appended to the wind speed followed by the highest expected gust (two or three digits if 100 knots or greater).

Calm winds (three knots or less) are encoded as 00000KT.

Variable winds are encoded when it is impossible to forecast a wind direction due to winds associated with convective activity or low wind speeds. A variable wind direction is noted byVRB where the three digit direction usually appears.

Examples:

- 18010KT - Wind one eight zero at one zero knots
- 35012G20KT - Wind three five zero at one two gust two zero knots
- 00000KT - Wind calm

Visibility: ie. (5SM)

The expected prevailing visibility is forecast in statute miles and fractions of statute miles followed by SM to note the units of measure. Statute miles followed by fractions of statute miles are separated with a space, for example, 1 1/2SM. Forecast visibility greater than 6 statute miles is indicated by coding P6SM. Directional or variable visibility is not forecasted and the visibility group is omitted if missing.

Examples:

- 1/2SM - Visibility one-half statute mile

- 2 1/4SM - Visibility two and one-quarter statute miles

- 5SM - Visibility five statute miles

- P6SM - Visibility more than six statute miles

Weather: ie. (BR)

The expected weather phenomenon or phenomena is coded in TAF reports using the same format, qualifiers, and phenomena contractions as METAR reports (except UP).

Qualifiers of Intensity or Proximity

- – Light

- Moderate (no qualifier)

- + Heavy or well-developed

- VC in the Vicinity

Qualifier Descriptor

- MI Shallow

- BC Patches

- DR Low Drifting

- BL Blowing

- SH Showers

- TS Thunderstorm

- FZ Freezing

- PR Partial

Precipitation

- DZ Drizzle

- RA Rain

- SN Snow

- SG Snow Grains

- IC Ice Crystals

- PL Ice Pellets

- GR Hail

- GS Small Hail or Snow Pellets (less than 1/4 inch in diameter)

- UP Unknown precipitation (automated stations only)

Obscuration

(Obscurations to vision will be forecast whenever the prevailing visibility is forecast to be 6 statute miles or less.)

- BR Mist (*Foggy* conditions with visibilities greater than 5/8 statute mile)

- FG Fog (visibility 5/8 statute mile or less)

- FU Smoke

- DU Dust

- SA Sand

- HZ Haze

- PY Spray

- VA Volcanic Ash

Other

- PO Well-Developed Dust/Sand Whirls

- SQ Squalls

- FC Funnel Cloud

- +FC Well-Developed Funnel Cloud, Tornado or Waterspout

- SS Sandstorm

- DS Duststorm

If no significant weather is expected to occur during a specific time period in the forecast, the weather group is omitted for that time period. If, after a time period in which significant weather has been forecast, a change to a forecast of no significant weather occurs, the contraction NSW(No Significant Weather) will apear as the weather group in the new time period. However, NSW is only included in the BECMG or TEMPO groups.

Sky Condition: ie. (BKN030)

TAF sky condition forecasts use the METAR format. Cumulonimbus clouds (CB) are the only cloud type forecast in TAFs.

When the sky is obscured due to a surface-based phenomenon, vertical visibility (VV) into the obscuration is forecast. The format for vertical visibility is VV followed by a three-digit height in hundreds of feet.

Note: Ceiling layers are not designated in the TAF code. For aviation purposes, the ceiling is the lowest broken or overcast layer or vertical visibility into a complete obscuration.

Examples:

- SKC - Sky clear

- SCT005 BKN025CB BKN250 - Five hundred scattered, ceiling two thousand five hundred broken cumulonimbus clouds, two five thousand broken.

Optional Data (Wind Shear)

Wind shear is the forecast of non-convective low level winds (up to 2000 feet) and is entered after the sky conditions when wind shear is expected. The forecast includes the height of the wind shear followed by the wind direction and wind speed at the indicated height. Height is given in hundreds of feet AGL up to and including 2,000 feet. Wind shear is encoded with the contraction WS followed by a three-digit height, slant character, and winds at the height indicated in the same format as surface winds. The wind shear element is omitted if not expected to occur.

Example:

WS010/18040KT - Low level wind shear at one thousand, wind one eight zero at four zero.

Probability Forecast: ie. (PROB40 0006)

The probability or chance of thunderstorms or other precipitation events occuring, along with associated weather conditions (wind, visibility, and sky conditions).

The PROB40 group is used when the occurrence of thunderstorms or precipitation is in the 30% to less than 50% range, thus the probability value 40 is appended to the PROB contraction. This is followed by a four-digit group giving the beginning hour and ending hour of the time period during which the thunderstorms or precipitation is expected.

Note: PROB40 will not be shown during the first six hours of a forecast.

Examples:

- PROB40 2102 1/2SM +TSRA - Chance between 2100Z and 0200Z of visibility one-half thunderstorm, heavy rain.
- PROB40 1014 1SM RASN - Chance between 1000Z and 1400Z of visibility one rain and snow.
- PROB40 2024 2SM FZRA - Chance between 2000Z and 0000Z of visibility two freezing rain.

Forecast Change Indicators

The following change indicators are used when either a rapid, gradual, or temporary change is expected in some or all of the forecast meteorological conditions. Each change indicator marks a time group within the TAF report.

FROM Group: ie. (FM1600)

The FM group is used when a rapid change, usually occuring in less than one hour, in prevailing conditions is expected. Typically, a rapid change of prevailing conditions to more or less a completely new set of prevailing conditions is associated with a synoptic feature passing through the terminal area (cold or warm frontal passage). Appended to the FMindicator is the four-digit hour and minute the change is expected to begin and continues until the next change group or until the end of the current forecast.

A FM group will mark the beginning of a new line in a TAF report. Each FM group contains all the required elements -- wind, visibility, weather, and sky condition. Weather will be omitted inFM groups when it is not significant to aviation. FM groups will not include the contraction NSW.

Examples:

- FM0100 SKC - After 0100Z sky clear
- FM1430 OVC020 - After 1430Z ceiling two thousand overcast

BECOMING Group: ie. (BECMG 2224)

The BECMG group is used when a gradual change in conditions is expected over a longer time period, usually two hours. The time period when the change is expected is a four-digit group with the beginning hour and ending hour of the change period which follows the BECMGindicator. The gradual change will occur at an unspecified time within this time period. Only the conditions are carried over from the previous time group.

Example:

OVC012 BECMG 1416 BKN020 - Ceiling one thousand two hundred overcast. Then a gradual change to ceiling two thousand broken between 1400Z and 1600Z.

TEMPORARY Group: ie. (TEMPO 1316)

The TEMPO group is used for any conditions in wind, visibility, weather, or sky condition which are expected to last for generally less than an hour at a time (occasional), and are expected to occur during less than half the time period. The TEMPO indicator is followed by a four-digit group giving the beginning hour and ending hour of the time period during which the temporary conditions are expected. Only the changing forecast meteorological conditions are included in TEMPO groups. The omitted conditions are carried over from the previous time group.

Examples:

- SCT030 TEMPO 1923 BKN030 - Three thousand scattered with occasional ceilings three thousand broken between 1900Z and 2300Z.

- 4SM HZ TEMPO 0006 2SM BR HZ - Visibility four in haze with occasional visibility two in mist and haze between 0000Z and 0600Z.

- The = indicates the end of the individual TAF transmission. TAFs are bundled together and transmitted as a single document. The = provides a convenient means of separating this document into the individual TAF reports.

Appendix C

 **UAV Flight Risk Assessment**

Before each flight, assess each of the following conditions and assign a numerical rating of 1 to 5 in the right-hand (Rating) column. Add up the entries in the Rating column to obtain an overall risk estimate, and see where it falls in the Green/Yellow/Red Risk Chart.

Add up the entries in the Rating column to obtain an overall risk estimate, and see where it falls in the Green/Yellow/Red Risk Chart.

Pilot_____Observer_____Observer_____

Points	1	2	3	4	5	Rating
Location	Wide Open & Remote		Open Space but Suburbs	Confined Space & Suburbs	Congested & Urban	
Crewmembers	Pilot & Observers		Pilot & 1 Observer		Pilot Only	
Drone Experience	Primary Drone & > 100 hours	Primary Drone & < 100 hours	Primary Drone & < 50 hours Unfamiliar	Drone Testing	Drone Unfamiliar	
Sleep in last 24 hrs	>7 hrs	6-7 hrs		3-5 hrs	<3 hrs	
Alcohol in previous 8 hours	0 drinks	**See Note below**				
UAS Condition	No Defects	Minor or cosmetic defects only.	1 system INOP, Inspected, Does not prevent safe flight		>1 System INOP.	
Visibility	> 3miles	>2 miles	>1 mile	< 1 mile	<1/2 mile	

Ceiling	> 1,000 ft.		500 – 1,000 ft		< 500 ft.	
Wind	<5 Kts	5-10 Kts	10-15 Kts	15-20 Kts	>20 Kts	
90 Day Currency	>20 hrs	15-20 hrs.	10-15 hrs	< 10 hrs	<5 hrs	
					TOTAL	

No unusual hazards. Use normal flight planning and established personal minimums and operating procedures.	< 20
Somewhat riskier than usual. Conduct flight planning with extra care. Review personal minimums and operating procedures to ensure that all standards are being met. Consider alternatives to reduce risk	20-33
Conditions present much higher than normal risk. Conduct flight planning with extra care and review all elements to identify those that could be modified to reduce risk. If available, consult with more experienced pilot or instructor for guidance before flight. Develop contingency plans before flight to deal with high risk items. Decide beforehand on alternates and brief passengers and other crewmembers on special precautions to be taken during the flight. Consider delaying flight until conditions improve and risk is reduced.	33+

Appendix D
Practice Exam

Question 1

A stable air mass is most likely to have which characteristic?

<u>A</u>   Showery precipitation

<u>B</u>   Turbulent air

<u>C</u>   Poor surface visibility

Question 2

To get a complete weather overview for the planned flight, the Remote Pilot in Command should obtain a:

<u>A</u>   An outlook briefing

<u>B</u>   An abbreviated briefing

<u>C</u>   A standard briefing

Question 3

What are characteristics of a moist, unstable air mass?

<u>A</u>   Turbulence and showery precipitation

<u>B</u>   Poor visibility and smooth air

<u>C</u>   Haze and smoke

Question 4

Who holds the responsibility to ensure all crewmembers who are participating in the operation are not impaired by drugs or alcohol?

<u>A</u>   Remote Pilot in Command

<u>B</u>   Contractor

<u>C</u>   Aircraft Owner

Question 5

Identify the hazardous attitude or characteristic a Remote Pilot in Command displays while taking risks in order to impress others?

<u>A</u>   Impulsivity

<u>B</u>   Invulnerability

<u>C</u>   Machoism

Question 6

You are a Remote Pilot in Command for a co-op energy service provider. You plan to use your unmanned aircraft to inspect powerlines in the remote area 15 hours away from your home office. After the drive, fatigue impacts your abilities to complete your assignment on time.

Fatigue can be recognized:

<u>A</u>   Easily by an experienced pilot.

<u>B</u>   As being in an impaired state.

<u>C</u>   By an ability to overcome sleep deprivation.

Question 7

The most comprehensive information on a given airport is provided by:

<u>A</u>   The Chart Supplements U.S. (formerly Airport/Facility Directory)

<u>B</u>   Notices to Airmen (NOTAMs)

<u>C</u>   Terminal Area Chart (TAC)

Question 8

Refer to Figure 12 below, *Aviation Routine Weather Reports (METAR)*.

The wind direction and velocity at KJFK is from:

<u>A</u>   180° true at 4 knots

<u>B</u>   180° magnetic at 4 knots

<u>C</u>   040° true at 18 knots

METAR KINK 121845Z 11012G18KT 15SM SKC 25/17 A3000

METAR KBOI 121854Z 13004KT 30SM SCT150 17/6 A3015

METAR KLAX 121852Z 25004KT 6SM BR SCT007 SCT250 16/15 A2991

SPECI KMDW 121856Z 32005KT 1 1/2SM RA OVC007 17/16 A2980 RMK RAB35

SPECI KJFK 121853Z 18004KT 1/2SM FG R04/2200 OVC005 20/18 A3006

Figure 12.—Aviation Routine Weather Reports (METAR).

Question 9

Refer to <u>FAA-CT-8080-2G</u>, Figure 12.

What are the current conditions for Chicago Midway Airport (KMDW)?

<u>A</u>   Sky 700 feet overcast, visibility 1-1/2SM, rain

<u>B</u>   Sky 7000 feet overcast, visibility 1-1/2SM, heavy rain

<u>C</u>   Sky 700 feet overcast, visibility 11, occasionally 2SM, with rain

Question 10

Refer to FAA-CT-8080-2G, Figure 20(21), *Sectional Chart Excerpt*.

Why would the small flag at Lake Drummond in area 2 of the sectional chart be important to a Remote PIC?

A   The flag indicates a VFR check point for manned aircraft, and a higher volume of air traffic should be expected there.

B   The flag indicates a GPS check point that can be used by both manned and remote pilots for orientation.

C   The flag indicates that there will be a large obstruction depicted on the next printing of the chart.

Question 11

Refer to FAA-CT-8080-2G, Figure 20, area 3.

With ATC authorization, you are operating your small unmanned aircraft approximately 4 SM southeast of Elizabeth City Regional Airport (ECG).

What hazard is indicated to be in that area?

A   High density military operations in the vicinity

B   Unmarked balloon on a cable up to 3,008 feet AGL

C   Unmarked balloon on a cable up to 3,008 feet MSL

Question 12

Refer to FAA-CT-8080-2G, Figure 20, area 5.

Who would a Remote Pilot in Command contact to "CHECK NOTAMS" as it is noted in the CAUTION box regarding the unmarked balloon?

A   NTSB office

B   FAA district office

C   Flight Service

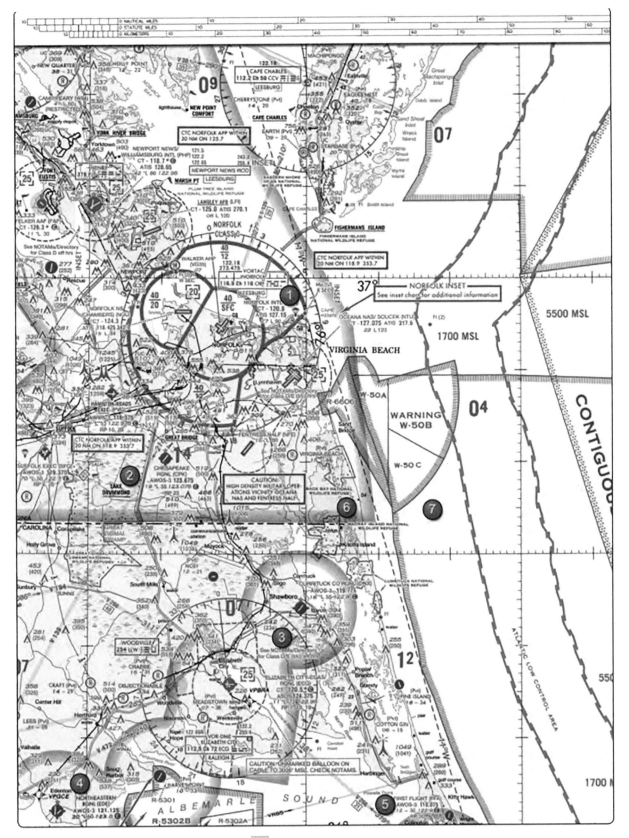

FIGURE 20.—Sectional Chart Excerpt.

NOTE: Chart is not to scale and should not be used for navigation. Use associated scale.

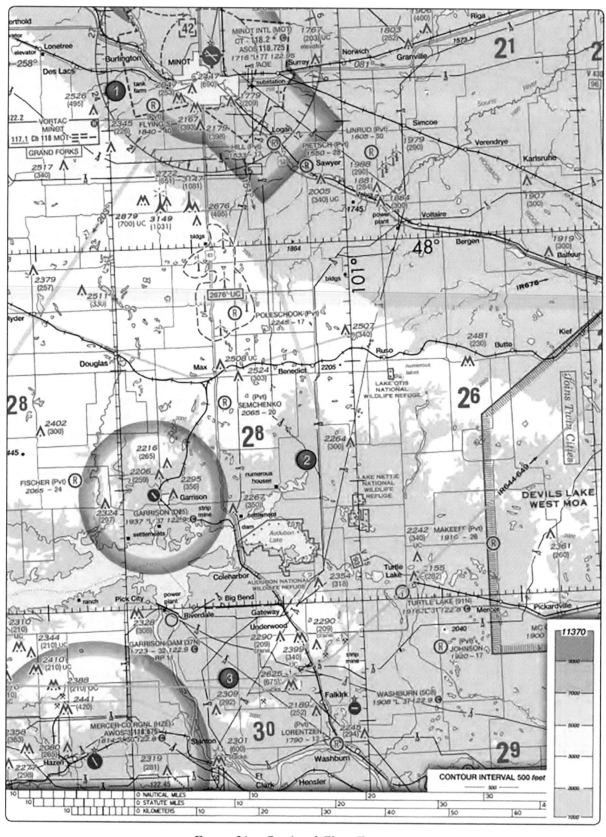

FIGURE 21.—Sectional Chart Excerpt.
NOTE: Chart is not to scale and should not be used for navigation. Use associated scale.

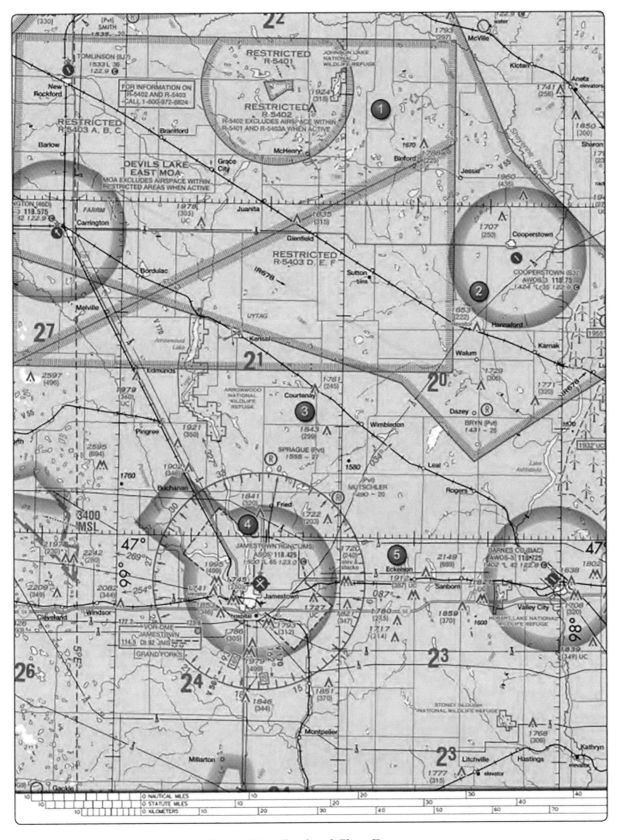

FIGURE 26.—Sectional Chart Excerpt.
NOTE: Chart is not to scale and should not be used for navigation. Use associated scale.

Question 13

Refer to FAA-CT-8080-2G, Figure 21, *Sectional Chart Excerpt*.

What airport is located approximately 47 (degrees) 40 (minutes) N latitude and 101 (degrees) 26 (minutes) W longitude?

A   Mercer County Regional Airport

B   Semshenko Airport

C   Garrison Airport

Question 14

Refer to FAA-CT-8080-2G, Figure 21.

You have been hired by a farmer to use your small unmanned aircraft to inspect his crops. The area that you are to survey is in the Devil`s Lake West MOA, east of area 2. How would you find out if the MOA is active?

A   Contact Flight Service.

B   Locate the information in the Small UAS database.

C   Refer to the Military Operations Directory.

Question 15

Refer to FAA-CT-8080-2G, Figure 26, *Sectional Chart Excerpt*.

What does the line of latitude at area 4 measure?

A   The degrees of latitude east and west of the Prime Meridian.

B   The degrees of latitude north and south from the equator.

C   The degrees of latitude east and west of the line that passes through Greenwich, England.

Question 16

Refer to FAA-CT-8080-2G, Figure 26, area 2.

While monitoring the Cooperstown Common Traffic Advisory Frequency (CTAF) you hear an aircraft announce that they are midfield left downwind to RWY 13. Where would the aircraft be relative to the runway?

A   The aircraft is East.

B   The aircraft is South.

C   The aircraft is West.

Question 17

Refer to FAA-CT-8080-2G, Figure 26, area 4.

You have been hired to inspect the tower under construction at 46.9N and 98.6W, near Jamestown Regional (JMS).

What must you receive prior to flying your unmanned aircraft in this area?

A   Authorization from the military

B   Authorization from ATC

C   Authorization from the National Park Service

Question 18

Which of the following individuals may process an application for a part 107 remote pilot certificate with an sUAS rating? [Sources: 14 CFR parts 107.63 and 61.56]

A   Commercial Balloon pilot

B   Remote Pilot in Command

C   Designated Pilot Examiner

Question 19

After receiving a part 107 remote pilot certificate with an sUAS rating, how often must you satisfy recurrent training requirements? [Sources: 14 CFR part 107.63 and 107.65; AC 107, Small UAS (as amended)]

A   Every 24 months

B   Every 6 months

C   Every 12 months

Question 20

According to 14 CFR part 107, an sUAS is a unmanned aircraft system weighing: [Sources: 14 CFR parts 107.1 and 107.3; AC 107, Small UAS (as amended)]

A   Less than 55 lbs

B   55kg or less

C   55 lbs or less

Question 21

Unmanned aircraft means an aircraft operated: [Sources: 14 CFR parts 107.1 and 107.3; AC 107, Small UAS (as amended)]

A   During search and rescue operations other than public

B   For hobby and recreational use when not certificated

C   Without the possibility of direct human intervention from within or on the aircraft

Question 22

Which of the following types of operations are excluded from the requirements in part 107? [Sources: 14 CFR parts 101.41 and 107.1]

A   Quadcopter capturing aerial imagery for crop monitoring

B   Model aircraft for hobby use

C   UAS used for motion picture filming

Question 23

Which of the following operations would be regulated by 14 CFR 107? [Sources: 14 CFR parts 101.41 and 107.1]

A   Operating your sUAS for an imagery company

B   Conducting public operations during a search mission

C   Flying for enjoyment with family and friends

Question 24

According to 14 CFR part 48, when would a small unmanned aircraft owner not be permitted to register it? [Source: 14 CFR 48.25(b)]

A   If the owner does not have a valid United States driver`s license

B   All persons are eligible to register a small unmanned aircraft

C   If the owner is less than 13 years of age

Question 25

Under what condition would a small unmanned aircraft not have to be registered before it is operated in the United States? [Source: 14 CFR 48.15]

A   When the aircraft has a takeoff weight that is more than .55 pounds, but less than 55 pounds, not including fuel and necessary attachments

B   All small unmanned aircraft need to be registered regardless of the weight of the aircraft before, during, or after the flight

C   When the aircraft weighs less than .55 pounds on takeoff, including everything that is on-board or attached to the aircraft

Question 26

When using a small unmanned aircraft in a commercial operation, who is responsible for informing the participants about emergency procedures? [Source: AC 107, Small UAS (as amended)]

A   The Remote Pilot in Command

B   The lead visual observer

C   The FAA Inspector-in-Charge

Question 27

A person without a part 107 remote pilot certificate may operate an sUAS for commercial operations: [Source: AC-107, Small UAS (as amended)]

A   Under the direct supervision of a Remote PIC

B   Only when visual observers participate in the operation

C   Alone, if operating during daylight hours

Question 28

A person whose sole task is watching the sUAS to report hazards to the rest of the crew is called: [Sources: 14 CFR part 107.3; AC 107, Small UAS (as amended)]

A   Visual observer

B   Remote PIC

C   Person manipulating the controls

Question 29

When adapting crew resource management (CRM) concepts to the operation of a small unmanned aircraft, CRM must be integrated into: [Source: FAA-H-8083-25, Pilot's Handbook of Aeronautical Knowledge (PHAK), 17-2]

A   All phases of the operation

B   The communications only

C   The flight portion only

Question 30

You have been hired as a Remote Pilot in Command by a local TV news station to film breaking news with a small unmanned aircraft. You expressed a safety concern and the station manager has instructed you to "fly first, ask questions later." What type of hazardous attitude does this attitude represent? [Source: FAA-H-8083-25, Pilot's Handbook of Aeronautical Knowledge (PHAK), 17-4]

A   Invulnerability

B   Impulsivity

C   Machoism

Question 31

Under what condition should the Remote Pilot in Command of a small unmanned aircraft establish a scheduled maintenance protocol? [Source: 14 CFR 107.8-2]

A   When the manufacturer does not provide a maintenance schedule

B   Small unmanned aircraft systems do not require maintenance

C   When the FAA requires you to, following an accident

Question 32

Scheduled maintenance should be performed in accordance with the: [Source: AC-107, Small UAS (as amended)]

A   Stipulations in 14 CFR part 43

B   Manufacturer's suggested procedures

C   Contractor requirements

Question 33

According to 14 CFR part 107, the responsibility to inspect the small unmanned aircraft system (sUAS) to ensure it is in a safe operating condition rests with the: [Source: 14 CFR 107.49(a)]

A   Remote Pilot in Command

B   Owner of the sUAS

C   Visual observer

Question 34

Before each flight, the Remote PIC must ensure that: [Source: AC-107, Small UAS (as amended)]

A   Objects carried on the sUAS are secure

B   ATC has granted clearance

C   The site supervisor has approved the flight

Question 35

When operating an unmanned aircraft, the Remote Pilot in Command should consider that the load factor on the wings or rotors may be increased anytime when: [Source: FAA-H-8083-25, Pilot's Handbook of Aeronautical Knowledge, Chapter 4-12]

A   The aircraft is subjected to maneuvers other than straight and level flight.

B   The gross weight is reduced

C   The center of gravity (CG) is shifted rearward to the aft CG limit

Question 36

A stall occurs when the smooth airflow over the unmanned airplane`s wing is disrupted, and the lift degenerates rapidly. This is caused when the wing: [Source: FAA-H-8083-3, Airplane Flying Handbook, 4 3]

A   Exceeds the maximum speed

B   Exceeds its critical angle of attack

C   Exceeds maximum allowable operating weight

Question 37

What could be a consequence of operating a small unmanned aircraft above its maximum allowable weight? [Source: Pilot's Handbook of Aeronautical Knowledge (PHAK), 9-2]

A   Faster speed

B   Increased maneuverability

C   Shorter endurance

Question 38

According to 14 CFR part 107, who is responsible for determining the performance of a small unmanned aircraft? [Source: 14 CFR 107.49]

A   Manufacturer

B   Owner or operator

C   Remote Pilot in Command

Question 39

To ensure that the unmanned aircraft center of gravity (CG) limits are not exceeded, follow the aircraft loading instructions specified in the: [Source: FAA-H-8083-1, Weight & Balance Handbook, 4-4-5]

A   Aircraft Weight and Balance Handbook

B   Aeronautical Information Manual (AIM)

C   Pilot's Operating Handbook or UAS Flight Manual

Question 40

How would high density altitude affect the performance of a small unmanned aircraft? [Source: Pilot's Handbook of Aeronautical Knowledge (PHAK), Chapter 10]

A   Increased performance

B   Decreased performance

C   No change in performance

Question 41

While operating around buildings, the Remote Pilot in Command should be aware of the creation of wind gusts that: [Source: Pilot's Handbook of Aeronautical Knowledge (PHAK), Chapter 11]

A   Enhance stability and imagery

B   Change rapidly in direction and speed causing turbulence

C   Increase performance of the aircraft

Question 42

According to 14 CFR part 107, what is required to operate a small unmanned aircraft within 30 minutes after official sunset? [Source: 14 CFR 107.29(b)]

A   Must be operated in a rural area

B   Use of lighted anti-collision lights

C   Use of a transponder

Question 43

According to 14 CFR part 107, how may a Remote Pilot in Command (Remote PIC) operate an unmanned aircraft in class C airspace? [Source: Aeronautical Information Manual (AIM), 3-2-6]

A   The Remote PIC must contact the Air Traffic Control (ATC) facility after launching the unmanned aircraft

B   The Remote PIC must have prior authorization from Air Traffic Control (ATC)

C   The Remote PIC must monitor the Air Traffic Control (ATC) frequency from launch to recovery

Question 44

In accordance with 14 CFR part 107, you may operate an sUAS from a moving vehicle when no property is carried for compensation or hire: [Sources: 14 CFR part 107.25; AC 107, Small UAS (as amended)]

A   Over a parade or other social events

B   Over suburban areas

C   Over a sparsely populated area

Question 45

In accordance with 14 CFR part 107, except when within a 400' radius of a structure, at what maximum altitude can you operate sUAS? [Source: 14 CFR part 107.51]

A   500 feet AGL

B   600 feet AGL

C   400 feet AGL

Question 46

The FAA may approve your application for a waiver of provisions in part 107 only when it has been determined that the proposed operation: [Sources: 14 CFR Parts 101.41. 107.1, 107.200, and 107.205; AC 107, Small UAS (as amended)]

A   Will be conducted outside of the United States

B   Involves public aircraft or air carrier operations

C   Can be safely conducted under the terms of that certificate of waiver

Question 47

When requesting a waiver, the required documents should be presented to the FAA at least how many days prior to the planned operation? [Source: AC 107, Small UAS (as amended)]

A   30 days

B   10 days

C   90 days

Question 48

To avoid a possible collision with a manned airplane, you estimate that your small unmanned aircraft climbed to an altitude greater than 600 feet AGL. To whom must you report the deviation? [Source: 14 CFR 107.21(b)]

A   The Federal Aviation Administration, upon request

B   Air Traffic Control

C   The National Transportation Safety Board

Question 49

Damaged lithium batteries can cause: [Source: Safety Alert for Operators (SAFO) 10017, Risks in Transporting Lithium Batteries in Cargo by Aircraft]

A   A change in aircraft center of gravity

B   Increased endurance

C   An inflight fire

Question 50

While operating a small unmanned aircraft system (sUAS), you experience a flyaway and several people suffer injuries. Which of the following injuries requires reporting to the FAA? [Source: 14 CFR 107.9 and 107(III)(I)(2); AC-107, Small UAS (as amended)]

A   Minor bruises

B   An injury requiring an overnight hospital stay

C   Scrapes and cuts bandaged on site

Answer Key

1. C
2. C
3. A
4. A
5. C
6. B
7. A
8. B
9. A
10. A
11. A
12. C
13. C
14. A
15. B
16. A
17. B
18. C
19. A
20. A
21. C
22. B
23. A
24. C
25. C

26. A
27. A
28. A
29. A
30. B
31. A
32. B
33. A
34. A
35. A
36. B
37. C
38. C
39. C
40. B
41. B
42. B
43. B
44. C
45. C
46. C
47. C
48. A
49. C
50. B

Federal Aviation Regulations Excerpt

The Amendment

In consideration of the foregoing, the Federal Aviation Administration amends

chapter I of title 14, Code of Federal Regulations as follows:

PART 21—CERTIFICATION PROCEDURES FOR PRODUCTS AND PARTS

The authority citation for part 21 is revised to read as follows:

Authority: 42 U.S.C. 7572; 49 U.S.C. 106(f), 106(g), 40101 note, 40105, 40113, 44701-44702, 44704, 44707, 44709, 44711, 44713, 44715, 45303; Sec. 333 of Pub. L. 112-95.

In § 21.1, revise paragraph (a) introductory text to read as follows:

§ 21.1 Applicability and definitions.

(a) Except for aircraft subject to the provisions of part 107 of this chapter, this part

prescribes—

* * * * *

PART 43—MAINTENANCE, PREVENTIVE MAINTENANCE, REBUILDING, AND ALTERATION

The authority citation for part 43 is revised to read as follows:

Authority: 49 U.S.C. 106(f), 106(g), 40113, 44701, 44703, 44705, 44707, 44711, 44713, 44717, 44725.

4. In § 43.1, revise paragraph (b) to read as follows:

§ 43.1 Applicability.

* * * * *

(b) This part does not apply to—

(1) Any aircraft for which the FAA has issued an experimental certificate, unless the FAA has previously issued a different kind of airworthiness certificate for that aircraft;

(2) Any aircraft for which the FAA has issued an experimental certificate under the provisions of §21.191(i)(3) of this chapter, and the aircraft was previously issued a special airworthiness certificate in the light-sport category under the provisions of §21.190 of this chapter; or

(3) Any aircraft subject to the provisions of part 107 of this chapter.

* * * * *

PART 61—CERTIFICATION: PILOTS, FLIGHT INSTRUCTORS, AND GROUND INSTRUCTORS

5. The authority citation for part 61 continues to read as follows:

Authority: 49 U.S.C. 106(f), 106(g), 40113, 44701-44703, 44707, 44709-44711, 44729, 44903, 45103-45103, 45301-45302.

6. In § 61.1, revise paragraph (a) introductory text to read as follows:

§ 61.1 Applicability and definitions.

(a) Except as provided in part 107 of this chapter, this part prescribes:

* * * * *

7. Add § 61.8 to read as follows:

§ 61.8 Inapplicability of unmanned aircraft operations.

Any action conducted pursuant to part 107 of this chapter or Subpart E of part 101 of this chapter cannot be used to meet the requirements of this part.

8. Revise § 61.193 to read as follows.

§ 61.193 Flight instructor privileges.

* * * * *

(b) A person who holds a flight instructor certificate is authorized, in a form and manner acceptable to the Administrator, to:

(1) Accept an application for a student pilot certificate or, for an applicant who holds a pilot certificate (other than a student pilot certificate) issued under part 61 of this chapter and meets the flight review requirements specified in § 61.56, a remote pilot certificate with a small UAS rating;

(2) Verify the identity of the applicant; and

(3) Verify that an applicant for a student pilot certificate meets the eligibility requirements in § 61.83 or an applicant for a remote pilot certificate with a small UAS rating meets the eligibility requirements in § 107.61.

9. Revise § 61.413 to read as follows:

§ 61.413 What are the privileges of my flight instructor certificate with a sport pilot rating?

* * * * *

(b) A person who holds a flight instructor certificate with a sport pilot rating is authorized, in a form and manner acceptable to the Administrator, to:

(1) Accept an application for a student pilot certificate or, for an applicant who holds a pilot certificate (other than a student pilot certificate) issued under part 61 of this chapter and meets the flight review requirements specified in § 61.56, a remote pilot certificate with a small UAS rating;;

(2) Verify the identity of the applicant; and

(3) Verify that an applicant for a student pilot certificate meets the eligibility requirements in § 61.83.

PART 91—GENERAL OPERATING AND FLIGHT RULES

10. The authority citation for part 91 continues to read as follows:

Authority: 49 U.S.C. 106(f), 106(g), 1155, 40101, 40103, 40105, 40113, 40120, 44101, 44111, 44701, 44704, 44709, 44711, 44712, 44715, 44716, 44717, 44722, 46306, 46315, 46316, 46504, 46506-46507, 47122, 47508, 47528-47531, 47534, articles 12 and 29 of the Convention on International Civil Aviation (61 Stat. 1180), (126 Stat. 11).

11. In § 91.1, revise paragraph (a) introductory text and add paragraph (e) to read as follows:

§ 91.1 Applicability.

(a) Except as provided in paragraphs (b), (c), (e), and (f) of this section and §§ 91.701 and 91.703, this part prescribes rules governing the operation of aircraft within the United States, including the waters within 3 nautical miles of the U.S. coast.

* * * * *

(e) This part does not apply to any aircraft or vehicle governed by part 103 of this chapter, or subparts B, C, or D of part 101 of this chapter.

(f) Except as provided in §§ 107.13, 107.27, 107.47, 107.57, and 107.59 of this chapter, this part does not apply to any aircraft governed by part 107 of this chapter.

PART 101—MOORED BALLOONS, KITES, AMATEUR ROCKETS, UNMANNED FREE BALLOONS, AND CERTAIN MODEL AIRCRAFT

12. The heading for part 101 is revised to read as set forth above.

13. The authority citation for part 101 is revised to read as follows:

Authority: 49 U.S.C. 106(f), 106(g), 40101 note, 40103, 40113-40114, 45302, 44502, 44514, 44701-44702, 44721, 46308, Sec. 336(b), Pub. L. 112-95.

14. In § 101.1, add paragraph (a)(5) to read as follows:

§ 101.1 Applicability.

(a) * * *

(5) Any model aircraft that meets the conditions specified in § 101.41. For purposes of this part, a model aircraft is an unmanned aircraft that is:

(i) Capable of sustained flight in the atmosphere;

(ii) Flown within visual line of sight of the person operating the aircraft; and

(iii) Flown for hobby or recreational purposes.

* * * * *

15. Add subpart E, consisting of §§ 101.41 and 101.43, to read as follows:

Subpart E – Special Rule for Model Aircraft

§ 101.41 Applicability.

This subpart prescribes rules governing the operation of a model aircraft (or an aircraft being developed as a model aircraft) that meets all of the following conditions as set forth in section 336 of Public Law 112-95:

(a) The aircraft is flown strictly for hobby or recreational use;

(b) The aircraft is operated in accordance with a community-based set of safety guidelines and within the programming of a nationwide community-based organization;

(c) The aircraft is limited to not more than 55 pounds unless otherwise certified through a design, construction, inspection, flight test, and operational safety program administered by a community-based organization;

(d) The aircraft is operated in a manner that does not interfere with and gives way to any manned aircraft; and

(e) When flown within 5 miles of an airport, the operator of the aircraft provides the airport operator and the airport air traffic control tower (when an air traffic facility is located at the airport) with prior notice of the operation.

§ 101.43 Endangering the safety of the National Airspace System.

No person may operate model aircraft so as to endanger the safety of the national airspace system.

16. Add part 107 to read as follows:

PART 107–SMALL UNMANNED AIRCRAFT SYSTEMS

Sec.

Subpart A—General

§ 107.1 Applicability.

§ 107.3 Definitions.

§ 107.5 Falsification, reproduction or alteration.

§ 107.7 Inspection, testing, and demonstration of compliance.

§ 107.9 Accident reporting.

Subpart B—Operating Rules

§ 107.11 Applicability.

§ 107.12 Requirement for a remote pilot certificate with a small UAS rating.

§ 107.13 Registration.

§ 107.15 Condition for safe operation.

§ 107.17 Medical condition.

§ 107.19 Remote pilot in command.

§ 107.21 In-flight emergency.

§ 107.23 Hazardous operation.

§ 107.25 Operation from a moving vehicle or aircraft.

§ 107.27 Alcohol or drugs.

§ 107.29 Daylight operation.

§ 107.31 Visual line of sight aircraft operation.

§ 107.33 Visual observer.

§ 107.35 Operation of multiple small unmanned aircraft.

§ 107.36 Carriage of hazardous material.

Authority: 49 U.S.C. 106(f), 40101 note, 40103(b), 44701(a)(5); Sec. 333 of Pub. L. 112-95.

Subpart A—General§ 107.1 Applicability.

(a) Except as provided in paragraph (b) of this section, this part applies to the

registration, airman certification, and operation of civil small unmanned aircraft systems within the United States.

(b) This part does not apply to the following:

(1) Air carrier operations;

(2) Any aircraft subject to the provisions of part 101 of this chapter; or

(3) Any operation that a remote pilot in command elects to conduct pursuant to an

exemption issued under section 333 of Public Law 112-95, unless otherwise specified in

the exemption.

§ 107.3 Definitions.

The following definitions apply to this part. If there is a conflict between the definitions of this part and definitions specified in § 1.1 of this chapter, the definitions in this part control for purposes of this part:

Control station means an interface used by the remote pilot to control the flight path of the small unmanned aircraft.

Corrective lenses means spectacles or contact lenses.

Small unmanned aircraft means an unmanned aircraft weighing less than 55 pounds on takeoff, including everything that is on board or otherwise attached to the aircraft.

Small unmanned aircraft system (small UAS) means a small unmanned aircraft and its associated elements (including communication links and the components that control the small unmanned aircraft) that are required for the safe and efficient operation of the small unmanned aircraft in the national airspace system.

Unmanned aircraft means an aircraft operated without the possibility of direct human intervention from within or on the aircraft.

Visual observer means a person who is designated by the remote pilot in command to assist the remote pilot in command and the person manipulating the flight controls of the small UAS to see and avoid other air traffic or objects aloft or on the ground.

§ 107.5 Falsification, reproduction or alteration.

(a) No person may make or cause to be made—

(1) Any fraudulent or intentionally false record or report that is required to be made, kept, or used to show compliance with any requirement under this part.

(2) Any reproduction or alteration, for fraudulent purpose, of any certificate, rating, authorization, record or report under this part.

(b) The commission by any person of an act prohibited under paragraph (a) of this section is a basis for any of the following:

(1) Denial of an application for a remote pilot certificate or a certificate of waiver,

(2) Suspension or revocation of any certificate or waiver issued by the Administrator under this part and held by that person; or

(3) A civil penalty.

§ 107.7 Inspection, testing, and demonstration of compliance.

(a) A remote pilot in command, owner, or person manipulating the flight controls of a small unmanned aircraft system must, upon request, make available to the Administrator:

(1) The remote pilot certificate with a small UAS rating; and

(2) Any other document, record, or report required to be kept under the regulations of this chapter.

(b) The remote pilot in command, visual observer, owner, operator, or person manipulating the flight controls of a small unmanned aircraft system must, upon request, allow the Administrator to make any test or inspection of the small unmanned aircraft system, the remote pilot in command, the person manipulating the flight controls of a small unmanned aircraft system, and, if applicable, the visual observer to determine compliance with this part.

§ 107.9 Accident reporting.

No later than 10 calendar days after an operation that meets the criteria of either paragraph (a) or (b) of this section, a remote pilot in command must report to the FAA, in a manner acceptable to the Administrator, any operation of the small unmanned aircraft involving at least:

(a) Serious injury to any person or any loss of consciousness; or

(b) Damage to any property, other than the small unmanned aircraft, unless one of the following conditions is satisfied:

(1) The cost of repair (including materials and labor) does not exceed $500; or

(2) The fair market value of the property does not exceed $500 in the event of total loss.

Subpart B—Operating Rules

§ 107.11 Applicability.

This subpart applies to the operation of all civil small unmanned aircraft systems subject to this part.

§ 107.12 Requirement for a remote pilot certificate with a small UAS rating.

(a) Except as provided in paragraph (c) of this section, no person may manipulate the flight controls of a small unmanned aircraft system unless:

(1) That person has a remote pilot certificate with a small UAS rating issued pursuant to Subpart C of this part and satisfies the requirements of § 107.65; or

(2) That person is under the direct supervision of a remote pilot in command and the remote pilot in command has the ability to immediately take direct control of the flight of the small unmanned aircraft.

(b) Except as provided in paragraph (c) of this section, no person may act as a remote pilot in command unless that person has a remote pilot certificate with a small UAS rating issued pursuant to Subpart C of this part and satisfies the requirements of § 107.65.

(c) The Administrator may, consistent with international standards, authorize an airman to operate a civil foreign-registered small unmanned aircraft without an FAA-issued remote pilot certificate with a small UAS rating.

§ 107.13 Registration.

A person operating a civil small unmanned aircraft system for purposes of flight must comply with the provisions of § 91.203(a)(2).

§ 107.15 Condition for safe operation.

(a) No person may operate a civil small unmanned aircraft system unless it is in a condition for safe operation. Prior to each flight, the remote pilot in command must check the small unmanned aircraft system to determine whether it is in a condition for safe operation.

(b) No person may continue flight of the small unmanned aircraft when he or she knows or has reason to know that the small unmanned aircraft system is no longer in a condition for safe operation.

§ 107.17 Medical condition.

No person may manipulate the flight controls of a small unmanned aircraft system or act as a remote pilot in command, visual observer, or direct participant in the operation of the small unmanned aircraft if he or she knows or has reason to know that he or she has a physical or mental condition that would interfere with the safe operation of the small unmanned aircraft system.

§ 107.19 Remote pilot in command.

(a) A remote pilot in command must be designated before or during the flight of the small unmanned aircraft.

(b) The remote pilot in command is directly responsible for and is the final authority as to the operation of the small unmanned aircraft system.

(c) The remote pilot in command must ensure that the small unmanned aircraft will pose no undue hazard to other people, other aircraft, or other property in the event of a loss of control of the aircraft for any reason.

(d) The remote pilot in command must ensure that the small UAS operation complies with all applicable regulations of this chapter.

(e) The remote pilot in command must have the ability to direct the small unmanned aircraft to ensure compliance with the applicable provisions of this chapter.

§ 107.21 In-flight emergency.

(a) In an in-flight emergency requiring immediate action, the remote pilot in command may deviate from any rule of this part to the extent necessary to meet that emergency.

(b) Each remote pilot in command who deviates from a rule under paragraph (a) of this section must, upon request of the Administrator, send a written report of that deviation to the Administrator.

§ 107.23 Hazardous operation.

No person may:

(a) Operate a small unmanned aircraft system in a careless or reckless manner so as to endanger the life or property of another; or

(b) Allow an object to be dropped from a small unmanned aircraft in a manner that creates an undue hazard to persons or property.

§ 107.25 Operation from a moving vehicle or aircraft.

No person may operate a small unmanned aircraft system -

(a) From a moving aircraft; or

(b) From a moving land or water-borne vehicle unless the small unmanned aircraft is flown over a sparsely populated area and is not transporting another person's property for compensation or hire.

§ 107.27 Alcohol or drugs.

A person manipulating the flight controls of a small unmanned aircraft system or acting as a remote pilot in command or visual observer must comply with the provisions of §§ 91.17 and 91.19 of this chapter.

§ 107.29 Daylight operation.

(a) No person may operate a small unmanned aircraft system during night.

(b) No person may operate a small unmanned aircraft system during periods of civil twilight unless the small unmanned aircraft has lighted anti-collision lighting visible for at least 3 statute miles. The remote pilot in command may reduce the intensity of the anti-collision lighting if he or she determines that, because of operating conditions, it would be in the interest of safety to do so.

(c) For purposes of subsection (b) of this section, civil twilight refers to the following:

(1) Except for Alaska, a period of time that begins 30 minutes before official sunrise and ends at official sunrise;

(2) Except for Alaska, a period of time that begins at official sunset and ends 30 minutes after official sunset; and

(3) In Alaska, the period of civil twilight as defined in the Air Almanac.

§ 107.31 Visual line of sight aircraft operation.

(a) With vision that is unaided by any device other than corrective lenses, the remote pilot in command, the visual observer (if one is used), and the person manipulating the flight control of the small unmanned aircraft system must be able to see the unmanned aircraft throughout the entire flight in order to:

(1) Know the unmanned aircraft's location;

(2) Determine the unmanned aircraft's attitude, altitude, and direction of flight;

(3) Observe the airspace for other air traffic or hazards; and

(4) Determine that the unmanned aircraft does not endanger the life or property of another.

(b) Throughout the entire flight of the small unmanned aircraft, the ability described in subsection (a) of this section must be exercised by either:

(1) The remote pilot in command and the person manipulating the flight controls of the small unmanned aircraft system; or

(2) A visual observer.

§ 107.33 Visual observer.

If a visual observer is used during the aircraft operation, all of the following requirements must be met:

(a) The remote pilot in command, the person manipulating the flight controls of the small unmanned aircraft system, and the visual observer must maintain effective communication with each other at all times.

(b) The remote pilot in command must ensure that the visual observer is able to see the unmanned aircraft in the manner specified in § 107.31.

(c) The remote pilot in command, the person manipulating the flight controls of the small unmanned aircraft system, and the visual observer must coordinate to do the following:

(1) Scan the airspace where the small unmanned aircraft is operating for any potential collision hazard; and

(2) Maintain awareness of the position of the small unmanned aircraft through direct visual observation.

§ 107.35 Operation of multiple small unmanned aircraft.

A person may not operate or act as a remote pilot in command or visual observer in the operation of more than one unmanned aircraft at the same time.

§ 107.36 Carriage of hazardous material.

A small unmanned aircraft may not carry hazardous material. For purposes of this section, the term hazardous material is defined in 49 CFR 171.8.

§ 107.37 Operation near aircraft; right-of-way rules.

(a) Each small unmanned aircraft must yield the right of way to all aircraft, airborne vehicles, and launch and reentry vehicles. Yielding the right of way means that the small unmanned aircraft must give way to the aircraft or vehicle and may not pass over, under, or ahead of it unless well clear.

(b) No person may operate a small unmanned aircraft so close to another aircraft as to create a collision hazard.

§ 107.39 Operation over human beings.

No person may operate a small unmanned aircraft over a human being unless that human being is:

(a) Directly participating in the operation of the small unmanned aircraft; or

(b) Located under a covered structure or inside a stationary vehicle that can provide reasonable protection from a falling small unmanned aircraft.

§ 107.41 Operation in certain airspace.

No person may operate a small unmanned aircraft in Class B, Class C, or Class D airspace or within the lateral boundaries of the surface area of Class E airspace designated for an airport unless that person has prior authorization from Air Traffic Control (ATC).

§ 107.43 Operation in the vicinity of airports.

No person may operate a small unmanned aircraft in a manner that interferes with operations and traffic patterns at any airport, heliport, or seaplane base.

§ 107.45 Operation in prohibited or restricted areas.

No person may operate a small unmanned aircraft in prohibited or restricted areas unless that person has permission from the using or controlling agency, as appropriate.

§ 107.47 Flight restrictions in the proximity of certain areas designated by notice to airmen.

A person acting as a remote pilot in command must comply with the provisions of §§ 91.137 through 91.145 and 99.7 of this chapter.

§ 107.49 Preflight familiarization, inspection, and actions for aircraft operation.

Prior to flight, the remote pilot in command must:

(a) Assess the operating environment, considering risks to persons and property in the immediate vicinity both on the surface and in the air. This assessment must include:

(1) Local weather conditions;

(2) Local airspace and any flight restrictions;

(3) The location of persons and property on the surface; and

(4) Other ground hazards.

(b) Ensure that all persons directly participating in the small unmanned aircraft operation are informed about the operating conditions, emergency procedures, contingency procedures, roles and responsibilities, and potential hazards;

(c) Ensure that all control links between ground control station and the small unmanned aircraft are working properly;

(d) If the small unmanned aircraft is powered, ensure that there is enough available power for the small unmanned aircraft system to operate for the intended operational time; and

(e) Ensure that any object attached or carried by the small unmanned aircraft is secure and does not adversely affect the flight characteristics or controllability of the aircraft.

§ 107.51 Operating limitations for small unmanned aircraft.

A remote pilot in command and the person manipulating the flight controls of the small unmanned aircraft system must comply with all of the following operating limitations when operating a small unmanned aircraft system:

(a) The groundspeed of the small unmanned aircraft may not exceed 87 knots (100 miles per hour).

(b) The altitude of the small unmanned aircraft cannot be higher than 400 feet above ground level, unless the small unmanned aircraft:

(1) Is flown within a 400-foot radius of a structure; and

(2) Does not fly higher than 400 feet above the structure's immediate uppermost limit.

(c) The minimum flight visibility, as observed from the location of the control station must be no less than 3 statute miles. For purposes of this section, flight visibility means the average slant distance from the control station at which prominent unlighted objects may be seen and identified by day and prominent lighted objects may be seen andidentified by night.

(d) The minimum distance of the small unmanned aircraft from clouds must be no less than:

(1) 500 feet below the cloud; and

(2) 2,000 feet horizontally from the cloud.

Subpart C—Remote Pilot Certification

§ 107.53 Applicability.

This subpart prescribes the requirements for issuing a remote pilot certificate with a small UAS rating.

§ 107.57 Offenses involving alcohol or drugs.

(a) A conviction for the violation of any Federal or State statute relating to the growing, processing, manufacture, sale, disposition, possession, transportation, or importation of narcotic drugs, marijuana, or depressant or stimulant drugs or substances is grounds for:

(1) Denial of an application for a remote pilot certificate with a small UAS rating for a period of up to 1 year after the date of final conviction; or

(2) Suspension or revocation of a remote pilot certificate with a small UAS rating.

(b) Committing an act prohibited by § 91.17(a) or § 91.19(a) of this chapter is grounds for:

(1) Denial of an application for a remote pilot certificate with a small UAS rating for a period of up to 1 year after the date of that act; or

(2) Suspension or revocation of a remote pilot certificate with a small UAS rating.

§ 107.59 Refusal to submit to an alcohol test or to furnish test results.

A refusal to submit to a test to indicate the percentage by weight of alcohol in the blood, when requested by a law enforcement officer in accordance with § 91.17(c) of this chapter, or a refusal to furnish or authorize the release of the test results requested by the Administrator in accordance with § 91.17(c) or (d) of this chapter, is grounds for:

(a) Denial of an application for a remote pilot certificate with a small UAS rating for a period of up to 1 year after the date of that refusal; or

(b) Suspension or revocation of a remote pilot certificate with a small UAS rating.

§ 107.61 Eligibility.

Subject to the provisions of §§ 107.57 and 107.59, in order to be eligible for a remote pilot certificate with a small UAS rating under this subpart, a person must:

(a) Be at least 16 years of age;

(b) Be able to read, speak, write, and understand the English language. If the applicant is unable to meet one of these requirements due to medical reasons, the FAA may place such operating limitations on that applicant's certificate as are necessary for the safe operation of the small unmanned aircraft;

(c) Not know or have reason to know that he or she has a physical or mental condition that would interfere with the safe operation of a small unmanned aircraft system; and

(d) Demonstrate aeronautical knowledge by satisfying one of the following conditions:

(1) Pass an initial aeronautical knowledge test covering the areas of knowledge specified in § 107.73(a); or

(2) If a person holds a pilot certificate (other than a student pilot certificate) issued under part 61 of this chapter and meets the flight review requirements specified in § 61.56, complete an initial training course covering the areas of knowledge specified in § 107.74(a) in a manner acceptable to the Administrator.

§ 107.63 Issuance of a remote pilot certificate with a small UAS rating.

An applicant for a remote pilot certificate with a small UAS rating under this subpart must make the application in a form and manner acceptable to the Administrator.

(a) The application must include either:

(1) Evidence showing that the applicant passed an initial aeronautical knowledge test. If applying using a paper application, this evidence must be an airman knowledge test report showing passage of the knowledge test; or

(2) If a person holds a pilot certificate (other than a student pilot certificate) issued under part 61 of this chapter and meets the flight review requirements specified in § 61.56, a certificate of completion of a part 107 initial training course.

(b) If the application is being made pursuant to paragraph (a)(2) of this section:

(1) The application must be submitted to a Flight Standards District Office, a designated pilot examiner, an airman certification representative for a pilot school, a certificated flight instructor, or other person authorized by the Administrator;

(2) The person accepting the application submission must verify the identity of the applicant in a manner acceptable to the Administrator; and

(3) The person making the application must, by logbook endorsement or other manner acceptable to the Administrator, show the applicant meets the flight review requirements specified in § 61.56 of this chapter.

§ 107.64 Temporary Certificate

(a) A temporary remote pilot certificate with a small UAS rating is issued for up to 120 calendar days, at which time a permanent certificate will be issued to a person whom the Administrator finds qualified under this part.

(b) A temporary remote pilot certificate with a small UAS rating expires:

(1) On the expiration date shown on the certificate;

(2) Upon receipt of the permanent certificate; or

(3) Upon receipt of a notice that the certificate sought is denied or revoked.

§ 107.65 Aeronautical knowledge recency.

A person may not operate a small unmanned aircraft system unless that person has completed one of the following, within the previous 24 calendar months:

(a) Passed an initial aeronautical knowledge test covering the areas of knowledge specified in § 107.73(a);

(b) Passed a recurrent aeronautical knowledge test covering the areas of knowledge specified in § 107.73(b); or

(c) If a person holds a pilot certificate (other than a student pilot certificate) issued under part 61 of this chapter and meets the flight review requirements specified in § 61.56, passed either an initial or recurrent training course covering the areas of knowledge specified in § 107.74(a) or (b) in a manner acceptable to the Administrator.

§ 107.67 Knowledge tests: General procedures and passing grades.

(a) Knowledge tests prescribed by or under this part are given by persons and in the manner designated by the Administrator.

(b) An applicant for a knowledge test must have proper identification at the time of application that contains the applicant's:

(1) Photograph;

(2) Signature;

(3) Date of birth, which shows the applicant meets or will meet the age requirements of this part for the certificate and rating sought before the expiration date of the airman knowledge test report; and

(4) Permanent mailing address. If the applicant's permanent mailing address is a post office box number, then the applicant must also provide a current residential address.

(c) The minimum passing grade for the knowledge test will be specified by the Administrator.

§ 107.69 Knowledge tests: Cheating or other unauthorized conduct.

(a) An applicant for a knowledge test may not:

(1) Copy or intentionally remove any knowledge test;

(2) Give to another applicant or receive from another applicant any part or copy of a knowledge test;

(3) Give or receive assistance on a knowledge test during the period that test is being given;

(4) Take any part of a knowledge test on behalf of another person;

(5) Be represented by, or represent, another person for a knowledge test;

(6) Use any material or aid during the period that the test is being given, unless specifically authorized to do so by the Administrator; and

(7) Intentionally cause, assist, or participate in any act prohibited by this paragraph.

(b) An applicant who the Administrator finds has committed an act prohibited by paragraph (a) of this section is prohibited, for 1 year after the date of committing that act, from:

(1) Applying for any certificate, rating, or authorization issued under this chapter; and

(2) Applying for and taking any test under this chapter.

(c) Any certificate or rating held by an applicant may be suspended or revoked if the Administrator finds that person has committed an act prohibited by paragraph (a) of this section.

§ 107.71 Retesting after failure.

An applicant for a knowledge test who fails that test may not reapply for the test for 14 calendar days after failing the test.

§ 107.73 Initial and recurrent knowledge tests.

(a) An initial aeronautical knowledge test covers the following areas of knowledge:

(1) Applicable regulations relating to small unmanned aircraft system rating privileges, limitations, and flight operation;

(2) Airspace classification, operating requirements, and flight restrictions affecting small unmanned aircraft operation;

(3) Aviation weather sources and effects of weather on small unmanned aircraft performance;

(4) Small unmanned aircraft loading;

(5) Emergency procedures;

(6) Crew resource management;

(7) Radio communication procedures;

(8) Determining the performance of small unmanned aircraft;

(9) Physiological effects of drugs and alcohol;

(10) Aeronautical decision-making and judgment;

(11) Airport operations; and

(12) Maintenance and preflight inspection procedures.

(b) A recurrent aeronautical knowledge test covers the following areas of knowledge:

(1) Applicable regulations relating to small unmanned aircraft system rating privileges, limitations, and flight operation;

(2) Airspace classification and operating requirements and flight restrictions affecting small unmanned aircraft operation;

(3) Emergency procedures;

(4) Crew resource management;

(5) Aeronautical decision-making and judgment;

(6) Airport operations; and

(7) Maintenance and preflight inspection procedures.

§ 107.74 Initial and recurrent training courses.

(a) An initial training course covers the following areas of knowledge:

(1) Applicable regulations relating to small unmanned aircraft system rating privileges, limitations, and flight operation;

(2) Effects of weather on small unmanned aircraft performance;

(3) Small unmanned aircraft loading;

(4) Emergency procedures;

(5) Crew resource management;

(6) Determining the performance of small unmanned aircraft; and

(7) Maintenance and preflight inspection procedures.

(b) A recurrent training course covers the following areas of knowledge:

(1) Applicable regulations relating to small unmanned aircraft system rating privileges, limitations, and flight operation;

(2) Emergency procedures;

(3) Crew resource management; and

(4) Maintenance and preflight inspection procedures.

§ 107.77 Change of name or address.

(a) Change of Name. An application to change the name on a certificate issued under this subpart must be accompanied by the applicant's:

(1) Remote pilot certificate with small UAS rating; and

(2) A copy of the marriage license, court order, or other document verifying the name change.

(b) The documents in paragraph (a) of this section will be returned to the applicant after inspection.

(c) Change of address. The holder of a remote pilot certificate with small UAS rating issued under this subpart who has made a change in permanent mailing address may not, after 30 days from that date, exercise the privileges of the certificate unless the holder has notified the FAA of the change in address using one of the following methods:

(1) By letter to the FAA Airman Certification Branch, P.O. Box 25082, Oklahoma City, OK 73125 providing the new permanent mailing address, or if the permanent mailing address includes a post office box number, then the holder's current residential address; or

(2) By using the FAA website portal at www.faa.gov providing the new permanent mailing address, or if the permanent mailing address includes a post office box number, then the holder's current residential address.

§ 107.79 Voluntary surrender of certificate.

(a) The holder of a certificate issued under this subpart may voluntarily surrender it for cancellation.

(b) Any request made under paragraph (a) of this section must include the following signed statement or its equivalent: "I voluntarily surrender my remote pilot certificate with a small UAS rating for cancellation. This request is made for my own reasons, with full knowledge that my certificate will not be reissued to me unless I again complete the requirements specified in §§ 107.61 and 107.63."

Subpart D – Waivers

§ 107.200 Waiver policy and requirements.

(a) The Administrator may issue a certificate of waiver authorizing a deviation from any regulation specified in § 107.205 of this subpart if the Administrator finds that a proposed small UAS operation can safely be conducted under the terms of that certificate of waiver.

(b) A request for a certificate of waiver must contain a complete description of the proposed operation and justification that establishes that the operation can safely be conducted under the terms of a certificate of waiver.

(c) The Administrator may prescribe additional limitations that the Administrator considers necessary.

(d) A person who receives a certificate of waiver issued under this section:

(1) May deviate from the regulations of this part to the extent specified in the certificate of waiver; and

(2) Must comply with any conditions or limitations that are specified in the certificate of waiver.

§ 107.205 List of regulations subject to waiver.

A certificate of waiver issued pursuant to § 107.200 of this subpart may authorize a deviation from the following regulations of this part:

Sec.

107.25 – Operation from a moving vehicle or aircraft. However, no waiver of this provision will be issued to allow the carriage of property of another by aircraft for compensation or hire.

107.29 – Daylight operation.

107.31 – Visual line of sight aircraft operation. However, no waiver of this provision will be issued to allow the carriage of property of another by aircraft for compensation or hire.

107.33 – Visual observer.

107.35 – Operation of multiple small unmanned aircraft systems.

107.37(a) – Yielding the right of way.

107.39 – Operation over people.

107.41 – Operation in certain airspace.

107.51 – Operating limitations for small unmanned aircraft.

PART 119—CERTIFICATION: AIR CARRIERS AND COMMERCIAL OPERATORS

17. The authority citation for part 119 continues to read as follows:

Authority: 49 U.S.C. 106(g), 1153, 40101, 40102, 40103, 40113, 44105, 44106, 44111, 44701-44717, 44722, 44901, 44903, 44904, 44906, 44912, 44914, 44936, 44938, 46103, 46105.

18. In § 119.1, revise paragraphs (e)(9) and (e)(10) and add paragraph (e)(11) to

read as follows:

§ 119.1 Applicability.

* * * * *

(e) * * *

(9) Emergency mail service conducted under 49 U.S.C. 41906;

(10) Operations conducted under the provisions of § 91.321 of this chapter; or

(11) Small UAS operations conducted under part 107 of this chapter.

PART 133—ROTORCRAFT EXTERNAL-LOAD OPERATIONS

19. The authority citation for part 133 continues to read as follows:

Authority: 49 U.S.C. 106(g), 40113, 44701-44702.

20. In § 133.1, revise the introductory text to read as follows:

§ 133.1 Applicability.

Except for aircraft subject to part 107 of this chapter, this part prescribes-

* * * * *

PART 183—REPRESENTATIVES OF THE ADMINISTRATOR

21. The authority citation for part 183 is revised to read as follows:

Authority: 31 U.S.C. 9701; 49 U.S.C. 106(f), 106(g), 40113, 44702, 45303.

22. In § 183.23, revise paragraphs (b) and (c) and ad paragraph (d) to read as

follows:

§ 183.23 Pilot examiners.

* * * * *

(b) Under the general supervision of the appropriate local Flight Standards Inspector, conduct those tests;

(c) In the discretion of the appropriate local Flight Standards Inspector, issue temporary pilot certificates and ratings to qualified applicants; and

(d) Accept an application for a remote pilot certificate with a small UAS rating and verify the identity of the applicant in a form and manner acceptable to the Administrator.

Index

CPSIA information can be obtained at www.ICGtesting.com
Printed in the USA
BVIW12n0502031117
499440BV00029B/51